Mc
Graw
Hill
Education

Cover and Title Page: Nathan Love

www.mheonline.com/readingwonders

Copyright © 2016 McGraw-Hill Education

Send all inquiries to:
McGraw-Hill Education
2 Penn Plaza
New York, NY 10121

ISBN: 978-0-02-131049-4
MHID: 0-02-131049-1

Printed in the United States of America.

2 3 4 5 6 7 8 9 QVS 20 19 18 17 16

B

ELD
Companion Worktext

Program Authors

Diane August

Jana Echevarria

Josefina V. Tinajero

Mc
Graw
Hill
Education

Unit 1

EUREKA! I've Got It!

The Big Idea

Week 1 • Meeting a Need   14

Week 2 • Trial and Error   26

(t) Valeria Docampo; (b) James Bernardin

Unit 2

Taking the Next Step

The Big Idea

(t) J.S. Peterson/USDA NRCS NPDC; (c) Shawna Tenney; (b) Fancy/Alamy

Unit 3

Getting from Here to There

The Big Idea

(tl) Photodisc/Getty Images; (tr) Westend61/Getty Images; (b) Maryn Roos

4

Unit 4

IT'S UP TO YOU

The Big Idea

What's Next?

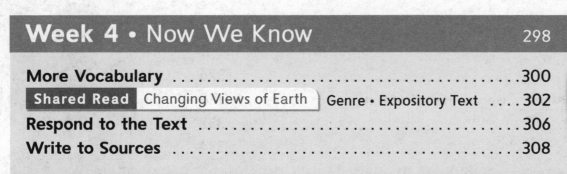

(t) age fotostock/SuperStock; (c) NASA-GFSC Image created by Reto Stockli with the help of Alan Nelson, under the leadership of Fritz Hasler; (b) Kirk Weddle/Photodisc/Getty Images

Linked In

The Big Idea

Week 1 • Joining Forces 324

Week 2 • Getting Along 336

EUREKA!
I've Got It!

THE BIG Idea

Where can an idea begin?

TALK ABOUT IT

Weekly Concept Meeting a Need

? **Essential Question**
How do we get the things we need?

>> *Go Digital*

COLLABORATE

Why is the woman in the rice field? How does the woman get what she needs? What other things does she need to live? Write the needs in the chart.

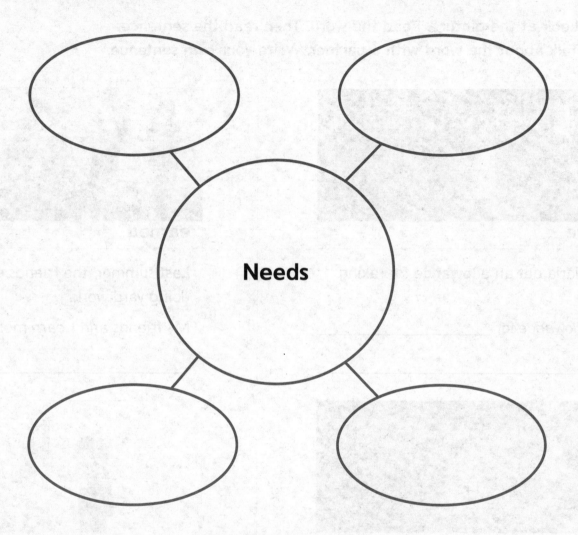

Needs

Discuss how the woman gets the things she needs to live. Use the words from the chart. Complete the sentence:

The woman meets her _____ by

_____.

More Vocabulary

Look at the picture. Read the word. Then read the sentence.
Talk about the word with a partner. Write your own sentence.

COLLABORATE

allowance

Sue and Maria get an **allowance** for raking the leaves.

I get an *allowance* for _____

_____.

earned

Last summer, the friends **earned** money by doing yard work.

My friends and I *earn* money by _____

_____.

budding

The **budding** roses will bloom soon.

A *budding* rose looks like _____

_____.

realized

Finally, they **realized** the answer to the question.

We _____ when we *realized*

_____.

ripened

After the tomatoes **ripened,** the farmers picked them from the vines.

Fruits taste better when they have *ripened*

because _____.

stand

We buy vegetables at the farm **stand**.

A farm *stand* sells _____

_____.

Words and Phrases
Connecting Words

especially = **for a specific person or purpose**
Mom baked a cake especially for me.

though = **however or but**
Grandpa's computer is old, though it still works.

Read the sentences below. Write the word that completes each sentence.

Our neighbors are quiet, _____ they are fun.

The pet store sells toys _____ for puppies.

Donald ran quickly, _____ he did not win the race.

Mia drew a picture _____ for her dad to hang on the wall.

>> *Go Digital* **Add the words *especially* and *though* to your New Words notebook. Write a sentence to show the meaning of each.**

COLLABORATE

1 Talk About It

Look at the picture. Read the title. Talk about what you see. Write your ideas.

Who is in the picture?

_____

_____

Where does the story take place?

_____

_____

What do you think is a fresh idea?

_____

_____

Take notes as you read the story.

A Fresh Idea

Essential Question

? **How do we get the things we need?**

Read about how one girl meets a need in her neighborhood.

18

One bright Saturday morning, Mali and her mom walked around the neighborhood. That is, her mom walked, but Mali ran, skipped, jumped over puddles, and visited the neighbors' dogs. Mali paused to look at the **budding** trees on her block. "I can't wait until summer," she said, "especially for Mrs. Fair's great tomatoes at her market **stand**." She pointed.

Mali's mom stood looking at the empty lot where the market set up every summer weekend. She looked at Mali. "Honey, Mrs. Fair told me last week that she had to close her stand. She's really getting too old to run it anymore."

Mali turned, stared, and put her hands on her hips. "But Mrs. Fair's stand can't close!" she said. "It's the only place in the neighborhood we can buy fresh, delicious tomatoes." Then she added, to show she wasn't being selfish, "Everyone needs fruits and vegetables for a healthy diet."

After they got home, Mali headed out to her backyard swing to think. "If only I could plant a garden," she thought, "but our yard is way too small." Just then, she noticed her neighbor, Mr. Taylor, looking at his daffodils. Mali knew he was thinking about how he had planted those flowers with his wife. This was the first spring since his wife had died, and Mali saw the sadness on his face. Then she had an idea.

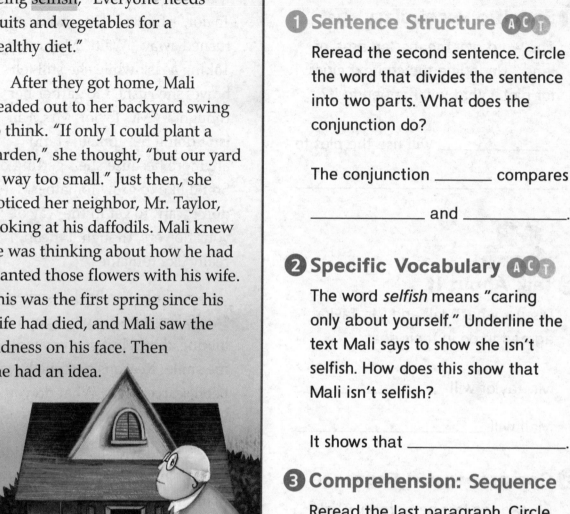

Valerie Decampo

1 Sentence Structure Ⓐ🅒🆃

Reread the second sentence. Circle the word that divides the sentence into two parts. What does the conjunction do?

The conjunction _____ compares

_____ and _____.

2 Specific Vocabulary Ⓐ🅒🆃

The word *selfish* means "caring only about yourself." Underline the text Mali says to show she isn't selfish. How does this show that Mali isn't selfish?

It shows that _____.

3 Comprehension: Sequence

Reread the last paragraph. Circle the words that tell sequence. Write about the events in sequence.

First, Mali _____.

Next, she _____.

Then, _____.

1 Specific Vocabulary

The word *plot* means "an area of land." Underline the context clues for plot. What will happen to it?

_____ will use the plot to

_____.

COLLABORATE

2 Talk About It

Discuss what Mali and Mr. Taylor agreed to do in their deal.

Mr. Taylor will _____.

Mali will _____.

3 Comprehension Sequence

Reread the last paragraph. Circle the words that show sequence. Explain when the event in the fourth sentence will happen.

Based on the sentence, the event

will happen _____

because _____.

Mali cleared her throat, and Mr. Taylor looked up. Mali decided to walk over to the fence. "Hi, Mr. Taylor," she said. He waved, and turned away. "Wait!" Mali cried. Taking a risk while she still felt brave, she rushed to gather her thoughts: "Mr. Taylor, Mrs. Fair isn't doing her tomato stand anymore because she's getting old. So I'd like to grow tomatoes. I don't want to get in the way of your flowers, though. I mean, I really like tomatoes."

Suddenly, Mr. Taylor smiled. "Mali, I'm not sure what you're talking about, but you've made me smile. Reasons to smile have been scarce lately. What do you want to do?"

As Mr. Taylor listened, an idea came to him. "I still need a place to plant my flowers, but there's room for tomatoes. How about I make you a loan? I'll let you use a plot of land in my yard. I'll help you, and when your garden starts to prosper, you can repay me with a few tomatoes."

Mali and Mr. Taylor shook hands on this deal. "But first," Mr. Taylor said, "you'll have to make an investment by buying some tomato plants at the nursery."

Mali thought. "Well, I have some savings from my **allowance**, and I was saving to buy a computer game." She paused. "But I'd rather have tomatoes, so let's start right away!"

The next day, Mali bought all the tomato plants she could afford. Mr. Taylor taught Mali how to prepare the soil and place the plants. Finally, Mali placed stakes in the ground to help hold the plants up. Mr. Taylor explained, "Once the tomatoes come, the heavy fruit makes the branches bend." Then all they could do was water, pull weeds, and wait.

When the fruit **ripened**, there were more juicy, red tomatoes than even Mali could have imagined. "There is no way I can eat all these," she **realized**. On Saturday, Mali and Mr. Taylor carried several crates of ripe tomatoes to the market, and by the day's end they had sold them all. "Not only did I get back the money I invested," said Mali, "but I also made a profit of twenty dollars!"

Mr. Taylor said, "Those are also your wages! You've **earned** that money."

Mali beamed and said, "Mr. Taylor, maybe you could sell some of your flowers, and we could run a market stand together!" Mr. Taylor, picturing a garden of zinnias and marigolds, was already looking forward to next summer.

Valerie Decampo

Make Connections

? How did Mali and Mr. Taylor each get something they needed? **ESSENTIAL QUESTION**

How has someone helped you get something you needed? **TEXT TO SELF**

Text Evidence 🔍

1 Sentence Structure Ⓐ Ⓒ Ⓣ

Reread the third sentence. Circle the pronoun *they*. Then underline the two people *they* refers to. What did they do?

They_____

and _____.

2 Specific Vocabulary Ⓐ Ⓒ Ⓣ

The phrase *looking forward to* means "being excited about something that is going to happen." Circle what Mr. Taylor looking forward to next summer.

Mr. Taylor is looking forward to

_____

next summer.

COLLABORATE

3 Talk About It

How do Mali and Mr. Taylor feel about each other? Use words from the story to support your ideas.

21

Respond to the Text

Partner Discussion Work with a partner. Answer the questions. Discuss what you read in "A Fresh Idea." Write the page numbers where you found text evidence.

How did Mali get what she needed?

Text Evidence 🔍

I read that Mali wanted _____.

Page(s): _____

Mali needed help because _____.

Page(s): _____

Mr. Taylor helped Mali by _____.

Page(s): _____

How did Mr. Taylor get what he needed?

Text Evidence 🔍

Mr. Taylor was sad and lonely because _____.

Page(s): _____

Mr. Taylor needed help because _____.

Page(s): _____

Mali helped Mr. Taylor by _____.

Page(s): _____

Group Discussion Present your answers to the group. Cite text evidence to justify your thinking. Listen to and discuss the group's opinions about your answers.

Write Review your notes about "A Fresh Idea." Then write your answer to the Essential Question. Use text evidence to support your answer. Use vocabulary words from this week's reading in your writing.

How did Mali and Mr. Taylor help each other get the things they need?

Mali and Mr. Taylor worked together to _____

_____.

Mali needed _____,

so Mr. Taylor _____

_____.

Mr. Taylor needed _____,

so Mali _____

_____.

Share Writing Present your writing to the class. Discuss their opinions. Think about what the class has to say. Did they justify their claims? Explain why you agree or disagree with their claims.

I agree with _____ because _____.

I disagree because _____.

Write to Sources

Jupiterimages/Creatas/360/Getty Images

José

Take Notes About the Text I took notes about the text to answer the question: *What does Mali want to plant next summer?*

pages 18–21

Detail
This year, Mali grew and sold tomatoes.

Detail
This year, Mr. Taylor grew daffodils.

Topic
Mali wants to plant a garden next year.

Detail
Next year, Mali wants to run a market stand with Mr. Taylor.

Detail
Next year, Mr. Taylor wants to grow zinnias and marigolds.

24

Write About the Text I used my notes to write a diary entry that describes Mali's plans for the garden.

Student Model: *Narrative Text*

August 15

    Today, I picked ripened tomatoes in the garden. Then I sold them at the market and made a profit. Everyone loves red, juicy tomatoes. Mr. Taylor grew daffodils this year, but he didn't sell any. I'm already looking forward to the next year.

    I want to plant more tomatoes next year. Mr. Taylor wants to plant zinnias and marigolds. I think people would love bright marigolds and zinnias at the market. I want to run a market stand with Mr. Taylor next year. We can sell his beautiful flowers and my ripe tomatoes.

TALK ABOUT IT
COLLABORATE

Text Evidence
Draw a box around a sentence that comes from the notes. Why did José use this detail?

Grammar
Circle adjectives. What senses do the adjectives describe?

Connect Ideas
Underline two sentences about running a market stand with Mr. Taylor. How can you combine these sentences to connect the ideas?

Your Turn
COLLABORATE

What does Mr. Taylor plan to do with the garden next year? Write a diary entry. Use text evidence in the writing.

>> *Go Digital!*
Write your response online. Use your editing checklist.

25

TALK ABOUT IT

Weekly Concept Trial and Error

 Essential Question
What can lead us to rethink an idea?

>> *Go Digital*

26

COLLABORATE

What happened when the surfer tried to ride the wave? How can the surfer learn from his mistake? Write what he can do in the chart.

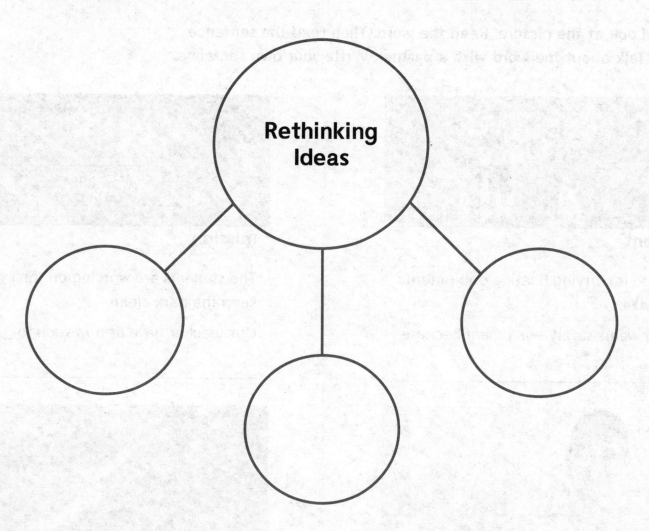

Rethinking Ideas

Discuss why the surfer needs to rethink his idea to achieve his goal. Use words from the chart. You can say:

The surfer needs to rethink his idea because _____.

One idea he can try is _____.

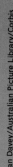

More Vocabulary

COLLABORATE

Look at the picture. Read the word. Then read the sentence.
Talk about the word with a partner. Write your own sentence.

equipment

Each person is carrying boating **equipment** from the lake.

The family wears safety *equipment* because

_____.

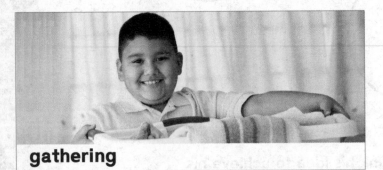

gathering

Diego is **gathering** laundry in a basket.

Another word for *gathering* is _____

_____.

mission

The students are working on their **mission** to keep the park clean.

Our teacher gave us a *mission* to _____

_____.

novice

The children are learning to swim because they are **novices**.

A *novice* is a person who _____

_____.

shift

Ann **shifts** her body to swing the bat.

When I *shift* my body, I _____

_____.

suction

The vacuum cleaner has **suction** to pick up dust on the floor.

I can create *suction* with a straw to _____

_____.

Words and Phrases
Connecting Words

either = also or too

Maria doesn't like tomatoes. Lucy doesn't like tomatoes <u>either</u>.

although = but or though

Jaime is going to the park, <u>although</u> he has homework to do.

Read the sentences below. Write the word that means the same as the underlined words.

Sue doesn't play basketball. Jan <u>also</u> doesn't play basketball.

Sue doesn't play basketball. Jan doesn't play basketball _____.

Anna is playing outside, <u>but</u> it is raining.

Anna is playing outside, _____ it is raining.

» Go Digital Add the words *either* and *although* to your New Words notebook. Write a sentence to show the meaning of each.

COLLABORATE

1 Talk About It

Look at the picture. Read the title. Talk about what you see. Write your ideas.

What does the title tell you?

_____

_____

_____

_____

What are the people doing?

_____

_____

_____

_____

Take notes as you read the story.

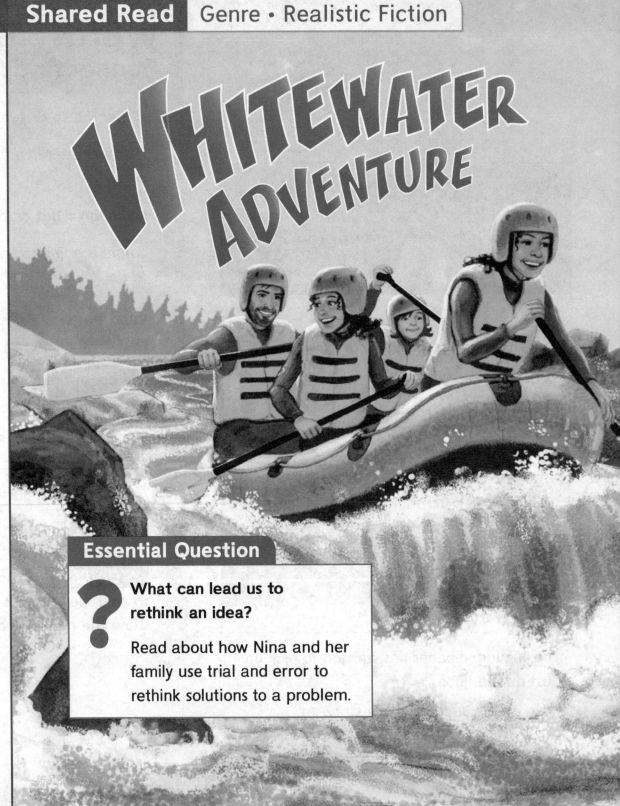

WHITEWATER ADVENTURE

Essential Question

? **What can lead us to rethink an idea?**

Read about how Nina and her family use trial and error to rethink solutions to a problem.

I don't know about you, but I never pictured my family on a whitewater rafting vacation in Colorado. We had tried rafting several times before with instructors and guides. All of us liked it! I come from a family of excellent athletes, and I sometimes have to work hard at holding my own. I didn't even mind when my sister, Marta, who is fourteen, kept correcting my technique. Because she's three years older, Marta believes it's her **mission** in life to make sure I do everything perfectly. "Nina, hold your paddle this way. Nina, plant your feet firmly," she corrects. Honestly, sometimes she's full of herself, although I guess she means well.

That morning, Dad had us assemble our **equipment**, as we had learned. He then took us through his checklist. Only Dad could read his checklist because his handwriting was so hard to decipher. "Paddles – check, helmets – check, life jackets – check, buckets – check," until everything was accounted for. Then we boarded our raft for our second solo trip and headed down the beautiful Colorado River.

Mom had mapped out our route—a **novice's** course with just enough whitewater to make it exciting. It felt great to navigate the raft, paddling in rhythm with everyone else. Dad and I sat in the rear, or stern, of the raft. Mom and Marta sat in the front, or the bow. From time to time, waves slapped against the sides of the raft, spraying water in our faces.

James Bernardin

Text Evidence

1 Specific Vocabulary Ⓐ Ⓒ Ⓣ

The phrase *holding my own* means "being equally good as others." Why does Nina want to hold her own against Marta?

Nina wants to hold her own against

Marta because _____

_____.

2 Sentence Structure Ⓐ Ⓒ Ⓣ

Reread the fifth sentence in the first paragraph. Underline what Marta does. Write what the sentence tells about Marta.

Marta is _____

_____.

COLLABORATE

3 Talk About It

How does Marta act toward Nina? Write about it.

_____

_____

❶ Comprehension
Problem and Solution

Reread the fourth paragraph. Circle the text that tells Marta's solution to the problem. Describe the results of Marta's solution.

Marta's solution _____

the problem because _____

_____.

❷ Specific Vocabulary Ⓐ Ⓒ Ⓣ

The idiom *there wasn't a soul in sight* means "nobody was around." Underline the text that provides context clues to the meaning.

❸ Sentence Structure Ⓐ Ⓒ Ⓣ

Reread the second sentence in the fifth paragraph. Underline the text that tells Dad's idea. What does he suggest?

Dad suggests that _____

_____.

Suddenly, I was distracted by a bear coming out of the trees, but it turned around and began to retrace its steps. All of us must have been distracted by that bear because, in the blink of an eye, we ran into a problem! Our raft came to a complete halt.

"What's wrong?" I asked, hoping I didn't sound nearly as anxious as I felt.

"Yikes!" exclaimed Mom. "We're stuck on some rocks!"

"Maybe a river guide will come by and give us a shove," suggested Marta. However, there wasn't a soul in sight. She tried shouting, "HELLO, OUT THERE!" All we heard back was an echo. To make matters worse, storm clouds were **gathering**. The last thing we needed now was a rainstorm.

"Don't worry, folks, I know what we can do," said Dad. "It's the front of the raft that's stuck, so let's all sit in the stern. Our weight will probably **shift** the raft off the rocks." Carefully, Mom and Marta moved to the rear. Nothing happened.

"Let's try swaying from side to side," urged Mom, looking up at the darkening sky. So we swayed and swayed, but the raft didn't move an inch. Dad even tried jumping a couple of times, but that didn't work either. Now it started to drizzle, and although no one wanted to admit it, we were running out of options.

"Wait!" I yelled. I thought back to our rafting lessons. "What if we tried to lift the side of the raft away from the rocks?" I asked hesitantly.

"Quick, let's try it!" said Mom. We went to the front of the raft and lifted the side away from the rocks. Then we heard a little popping noise. We held our breath.

"Did we tear the raft?" cried Marta.

"No, we broke the **suction** between the raft and the rocks!" said Dad, as he pushed off the rocks with his paddle.

"We did it!" yelled Marta. "I mean, you did it, Nina—that was truly brilliant!"

"Good thinking, Nina!" cheered Mom and Dad.

By this time, it was raining steadily, so we paddled really hard to return to land and wait indoors for the rain to stop. And how was I feeling? It's kind of hard to describe. I was on cloud nine! I felt like I could accomplish anything I wanted.

Make Connections

? Talk about why Nina and her family had to rethink solutions to the problem of being stuck on the rocks. Compare the different ideas they came up with. **ESSENTIAL QUESTION**

When have you had to rethink an idea in order to solve a problem? **TEXT TO SELF**

James Bernard

❶ Specific Vocabulary Ⓐ Ⓒ Ⓣ

Reread the first paragraph. The phrase *running out* means "not having any more of something." What are the options the family was running out of? Underline the text in the first paragraph.

❷ Sentence Structure Ⓐ Ⓒ Ⓣ

Reread the last sentence in the first paragraph. The pronoun *it* refers to different things in the sentence. What does *it* in the second part refer to? Underline the text that tells what no one wanted to admit.

No one wanted to admit that

_____.

COLLABORATE

❸ Talk About It

How did Marta react when Nina solved the problem?

Marta was _____

_____.

33

Respond to the Text

COLLABORATE

Partner Discussion Work with a partner. Answer the questions. Discuss what you read in the story. Write the page numbers where you found text evidence.

What ideas did Nina's family have to solve the problem?

I read that Marta's idea was to _____.

Dad's idea was to _____.

Mom's idea was to _____.

Their ideas did not solve the problem because _____

_____.

Text Evidence 🔍

Page(s): _____

Page(s): _____

Page(s): _____

Page(s): _____

What idea did Nina have? How did she get her idea?

I read that Nina's idea was to _____.

She got her idea by _____.

Nina's idea solved the problem because _____

_____.

Text Evidence 🔍

Page(s): _____

Page(s): _____

Page(s): _____

COLLABORATE

Group Discussion Present your answers to the group. Cite text evidence to justify your thinking. Listen to and discuss the group's opinions about your answers.

Write Review your notes about "Whitewater Adventure." Then write your answer to the Essential Question. Use text evidence to support your answer. Use vocabulary words from this week's reading in your writing.

How did Nina and her family rethink their solutions?

Nina's family had many ideas to _____, but

they did not _____

because_____.

One idea was to _____, but

_____.

However, Nina looked for a solution differently. She thought back to _____

_____.

Her solution was to _____,

and _____.

Share Writing Present your writing to the class. Discuss their opinions. Think about what the class has to say. Did they justify their claims? Explain why you agree or disagree with their claims.

I agree with _____ because _____.

I disagree because _____.

Write to Sources

Maddy

Take Notes About the Text I took notes about the text on the chart to answer the prompt: *How might Nina respond to a new problem, such as a leak in the raft?*

pages 30–33

Text Clues	Conclusion
Problem The raft gets stuck on rocks.	**Problem** The raft has a leak.
Events Marta calls for help. Mom and Marta move to the back and the family sways the raft. Dad jumps inside the raft.	**Events** Marta, Mom and Dad have ideas, but the ideas don't work.
Solution Nina tells her family to lift the side of the raft.	**Solution** Nina rethinks the problem and solves it.

Write About the Text I used my notes to write about how Nina's family reacts if the raft leaks.

Student Model: *Narrative Text*

I looked down and realized that the raft had a leak! "There's water coming in!" I cried. Immediately, everyone knew what to do.

"Look for the leak," Marta ordered. Mom found the hole. She put tape over it, but water soaked through the tape.

"Someone help us!" Dad yelled out but no one responded. Suddenly, I saw a large tree hunched over the river. "We can climb the tree over there!" I yelled. Dad and Marta paddled as Mom and I grabbed the tree's limbs. We pulled ourselves onto land. We were safe!

TALK ABOUT IT

Essential Question

How can experiencing nature change the way you think about it?

>> *Go Digital*

Where is the hiker? What does the hiker discover? Where can people experience nature? What can people experience there? Write about the places in the chart.

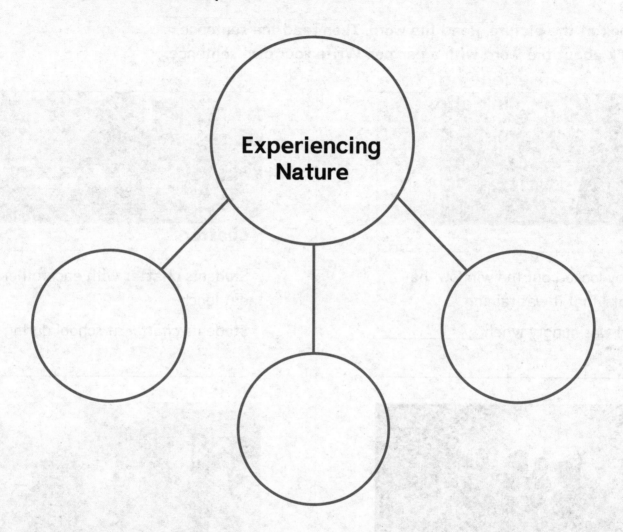

Experiencing Nature

Discuss how experiencing nature affects you. Complete the sentence:

One result of an experience with nature is _____

_____.

More Vocabulary

Look at the picture. Read the word. Then read the sentence. Talk about the word with a partner. Write your own sentence.

aware

When the boy looked out the window, he became **aware** that it was raining.

I was *aware* I was hungry when _____

_____ .

awe

The people watched the fireworks in **awe**.

When I feel in *awe* of something, I feel like

_____

_____ .

chatter

Students **chatter** with each other while they eat lunch.

Students *chatter* at school during _____

_____ .

company

My family spent the afternoon talking with our **company**.

When my family has *company* we usually _____

_____ .

40

habits

Todd has daily study **habits** of reading and writing after school.

I always complete my morning *habits* of

_____ before I go to school.

rustling

The wind caused a **rustling** of the leaves.

The leaves make *rustling* noise when the

wind _____

_____ .

Words and Phrases
Prepositions

The phrases *as though* and *as if* have the same meaning. They describe something that seems to be true.

The phrases *as though* and *as if* mean "like."

The puppy runs <u>as though</u> it never gets tired.

The puppy runs <u>as if</u> it never gets tired.

Read the sentence. Then answer the questions.

The wind howls as though it is angry.

What phrase tells you that the wind is not really angry?

_____

The cat yawns as if it is bored.

What phrase tells you that the cat is not really bored?

_____

>> *Go Digital*   Add the phrases *as though* and *as if* to your New Words notebook. Write sentences to show the meaning of each.

COLLABORATE

1 Talk About It

Read the title. Talk about what you see. Write your ideas.

What does the title tell you?

_____

_____

_____

What does the photograph show?

_____

_____

_____

Which season is it? How do you know?

_____

_____

_____

Take notes as you read the text.

A Life in the Woods

Essential Question

? How can experiencing nature change the way you think about it?

Read about how Thoreau's stay in the woods changed his view of nature.

(bkgd) Galen Rowell/Mountain Light/Alamy, (inset) Aaron Roth Photography

Into the Woods

Henry David Thoreau raised his pen to write, but the **chatter** of guests in the next room filled his ears. He stared at the page. "Concord, 1841" was all that he had written. How would he write a book with such noise in his family's house? Thoreau headed outside, shutting the door with emphasis. He would have to find a place of his own.

Thoreau walked out of town. Tall white pines soon replaced the painted houses. He listened to the **rustling** of the leaves. What if I could stay here, he thought. He could live off the land, close to nature, and begin his book. It would take work, but he could do it.

Years passed, but Thoreau still did not have a place in the woods. One day, his friend Ralph Waldo Emerson had an idea. Emerson was a well-known writer who had bought some land near Walden Pond. Because he and Thoreau shared the same interest in nature, Emerson decided to let Thoreau use part of this land.

In March of 1845, Thoreau began to build a cabin. By July, it was ready. He could live and write in the woods.

❶ Specific Vocabulary Ⓐ Ⓒ Ⓣ

The phrase *live off the land* means to "use things found in nature to live." Why did Thoreau want to live off the land? Put a box around the text that tells the reason.

❷ Sentence Structure Ⓐ Ⓒ Ⓣ

Reread the third sentence in the third paragraph. What person does the word *who* refer to? Circle the text that tells you.

The person is _____

_____.

❸ Comprehension
Cause and Effect

Reread the last sentence in the third paragraph. Underline the text that tells why Emerson let Thoreau use his land. What does the word *because* tell you?

The word *because* _____

_____.

COLLABORATE

❶ Talk About It

Reread the first paragraph. Discuss the company Thoreau had in the woods. Write about it.

_____

_____

❷ Sentence Structure ⒶⒸⓉ

Reread the sixth sentence in the second paragraph. What did Thoreau do? Underline the text. What did the loon do? Circle the text. What did the loon sound like?

The loon _____

_____.

❸ Comprehension
Cause and Effect

Reread the second paragraph. Why did Thoreau think the loon was laughing at him? Put a box around the text.

Cabin Life

Thoreau's move to the woods indicated that he liked to be alone. But Thoreau did not feel that way. "I have a great deal of **company** in my house," he wrote. Red squirrels woke him by running up and down the sheer sides of his cabin. A snowshoe hare lived in the debris under his cabin, thumping against the floorboards. A sparrow once perched on his shoulder. Thoreau recorded these experiences in his journal. How easily writing came to him with the beauty of nature around him!

On Walden Pond

Thoreau was a naturalist. He noticed the **habits** of animals. Each encounter showed him something new. One afternoon, Thoreau tried to get a close look at a loon, but the bird quickly dove into the pond. He knew loons could travel long distances under water, so he guessed where it would come up. But every time Thoreau paddled to one spot, the loon came up somewhere else and let out a call—a howling laugh. What a silly loon, Thoreau thought. But after a while, Thoreau felt as though the bird was laughing at him because he still could not catch up to it. Thoreau wrote in his journal:

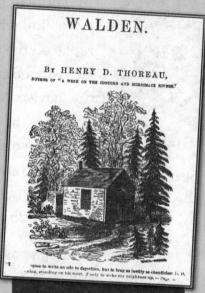

WALDEN.

By HENRY D. THOREAU,

AUTHOR OF "A WEEK ON THE CONCORD AND MERRIMACK RIVERS."

Thoreau published his book *Walden* in 1854.

His white breast, the stillness of the air, and the smoothness of the water were all against him. At length he uttered one of those prolonged howls, as if calling on the god of the loons to aid him, and immediately there came a wind from the east and rippled the surface, and filled the whole air with misty rain, and I was impressed.

Bettmann/CORBIS

Loons are still a common sight on Walden Pond.

The spectacular scene made Thoreau wonder at the loon. It no longer seemed a silly animal, but one with some mysterious power. As months went by, Thoreau also became **aware** of each animal's ability to stay alive. "His power of observation seemed to indicate additional senses," Emerson once remarked. In winter, as he warmed his cabin by fire, he watched in **awe** as the moles warmed their nest by their own body heat. He understood forest life as never before.

Back to Concord

Like the geese that move to new ponds at the season's end, so too did Thoreau leave Walden. He had done what he had set out to do, and had learned much from the woods around him. He packed his few belongings and his stack of journals and returned to Concord. Now, he would turn his journal entries into a book. Generations to come would know life on Walden Pond!

Make Connections

? Talk about how Thoreau's experiences at Walden Pond changed his view of nature. ESSENTIAL QUESTION

Think about a time that you saw something in nature close-up. How did it change your idea about it? TEXT TO SELF

Text Evidence

❶ Sentence Structure A C T

Reread the second sentence in the first paragraph. The words *It* and *one* refer to the same thing. Circle the text that identifies it.

The words *It* and *one* refer to

_____.

❷ Comprehension
Cause and Effect

Reread the second paragraph. Why did Thoreau leave Walden Pond? Underline the text.

Thoreau left because _____

_____.

COLLABORATE

❸ Talk About It

How did the encounter with the loon change Thoreau? Justify your answer.

_____

_____

Respond to the Text

Partner Discussion Work with a partner. Answer the questions. Discuss what you learned about "A Life in the Woods." Write the page numbers where you found text evidence.

How did Thoreau experience nature at Walden Pond?   **Text Evidence** 🔍

In his cabin, Thoreau lived with _____.   Page(s): _____

When he chased a loon, Thoreau _____.   Page(s): _____

In the winter, Thoreau saw _____.   Page(s): _____

Thoreau wrote about _____.   Page(s): _____

Why did Thoreau write easily in nature? How did he feel about nature at the end of his experience?   **Text Evidence** 🔍

Thoreau wrote easily because _____.   Page(s): _____

Thoreau felt amazed by nature because _____.   Page(s): _____

Group Discussion Present your answers to the group. Cite text evidence to justify your thinking. Listen to and discuss the group's opinions about your answers.

Write Review your notes about "A Life in the Woods." Then write your answer to the Essential Question. Use text evidence to support your answer. Use vocabulary words from this week's reading in your writing.

How did experiencing nature change the way Thoreau thought about it?

In the woods, Thoreau encountered many _____

_____.

His experiences with a loon caused Thoreau to _____

_____.

After spending time in the words, Thoreau thought nature _____

_____.

After the experience in the woods, Thoreau _____.

Share Writing Present your writing to the class. Discuss their opinions. Think about what the class has to say. Did they justify their claims? Explain why you agree or disagree with their claims.

I agree with _____ because _____.

I disagree because _____.

Sofia

Take Notes About the Text I took notes about the text on the idea web to answer the question: *Why did Thoreau spend a summer at Walden Pond?*

pages 42–45

Detail
His home and town were too noisy.

Detail
He wanted to write a book.

Topic
Thoreau spent a summer at Walden Pond.

Detail
He observed squirrels and hares near the cabin. He chased a loon.

Detail
He found ideas for his writing by watching wildlife.

Write About the Text I used my notes to write about why Thoreau spent a summer at Walden Pond.

Student Model: *Informative Text*

Henry David Thoreau spent a summer at Walden Pond for many reasons. He thought his home and his town were too noisy and they did not allow him to write. He wanted a quiet place to write his book. Thoreau wanted to find peace in nature. He loved nature. He found ideas for his writing by watching wildlife that lived on Walden Pond. He watched the habits of red squirrels and snowshoe hares near his cabin and he chased a loon on the pond.

TALK ABOUT IT

COLLABORATE

Text Evidence
Draw a box around a sentence that comes from the notes. Why did Sofia use this information as a supporting detail?

Grammar
Circle a prepositional phrase that tells a location. What other prepositional phrase can Sofia add?

Condense Ideas
Underline two sentences that tell about Thoreau's feelings about nature. How can you combine the sentences to condense the ideas?

Your Turn

COLLABORATE

How did living in the woods change Thoreau? Use text evidence in your writing.

≫ *Go Digital!*
Write your response online. Use your editing checklist.

TALK ABOUT IT

?

Essential Question

How does technology lead to creative ideas?

>> *Go Digital*

49

COLLABORATE

What invention is the artist using? How is this way of drawing different? Describe how inventions, such as a computer, help people do different things. Write about them on the chart.

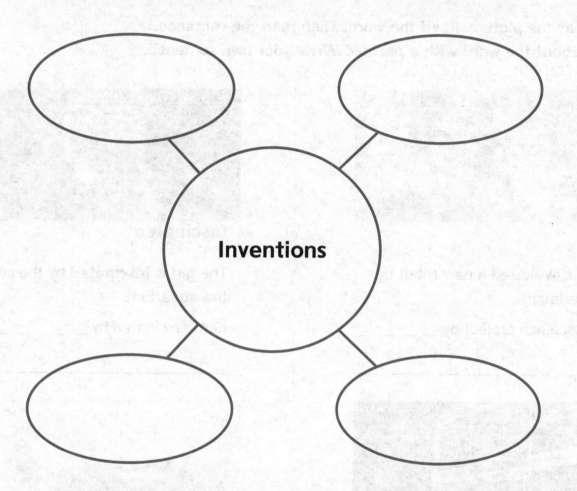

Inventions

Discuss how the artist uses inventions to draw. Use words from the chart. You can say:

The artist uses _____ to draw.

Inventions help people do different things, such as _____

_____.

More Vocabulary

COLLABORATE Look at the picture. Read the word. Then read the sentence.
Talk about the word with a partner. Write your own sentence.

developed

The researchers **developed** a new robot by conducting experiments.

I *developed* my science project by _____

_____.

fascinated

The girl is **fascinated** by the colorful fish in the aquarium.

I am *fascinated* by _____

_____.

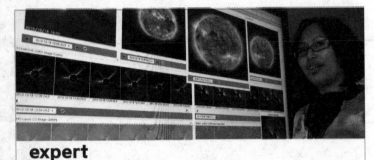

expert

An astronomer is an **expert** on stars, planets, and galaxies.

An *expert* is a person who _____

_____.

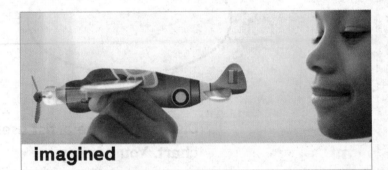

imagined

The boy **imagined** his model plane was soaring through the sky.

Another word for *imagined* is _____

_____.

system

The diagram shows the planets in our solar **system**.

The solar *system* has planets and _____

_____.

transmit

Special towers **transmit** electric power over long distances.

A computer can *transmit* _____

_____.

The International Astronomical Union/Martin Kornmesser - CC BY 3.0; Pixtal/age fotostock

Words and Phrases
Connecting Words and Adverbs

The word *since* gives a reason for what happens.

You can walk the dog <u>since</u> you are going outside.

The word *yet* means "up to now."

The show has not started <u>yet</u>. It will start in ten minutes.

Read the sentences below. Write the word that means the same as the underlined words.

I have not read the book <u>up to now</u>.

I have not read the book _____.

I will call you later <u>because</u> you are busy now.

I will call you later _____ you are busy now.

>> Go Digital **Add the words *since* and *yet* to your New Words notebook. Write a sentence to show the meaning of each.**

COLLABORATE

1 Talk About It

Read the title. Talk about what you see. Write your ideas.

The text is a biography. What does that tell you about the text?

_____

_____

_____

What do you think the title means?

_____

_____

_____

What does the image show?

_____

_____

_____

Take notes as you read the text.

Fantasy
Becomes Fact

Essential Question

?

How does technology lead to creative ideas?

Red about how a science fiction writer's ideas led to new technology.

Inventing the Future

Have you ever imagined ways of traveling into space? Or have you used a tool and wished it did something more? One person who thought just this way was the science fiction writer Arthur C. Clarke. Arthur is most famous for writing novels and stories about science and the future. But you may not know that real inventions came about as a result of things he first **imagined**!

In his writings, Arthur envisioned technologies that did not yet exist, but might. This was no accident. Arthur studied and used scientific knowledge all during his lifetime. Arthur wrote about advanced computers and spaceships. Years later, these technologies were **developed**.

Science at an Early Age

Even as a child, Arthur was passionate about science. Born in England in 1917 in a small town by the sea, Arthur spent his school years enthusiastically reading his favorite science fiction magazine. He was **fascinated** by astronomy and built a telescope when he was just 13. He also started writing his own science fiction stories. He even published them in a school magazine. Arthur loved imagining the future.

Arthur's own future became uncertain as a teenager, when his father died. Since his mother could not afford to send him to college, Arthur moved to London at the age of 19 and got an office job. In his free time, he worked at the subjects he loved. He also continued to write science fiction. His love of science and its possibilities would soon be useful.

Arthur C. Clarke's interest in science and space exploration lasted all his life. He sometimes constructed his own tools for his research.

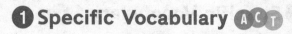

Text Evidence

1 Specific Vocabulary Ⓐ Ⓒ Ⓣ

The phrase *just this way* means "in the same way." Circle the text that tells what the phrase refers to. What did Arthur C. Clarke think?

He thought _____

_____.

2 Comprehension Sequence

Reread the third paragraph. Underline the signal words and phrases that tell the sequence of events. Write about the first event.

First, _____

_____.

3 Sentence Structure Ⓐ Ⓒ Ⓣ

Reread the second sentence of the fourth paragraph. Circle the word that signals the cause. Draw a box around the effect. Write about it.

_____

_____

55

Text Evidence

1 Specific Vocabulary ⒶⒸⓉ

The word *proposed* means "suggested an idea." Underline the text that tells you what Arthur proposed. Write about it.

Arthur proposed a new _____

_____.

2 Sentence Structure ⒶⒸⓉ

Reread the last two sentences on the page. Circle the signal words that tell cause and effect. Underline the text that tells why Arthur didn't make money.

3 Comprehension
Sequence

Reread the second paragraph. When was the idea for a satellite communication system proposed? Underline the text. Describe the invention of the communication system in sequence of events.

First, _____.

Next, _____.

Predicting the Future

In 1939 Arthur joined the Royal Air Force to help fight the Second World War. It was there that Arthur began to invent. Arthur became an **expert** in the radar **systems** used to guide planes and detect enemies. This technology gave Arthur ideas. He imagined an amazing breakthrough in communication systems. He **proposed** a wireless system using space stations. This system required rockets to carry satellites into space. Then the satellites would help **transmit** signals around the Earth. Since satellites and space stations did not exist, this idea was a demonstration of Arthur's imagination. He had learned much about space.

As with any inventor, Arthur built on technologies that already existed to create his system. For example, rockets had been invented but could not yet travel into space. In 1957, Russia used a rocket to launch *Sputnik 1*, which became the first manmade object to orbit Earth. In the 1960s, a satellite communications system was created. It was just like the one Arthur had envisioned years before. Years later, the same kind of satellite was used to make cell phone communication possible. Although Arthur claimed the communications system as his own idea, he did not apply for patents. As a result, he never made money from his idea.

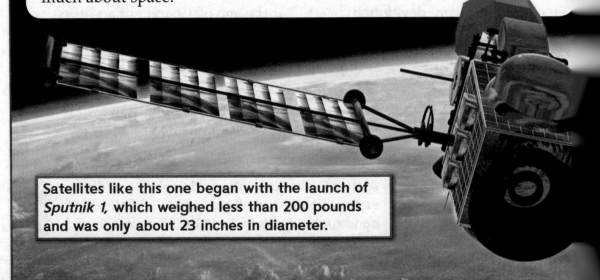

Satellites like this one began with the launch of *Sputnik 1*, which weighed less than 200 pounds and was only about 23 inches in diameter.

Can Science Fiction Come True?

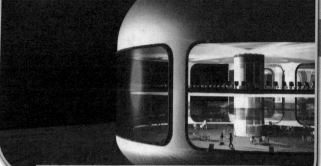

In 1968, Arthur published one of his best-known novels, *2001: A Space Odyssey*. In the novel, Arthur imagined a computer that controlled almost everything. Arthur's computer idea, HAL, could actually think for itself. Today, computers cannot think for themselves. However, they do control many of the devices in our homes, cars, planes, and spacecraft. HAL could recognize human voices as well as speak back. This technology did not exist when the book was written, but it is common today. Arthur's novel also predicted advances such as space stations and rocket-powered

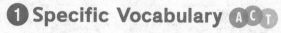

Inventors start out by imagining what the future will look like.

missions to far-off planets. He even predicted people reading news on electronic screens!

Arthur C. Clarke's science fiction books have captivated readers around the world. Many of the technologies he wrote about seemed like fantasy at the time, but they turned into fact. His creative ideas may have inspired others to invent the very technologies he imagined.

Make Connections

Talk about how existing technology helped Arthur C. Clarke imagine other inventions. **ESSENTIAL QUESTION**

What are some ways you would like to improve a machine or other object that you use in your everyday life? **TEXT TO SELF**

Text Evidence 🔍

❶ Specific Vocabulary Ⓐ🅒🅣

The word *advances* means "inventions, discoveries, or changes that make things better." Underline the text that tells what advances Arthur predicted.

❷ Comprehension Sequence

Reread the first paragraph. Circle the signal words that tell two different time periods.

The two time periods are _____

_____.

COLLABORATE

❸ Talk About It

Discuss how Arthur's ideas changed from fantasy to reality. Write about it.

_____

_____

_____

_____

57

Respond to the Text

Partner Discussion Work with a partner. Answer the questions. Discuss what you learned about "Fantasy Becomes Fact." Write the page numbers where you found text evidence.

How did Arthur get his ideas?	Text Evidence 🔍
During the Second World War, Arthur had an idea for _____ _____.	Page(s): _____
Arthur wrote about a computer that _____ _____.	Page(s): _____
His ideas came from _____.	Page(s): _____

How did Arthur think like an inventor?	Text Evidence 🔍
Arthur used existing technologies to _____.	Page(s): _____
He used radar to imagine _____.	Page(s): _____
Arthur imagined a computer that could _____.	Page(s): _____

COLLABORATE

Group Discussion Present your answers to the group. Cite text evidence to justify your thinking. Listen to and discuss the group's opinions about your answers.

Write Review your notes about "Fantasy Becomes Fact." Then write your answer to the Essential Question. Use text evidence to support your answer. Use vocabulary words from this week's reading in your writing.

How did Arthur C. Clarke use existing technology to create his ideas?

Arthur used technologies that existed to _____

_____.

He used radar to imagine _____

_____.

Arthur imagined a computer that could _____

_____.

Share Writing Present your writing to the class. Discuss their opinions. Think about what they have to say. Did they justify their claims? Explain why you agree or disagree with their claims.

I agree with _____ because _____.

I disagree because _____.

Write to Sources

Evan

Take Notes About the Text I took notes about the text on the chart to answer the question: *What was the author's purpose in writing "Fantasy Becomes Fact"?*

pages 54–57

Clue
Arthur wrote about science and the future.

Clue
Arthur wrote about computers and spaceships that didn't exist.
They developed years later.

Clue
In <u>*2001: A Space Odyssey,*</u> Arthur wrote about computers that talked to humans. This technology is common today.

Author's Purpose
Imagination creates real inventions.

60

Write About the Text I used my notes from my chart to write about the author's purpose in "Fantasy Becomes Fact."

The author wrote "Fantasy Becomes Fact" to show that imagination creates inventions. Arthur C. Clarke wrote science fiction stories about the future. He wrote about technologies that did not exist but developed years later. In his book *2001: A Space Odyssey,* he imagined a computer that talks to people. This technology is common today. The author showed that Arthur's imagination inspired real inventions.

TALK ABOUT IT

COLLABORATE

Text Evidence

Draw a box around a sentence that comes from a clue in the notes. How does the clue support the author's purpose?

Grammar

Circle the words *years later*. What do they tell you about technologies?

Condense Ideas

Underline two sentences that tell about the stories Arthur wrote. How can you combine these two sentences to condense the ideas?

Your Turn

COLLABORATE

How did the author help the reader understand Arthur's idea for a wireless system? Include text evidence.

>> *Go Digital!*
Write your response online. Use your editing checklist.

61

Essential Question

What are the positive and negative effects of new technology?

>> *Go Digital*

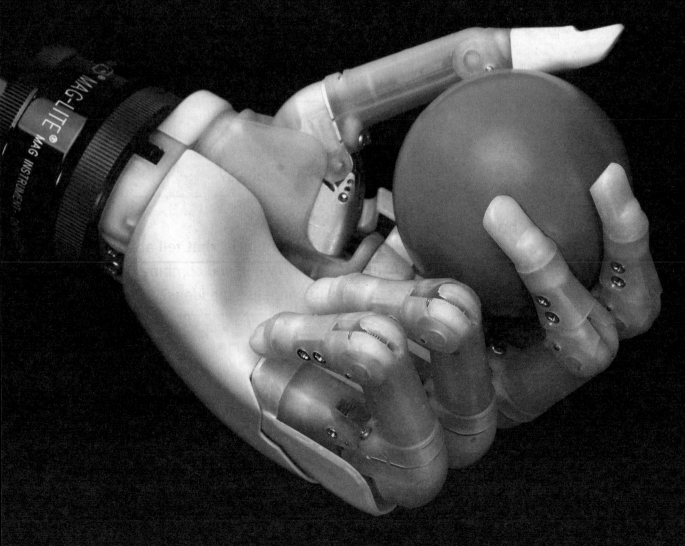

COLLABORATE

What does the bionic, or plastic, hand do? What are positive effects of using a bionic hand? Write your ideas in the chart.

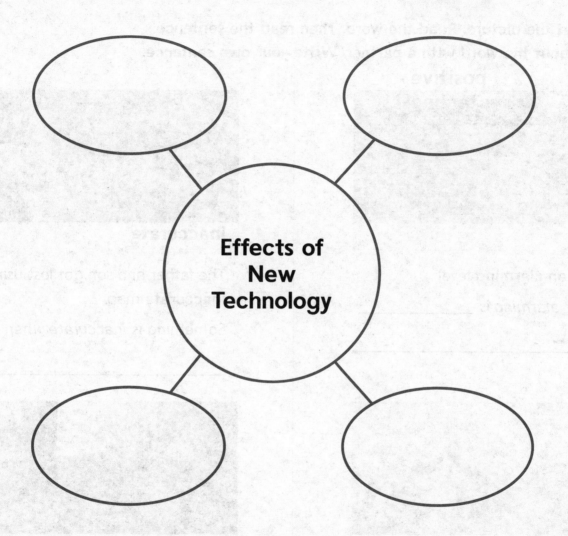

Effects of New Technology

Discuss the effects of using a bionic hand. Use words from the chart. Complete the sentence.

The positive effects of using a bionic hand are _____

More Vocabulary

COLLABORATE

Look at the picture. Read the word. Then read the sentence.
Talk about the word with a partner. Write your own sentence.

alarming

The river rose to an **alarming** level.

Another word for *alarming* is _____

_____.

inaccurate

The father and son got lost using an **inaccurate** map.

Something is *inaccurate* when _____

_____.

critics

The girl is a **critic** of tuba who thinks it is too loud.

Many people like the plan to build bike lanes, but the *critics* _____.

interactive

The father and son use the **interactive** screen to learn more about the exhibit.

Interactive websites are helpful because they

_____.

64

issue

These students think that recycling is an important **issue**.

Another word for *issue* is _____

_____.

tasks

The family members are doing **tasks** to help prepare a meal at home.

My *tasks* at home are _____

_____.

Words and Phrases
Connecting Word and Phrasal Verb

The phrase *in addition* tells that there is more information about a topic.

Many students do assignments online. <u>In addition</u>, they read newspapers online.

The phrase *plugged in* means "informed."

People use the internet to stay <u>plugged in</u> about current events.

Read the sentences below. Write the phrase that means the same as the underlined words.

I like to be <u>informed</u> about the weather.

I like to be _____ about the weather.

The museum is not open on Mondays. <u>Also</u>, the museum closes early on Saturday.

The museum is not open on Mondays. _____, the museum closes early on Saturday.

>> *Go Digital* Add the phrases *in addition* and *plugged in* to your New Words notebook. Write a sentence to show the meaning of each.

COLLABORATE

1 Talk About It

Look at the photograph. Read the title. Talk about what you see. Write your ideas.

What does the title tell you?

_____

_____

_____

_____

What are the girls in the photograph doing?

_____

_____

_____

_____

Take notes as you read the text.

Essential Question

? **What are the positive and negative effects of new technology?**

Read two different viewpoints about how technology affects kids.

JGI Jamie Grill/Blend Images/Getty Images

Are Electronic Devices Good for Us?

Plugged In

Kids need to spend time using electronic devices.

Do you love to surf the Internet, listen to music, IM, and talk on a cell phone? You are not alone. A recent study has some surprising news: Kids in the United States between the ages of 8 and 19 spend seven and a half hours a day on electronic devices. These include computers, smart phones, and video games. Some adults try to advance the idea that these devices waste kids' time. However, some research surveys say this idea is **inaccurate**. In fact, the data show that technology can benefit kids.

Critics say that kids stare at computers and TVs all day and do not get enough exercise. The facts stand in counterpoint to this belief. One study compared kids who use media a lot to those who do not. The "heavy" media users actually spent more time in physical activity than "light" media users.

One study by the National Institutes of Health says that action video games may help increase kids' visual attention. In addition, using **interactive** media can give kids good structure for learning. It can also help them learn to switch **tasks** effectively. Kids also need to use the Web to access information. Many argue that learning to use the Web responsibly sharpens kids' reasoning abilities.

Today's world is wired, and not just for fun. The jobs of the future depend on kids who plug in!

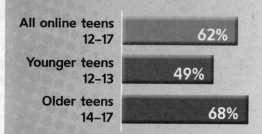

A Source of News for Teens

For the latest news, teens used to rely on newspapers, television, and magazines. See how many teens now get their news online.

All online teens 12–17	62%
Younger teens 12–13	49%
Older teens 14–17	68%

Text Evidence

1 Specific Vocabulary Ⓐ Ⓒ Ⓣ

The word *surveys* means "reports or descriptions about a subject." Underline the text that tells the subject of the surveys. Circle the text that tells the type of information that is in the survey.

2 Sentence Structure Ⓐ Ⓒ Ⓣ

Reread the sixth sentence in the first paragraph. Circle the text that the pronoun *this* refers to. What do the research surveys show?

The research surveys show _____

_____

_____.

3 Comprehension
Author's Point of View

Put a box around text that tells the author's point of view. Reread the third paragraph. Put a box around the text that supports the author's point of view.

67

Text Evidence

1 Specific Vocabulary ACT

The phrase *per day* means "each day." Circle what young people do each day. What is alarming?

2 Talk About It

Discuss the pie graphs. Who gets the best grades? Write about it.

The pie graphs show _____

_____.

I know because _____.

3 Comprehension

Author's Point of View

Reread the first paragraph. How are kids today different from kids 5 years ago? Circle the text that tells you. Write about it.

The differences are _____

_____.

Tuned Out

Electronic media is harming kids.

Are kids tuning out by tuning in to electronic devices? An **alarming** report states that young people spend an hour more **per day** on computers, smart phones, television, and other electronic media than they did 5 years ago. Nearly 7 out of 10 kids have cell phones. Just 5 years ago, 4 out of 10 had them. Are these devices harmless or hurtful to the well-being of young people? A close analysis of several studies shows that there are plenty of disadvantages to these devices.

The Internet is supposed to be a great tool for learning. Do kids who love computers do better in the classroom? To cite one report, access to electronic devices does not automatically bring high marks in school. See the graphs below.

Many young people use more than one electronic device at a time.

The Effect of Media Use on Grades

These pie graphs show how the use of media affects grades.

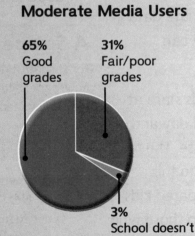

Heavy Media Users

51% Good grades

47% Fair/poor grades

Moderate Media Users

65% Good grades

31% Fair/poor grades

3% School doesn't use grades

Light Media Users

60% Good grades

23% Fair/poor grades

10% School doesn't use grades

The effects of using electronic devices on kids will continue to be studied. These devices seem to be here to stay.

Some argue that the devices get kids involved and help them make friends. Claims like these are incorrect. A study done by the Pew Research Center discusses teenagers' use of online social networks. Teens do this to keep in touch with friends they already have, not to make new ones. In addition, trying to meet people online can be dangerous.

There are other serious drawbacks to new technology.

One issue is multitasking, or trying to do many tasks at the same time. Is it possible to do more than one task at a time well? Some studies say kids' thinking improves when they do several tasks at once. Still, experts point out that much more research needs to be done on this.

New electronic devices hit stores every year. Kids should know that there is more to life than what they see on a screen.

Make Connections

Talk about the positive and negative effects of electronic devices on kids. **ESSENTIAL QUESTION**

What is your opinion of electronic devices? Compare your opinion to the views discussed in the two articles. **TEXT TO SELF**

Text Evidence

1 **Specific Vocabulary** Ⓐ Ⓒ Ⓣ

The word *claims* means "statements that something is true but without proof." Underline the text that *claims* refers to. What does the author think about the claims?

The author thinks _____

_____.

2 **Comprehension**
Author's Point of View

Reread the first paragraph. Put a box around the text that supports the author's point of view.

The author's point of view is that

_____

_____.

3 **Sentence Structure** Ⓐ Ⓒ Ⓣ

Reread the last sentence in the second paragraph. Circle the topic that experts say needs further research.

Respond to the Text

Partner Discussion Work with a partner. Answer the questions. Discuss what you learned about "Are Electronic Devices Good for Us?" Write the page numbers where you found text evidence.

How can using electronic devices have positive effects for kids?

Text Evidence 🔍

I read that kids who spend a lot of time using electronic devices _____

_____.

Page(s): _____

Video games can help _____.

Page(s): _____

Lerning to use technology is useful because _____.

Page(s): _____

How can using electronic devices have negative effects for kids?

Text Evidence 🔍

I read that kids who spend a lot of time using electronic devices _____

_____.

Page(s): _____

Kid use devices to talk to _____,

instead of _____.

Page(s): _____

Group Discussion Present your answers to the group. Cite text evidence to justify your thinking. Listen to and discuss the group's opinions about your answers.

Write Review your notes about "Are Electronic Devices Good for Us?" Then write your answer to the Essential Question. Use text evidence to support your answer. Use vocabulary words from this week's reading in your writing.

COLLABORATE

What are the positive and negative effects of new technology?

The positive effects of new technology are _____

_____

_____

_____

The negative effects of new technology are _____

_____

_____

_____

Share Writing Present your writing to the class. Discuss their opinions. Think about what the class has to say. Did they justify their claims? Explain why you agree or disagree with their claims.

COLLABORATE

I agree with _____ because _____.

I disagree because _____.

Write to Sources

Candice

Take Notes About the Text I took notes about the text on the chart to answer the question: *Is it good or bad for kids to spend a lot of time using electronic devices?*

pages 66–69

Topic	**Topic**
It is good for kids to use electronic devices.	It is bad for kids to use electronic devices.
Reason Kids spend more time doing physical activities.	**Reason** Kids don't get better grades.
Reason Video games may increase kids' visual attention.	**Reason** Kids use devices to talk to friends. They don't use devices to make new friends.
Reason Using interactive media can help students learn and sharpen reasoning abilities.	**Reason** It can be dangerous to meet people online.
Reason Kids need to know how to use technology for the future.	**Reason** Kids should learn to do other things than use electronic devices.

Write About the Text **I used my notes from my chart to write an opinion essay about the use of electronic devices.**

Student Model: *Opinion*

I think it is good for kids to spend time using electronic devices because there are many benefits. One study showed that kids who spend a lot of time on electronic devices do more physical activities. Action video games may increase kids' visual attention. Using interactive media can also help kids learn. Kids who use interactive media learn to sharpen their reasoning abilities. Finally, kids will need to use electronic devices for work in the future. It is very important that today's kids spend time using electronic devices.

TALK ABOUT IT

Text Evidence

Draw a box around a reason that comes from the notes. How does the reason support Candice's opinion?

Grammar

Underline a verb that is not in the present tense. Why did Candice use a different tense for this sentence?

Condense Ideas

Circle two sentences about interactive media. How can you combine these two sentences to condense the ideas?

Your Turn

Do you agree or disagree with the author of "Plugged In"? Why or why not? Use text evidence in your writing.

>> *Go Digital!*
Write your response online. Use your editing checklist.

Unit 2

Taking the Next Step

The Big Idea

What does it take to put a plan into action?

TALK ABOUT IT

? Essential Question

What do good problem solvers do?

>> *Go Digital*

COLLABORATE

What do you see on the flag? What did George Washington and Betsy Ross do to figure out what to put on a new flag? Describe what people can do to solve problems.

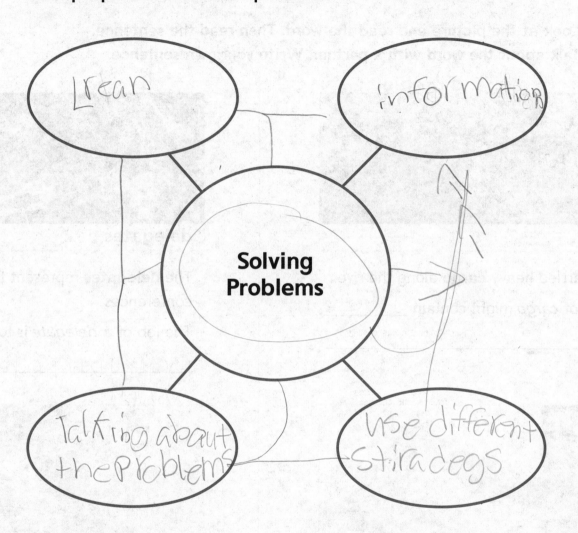

Lrean

information

Solving Problems

Talking about the Problems

Use different Stiradegs

Discuss what people need to do to be good problem solvers. Use the words from the chart. Complete the sentence:

A good way to solve a problem is by ___find more___ information

because ___you lream about it.___

77

More Vocabulary

COLLABORATE Look at the picture and read the word. Then read the sentence. Talk about the word with a partner. Write your own sentence.

cargo

The ship carried heavy **cargo** along the river.

The boxes of *cargo* might contain ___Food___

_____.

delegates

The **delegates** represent their country at conferences.

The job of a *delegate* is to ___what is happening and what people want.___

compromises

The partners make **compromises** by choosing colors they both like.

I make *compromises* with ___brother___

by ___cleaning___.

disguise

The boy wears a **disguise** for a costume party.

It's fun to wear a *disguise* on Halloween because ___you can get candy___.

78

Imported

The **imported** cars arrived on a ship from another country.

Imported means something comes from ____ _different country._

protests

Children attend **protests** to protect the environment.

People attend *protests* because they _want to show how they feel_ .

Words and Phrases
Transition Words

The transition words *consequently* and *therefore* tell why something happened and mean "as a result."

Tina broke her toe. <u>Consequently,</u> she cannot play soccer.

The grass is long. <u>Therefore,</u> Dad will cut the grass.

Read the sentences. Then answer the questions.

Adam likes to play soccer. *Therefore,* he will join a team.

Why will Adam join a soccer team? He will join as a result of _____ .

It is raining outside. *Consequently,* we are playing inside.

Why are we playing inside? We are playing inside as a result of _____ .

Complete the sentences using *consequently* and *therefore*.

My brother has the flu. _____,

he will not go to school.

Diego wore a disguise to the party. _____,

no one recognized him.

>> Go Digital Add the words *consequently* and *therefore* to your New Words notebook. Include your sentences.

COLLABORATE

1 Talk About It

Look at the picture. Read the title. Talk about what you see. Write your ideas.

What does the picture show?

_____

_____

What does the document show?

_____

_____

_____

What do the title and the document tell you the colonists are doing?

_____

_____

_____

Take notes as you read the text.

Creating a Nation

In CONGRESS, JULY 4, 1776.

Essential Question

?

What do good problem solvers do?

Read about how American colonists tried to solve their problems with Great Britain.

Peter Newark American Pictures/ Bridgeman Art Library

Taxes and Protests

In 1765, King George III of Great Britain needed money to rule his empire. How could he raise it? With taxes! Parliament, the law-making branch of the British government, passed a new tax called the Stamp Act. Every piece of paper sold in the American colonies had to carry a special stamp. Want to buy a newspaper? Stamp! Pay the tax.

To most colonists, the Stamp Act was unfair. The British had the right to choose representatives to speak for them in Parliament. The colonists had no such right. How could Parliament tax them if they had no voice in government?

The colonists held **protests** against the Stamp Act. Consequently, it was repealed, or canceled. But more taxes followed. Women protested a tax on cloth **imported** from Britain. How? They wove their own cloth at home.

Boston Tea Party: Some colonists disguised themselves as Native Americans.

Before long, the situation grew worse. In 1770, British soldiers fired into a disorderly crowd in Boston. Five colonists died. This tragedy is known as the Boston Massacre.

By 1773, most taxes had been repealed, or canceled, except the one on tea. One night, colonists held a protest called the Boston Tea Party. Dressed in **disguise**, they slipped onto three British ships in Boston Harbor and then they tossed the ships' **cargo**—tea—overboard.

Text Evidence

1 Comprehension

Problem and Solution

Reread the first paragraph. Underline the problem. Put a box around the solution.

The solution was _____

_____.

2 Specific Vocabulary Ⓐ Ⓒ Ⓣ

The phrase *speak for them* means "express the thoughts, feelings, and ideas of the group." Underline the text that tells who "speak for them." What do they do? Who does the pronoun *them* refer to?

_____

_____

3 Sentence Structure Ⓐ Ⓒ Ⓣ

Read the third sentence in the fifth paragraph. Circle the text that tells who the pronoun *they* refer to. What did they look like? Underline the text.

Text Evidence

1 Sentence Structure ACT

Reread the first sentence. Circle the text that tells what King George did to punish the colonists.

To punish the colonists, King

George _____

_____ .

2 Comprehension

Problem and Solution

Reread first and second paragraphs. Underline the text that tells the problem the First Continental Congress tried to solve.

The problem was _____

_____ .

COLLABORATE

3 Talk About It

Reread the third paragraph. Retell what happened at Lexington and Concord.

Revolution Begins

An angry King George punished the colonies by ordering the port of Boston closed and town meetings banned. Colonists called these harsh actions the "Intolerable Acts." However, they could not agree on how to resolve the problems with Great Britain. Patriots wanted to fight for independence. Loyalists wanted peace with the king. Many colonists were undecided.

Finally, colonists called for representatives from each colony to attend a convention. This important meeting, the First Continental Congress, took place in 1774 in Philadelphia. After discussion, the **delegates** decided to send a peace proposal to the king. Congress ended, but the trouble continued. In April 1775, there were rumors that the British were marching to Lexington and Concord, villages near Boston, to capture weapons that the patriots had hidden there.

The colonial militias were ready. Militias were groups of volunteers willing to fight. British troops attacked. The militias fired back. Surprisingly, the British retreated, or went back.

Now that war had begun, the patriots called for a Second Continental Congress in May. Delegates made George Washington commander of the new Continental Army. Congress also sent another peace proposal to King George.

As war continued, Congress formed committees to do important tasks. Five delegates were chosen to write a declaration of independence. This committee gave the job to one of its members—Thomas Jefferson.

Events of the American Revolution

1765	1766	1770	1773	1774	1775	1776	1778
Passage of Stamp Act		Boston Massacre		The First Continental Congress		Declaration of Independence	
	Repeal of Stamp Act		Boston Tea Party		• The Battle of Lexington and Concord		Alliance with France
					• Start of the Second Continental Congress		

Independence Declared

Jefferson knew he had to convince many colonists of the need for independence. As a result, he combined a variety of ideas to make his case. Individuals, he explained, had certain rights. These included life, liberty, and the pursuit of happiness. Governments were created to protect those rights. Instead, King George had taken away colonists' rights and freedoms. Therefore, the colonies had to separate from Britain.

Congress went on to debate Jefferson's points. As a result, his strong words against slavery were deleted. There were other **compromises**, too. But on July 4, 1776, Congress approved the Declaration of Independence. A nation was born. Washington's army fought on. Finally, in 1778, France joined the fight on America's side.

This was a turning point. In 1781, British troops surrendered in the war's last major battle. That year, Congress approved the Articles of Confederation. This document outlined a government for the former colonies. The United States was created as a confederation, or a union, of separate states. The Articles gave the states, rather than a central government, the power to make most decisions.

In 1783, King George finally recognized the nation's independence. By then, though, the United States government clearly wasn't working very well. The states often didn't agree with one another.

The revolution had ended. The work of shaping a government had just started. It would continue with a Constitutional Convention in 1787.

1781
- Last major battle of the War
- Approval of the Articles of Confederation

1783
King George recognizes independence of United States

1 Sentence Structure ACT

Reread the fourth sentence. Circle the text that the word *these* refer to. What does the sentence tell you?

The sentence tells about _____

_____.

2 Specific Vocabulary ACT

The words *turning point* mean "a time when important change happens." Underline the text that *turning point* refers to. What happened as a result? Put a box around the text that tells you.

3 Comprehension

Problem and Solution

Read the last paragraph. What problem still remained after the war ended? Write your answer.

_____

_____

_____

Make Connections

? Talk about some of the ways American colonists tried to solve their problems with Great Britain.
ESSENTIAL QUESTION

Think of a time you tried to solve a problem. How does your experience compare to the colonists'? **TEXT TO SELF**

(bkgd) Oleksiy Maksymenko/Alamy

83

Respond to the Text

Partner Discussion Work with a partner. Answer the questions. Discuss what you learned in "Creating a Nation." Write the page numbers where you found text evidence.

What problem did the colonists have?

I read that the British governent passed the Stamp Act which _____

_____.

The colonists held protests because _____

_____.

Text Evidence 🔍

Page(s): _____

Page(s): _____

How did the colonists solve the problem?

I learned that at the two meeting of Continental Congress, the

colonists tried _____

_____.

Congress asked Thomas Jefferson to _____

_____.

Text Evidence 🔍

Page(s): _____

Page(s): _____

Group Discussion Present your answers to the group. Cite text evidence to justify your thinking. Listen to and discuss the group's opinions about your answers.

84

COLLABORATE

Write Review your notes about "Creating a Nation." Then write your answer to the Essential Question. Use text evidence to support your answer. Use vocabulary words from this week's reading in your writing.

How were the colonists good at solving their problem?

The colonists had good problem solving skills because _____

_____.

The colonists protested in order to _____

_____.

When they decided to fight for independence, they _____

_____

_____

_____.

COLLABORATE

Share Writing Present your writing to the class. Discuss their opinions. Think about what the class has to say. Did they justify their claims? Explain why you agree or disagree with their claims.

I agree with _____ because _____.

I disagree because _____.

85

Write to Sources

Take Notes About the Text I took notes on the sequence chart to answer the question: *What sequence of events caused the colonies to declare independence from Britain?*

pages 80–83

Oscar

Event
The British government passed the Stamp Act and other taxes. Colonists thought these taxes were unfair.

Event
British soldiers killed five colonists in the Boston Massacre in 1770.

Event
King George closed Boston ports and banned town meetings. In 1775, British troops attacked militias near Boston.

Event
In 1776, Congress approved the Declaration of Independence.

Write About the Text I used notes from my chart to write about the events that caused the colonists to declare independence.

Student Model: *Informative Text*

A sequence of events caused the colonies to declare independence. First, the British government passed taxes. The colonists thought they were unfair. As a result, the colonists held protests. Next, in 1770, British soldiers killed five colonists during the Boston Massacre. Consequently, ports in Boston closed and town meeting were not allowed. Then in 1775, British troops attacked militias near Boston and fighting began. Finally, Congress approved the Declaration of Independence in 1776.

TALK ABOUT IT

COLLABORATE

Text Evidence
Draw a box around a sentence that comes from the notes. What words did Oscar use to show the information appears in sequence?

Grammar
Circle a past tense verb. Why did Oscar use past tense verbs to write the paragraph?

Connect Ideas
Underline the sentences about the first event. How can you combine the sentences to connect the ideas?

Your Turn
COLLABORATE

What is the author's point of view of the British? Use text evidence in your writing.

>> *Go Digital!*
Write your response online. Use your editing checklist.

TALK ABOUT IT

Weekly Concept Seeking the Answer

? **Essential Question**
What can you do to get the information you need?

>> *Go Digital*

COLLABORATE

What is the girl doing? What is she learning about? How can people get information? Write the ways people get information in the chart.

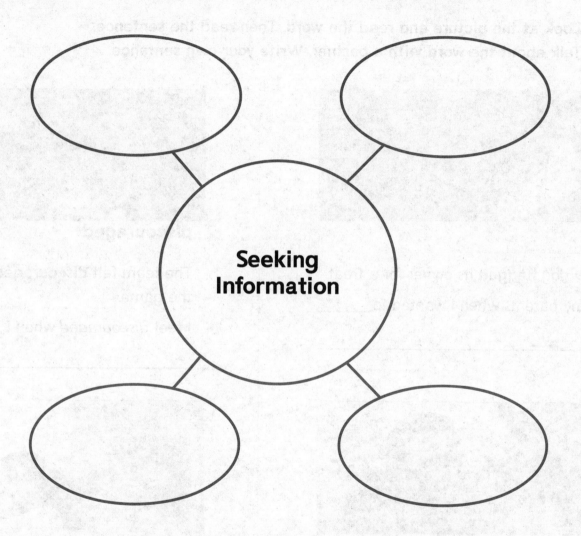

Seeking Information

Discuss the ways people get information. Use words from the chart. You can say:

People can get information by _____

_____.

More Vocabulary

Look at the picture and read the word. Then read the sentence.
Talk about the word with a partner. Write your own sentence.

begged

The hungry dog **begged** its owner for a treat.

I *begged* my parents when I wanted to _____

_____

compass

The hikers use a **compass** to check the direction.

Campers carry a *compass* when they _____

_____.

discouraged

The team felt **discouraged** when they lost the game.

I feel *discouraged* when I _____

_____.

eagerly

The students **eagerly** raised their hands to answer the teacher's question.

A puppy *eagerly* _____

when its owner comes home.

personally

The boy **personally** delivered newspapers to people in his neighborhood.

I will *personally* thank _____

_____.

quest

The swimmer had a **quest** to win the gold medal.

Another word for *quest* is _____.

Words and Phrases
Phrasal Verbs

powered up = **turned on or start**
Lee <u>powered up</u> her computer and searched the Web to gather information for her new project.

put up = **hung, as on a wall or ceiling**
The summer campers <u>put up</u> photos of their families in the cabins.

Read the sentences below. Write the phrasal verb that means the same as the underlined words.

Len <u>started</u> the model plane for take off.

Len _____ the model plane for take off.

Mrs. Zajac <u>hung</u> our solar system models.

Mrs. Zajac _____ our solar system models.

>> Go Digital Add the phrasal verbs to your New Words notebook. Write a sentence to show the meaning of each.

COLLABORATE

1 Talk About It

Look at the illustration. Talk about what you see. Write your ideas.

Based on the title, what do you think the story is about?

_____

_____

_____

_____

What are the girl and the boy doing?

_____

_____

_____

Take notes as you read the story.

A Modern Cinderella

Essential Question

? **What can you do to get the information you need?**

Read how a dancing Prince tries to get information about a mystery girl.

Once upon a time—the time being the other night—the Prince was as joyous as a gamer with the new highest score. He had just danced with an amazing young woman at the Royal Palace. It was during the taping of his weekly TV show, *Dancing with the Prince*. He had only agreed to do the show to help his mother, the Queen, raise money for charity. But when the prince twirled this lovely dancer in the presence of the audience and judges, he felt as if he were floating on a cloud.

However, circumstances changed as soon as the music stopped at midnight. As the applause began, the young woman's cell phone rang, and she rushed from the palace. All she left behind was a purple sneaker.

The Prince fell into a dungeon of despair. "I must find her again," he cried, "and in time for tomorrow night's final show!" How should he search? He clutched the purple sneaker in his hand.

Seeing the Prince's tears, the Queen advised, "He who consults the right sources will surely succeed." The Prince's mind raced like a galloping horse on his favorite game, "Horse Chaser." After much consideration, he made a plan. First, he interviewed everyone who had attended the show, but no one could help. Next, the Prince searched the Internet. He entered the phrase "great dancer with purple shoe," but he found no one. Then the Prince put up posters of the purple sneaker all over the kingdom's social network. Yet no one recognized the shoe or knew its owner.

Text Evidence

1 Sentence Structure Ⓐ Ⓒ Ⓣ

Reread the first sentence. Circle the text that tells when Prince was joyous. Why does the sentence include a gamer with new highest score?

The text describes _____

_____.

2 Specific Vocabulary Ⓐ Ⓒ Ⓣ

The word *despair* means "unhappiness." How does Prince feel? Underline text that provides clues to Prince's feelings.

I know that Prince feels _____

because _____.

COLLABORATE

3 Talk About It

Reread the fourth paragraph. What is the Queen's advice? Write about it.

_____

_____

93

Text Evidence

1 Specific Vocabulary Ⓐ Ⓒ Ⓣ

The phrase *even if* tells that something will still be true if Prince travels the entire kingdom. Underline the text that tells what will still be true.

2 Comprehension

Compare and Contrast

Reread the third paragraph. Put a box around the text that compares all of Prince's visits to the homes.

The result was similar because

_____.

The result was different because

_____.

COLLABORATE

3 Talk About It

Reread the fourth paragraph. Why did Prince grow sadder?

The Prince grew sadder because

_____.

The Prince held the purple sneaker in one hand and his computer **compass** in the other. "I will continue my **quest**," he cried, "even if I must **personally** travel the entire kingdom." With that, the Prince powered up his royal electric skateboard and set out!

At the first house, a woman came out to greet the Prince. He held out the sneaker and announced, "This shoe will tell me if you are my destiny." The excited woman struggled to jam her large foot into the shoe, but the sneaker was much too small.

At the next house, another woman **eagerly** tried on the sneaker. The shoe flopped and fell off. At every home the Prince visited, the purple sneaker seemed as big as a boat or as small as a seed. Every foot failed to meet his expectations.

As the day wore on, the Prince grew sadder. His **discouraged** heart was a cell phone in need of recharging. Finally, there was only one house left to visit. When the Prince arrived, three sisters stood in front, offering their feet. (They'd been following the newsfeed.) The shoe fit none of them.

"Does anyone else live here?" a weary Prince asked the sisters. From inside the house came a chime. The sisters' eyes became narrow slits. A young woman stepped outside and handed a phone to the oldest sister.

The Prince quickly held out the sneaker and requested, "Please try this on."

She did, and it fit her foot perfectly!

"You're my missing dancer!" the Prince cried. "Will you be my dance partner forever?"

The young woman smiled and replied, "Thanks, but not right now. I'll dance tomorrow, but I have a lot of plans. First I want to travel."

The Prince **begged**, "Please, say yes! After all, this is a fairy tale, where anything can happen."

"Sorry, Prince," the woman said. "You'll just have to wait."

"That's cool," the Prince sighed, "but at least reveal your name."

"It's Cinderella," the woman replied. She scribbled on a piece of paper. "Here's my number. Let's stay in touch. TTYLP."

The Prince looked puzzled and was unsure of how to reply.

"It means Talk To You Later, Prince," Cinderella explained.

"TTYLC," the Prince replied as he waved to Cinderella and rode away.

And they texted happily ever after.

Make Connections

? Talk about how the Prince got the information he needed. What things did he do? **ESSENTIAL QUESTION**

When have you had to search for something or someone? How did you search? **TEXT TO SELF**

Text Evidence

1 **Sentence Structure** (A)(C)(T)

Reread the fourth paragraph. Draw a box around the text that tells Cinderella's response to Prince's request. What is her reason?

Cinderella's response is _____

_____

because_____.

2 **Specific Vocabulary** (A)(C)(T)

The word *puzzled* means "confused." Circle the context clues for the word *puzzled*. Why is Prince puzzled?

He is puzzled because _____

_____.

3 **Comprehension**
Compare and Contrast

How do Cinderella and Prince decide to stay in touch? Underline the text. Why does Prince reply with TTYLC? Write your answer.

Prince replies with TTYLC because

_____.

Respond to the Text

Partner Discussion Work with a partner. Answer the questions. Discuss what you read in "A Modern Cinderella." Write the page numbers where you found text evidence.

How did the Prince meet the woman with the purple shoe?

Prince met the woman during _____.

He thought the woman was _____.

Text Evidence 🔍

Page(s): _____

Page(s): _____

What did the Prince do to find the girl with the purple shoe?

Prince visited _____.

At each house, he _____,

but _____.

Finally, at the last house Prince found _____

_____

Cinderella told Prince _____.

Text Evidence 🔍

Page(s): _____

Page(s): _____

Page(s): _____

Page(s): _____

Group Discussion Present your answers to the group. Cite text evidence to justify your thinking. Listen to and discuss the group's opinions about your answers.

COLLABORATE

Write Review your notes about "A Modern Cinderella." Then write your answer to the Essential Question. Use text evidence to support your answer. Use vocabulary words from this week's reading in your writing.

How did the Prince find Cinderella?

After the yound woman left, the Prince found a _____.

To find the woman, the Prince _____

_____.

Finally, he found the woman _____

_____.

When he found Cinderella, he asked _____.

Cinderella told Prince _____.

They decided to _____.

COLLABORATE

Share Writing Present your writing to the class. Discuss their opinions. Think about what the class has to say. Did they justify their claims? Explain why you agree or disagree with their claims.

I agree with _____ because _____.

I disagree because _____.

97

Write to Sources

Kara

Take Notes About the Text I took notes on the chart to answer the question: *What did Cinderella and the mysterious caller talk about after during the phone call?*

pages 92–95

Text Clue	Conclusion
At midnight Cinderella's cell phone rang.	The phone call reminds Cinderella or tells her to do something.
She ran from the palace.	Cinderella needed to go somewhere or do something quickly. The caller tells her to leave or go somewhere quickly.
She left behind a purple sneaker.	She ran so fast, she forgot her sneaker.

Write About the Text I used notes from my chart to write
a dialogue between Cinderella and the caller.

Student Model: *Narrative Text*

Cinderella heard the cell phone ring. At that
moment, she remembered something. She quickly
called back. "Hello. I already know why you called,"
Cinderella said.

"It's midnight! Don't forget that you promised
to meet me," the mysterious caller replied.

Cinderella said, "I know. I know. I'm leaving
right now. I will run so the Prince doesn't try to
stop me."

The caller yelled, "Hurry!"

Cinderella ran from the palace quickly. As
she ran, one purple sneaker came off her foot,
but she didn't stop.

TALK ABOUT IT

COLLABORATE

Text Evidence

Draw a box around a sentence that comes from
the notes. Is the information from a text clue or
a conclusion? How do you know?

Grammar

Circle a future-tense verb. Why did Kara use a
future-tense verb?

Condense Ideas

Underline the sentences that describe what
Cinderella did when the cell phone rang. How can
you condense ideas to create one detailed sentence?

Your Turn

COLLABORATE

Add an event to the beginning of
the story to tell what the Prince said
at the start of his TV show. Use text
evidence in your writing.

>> Go Digital!
Write your response online. Use your editing checklist.

Essential Question

How do we investigate questions about nature?

>> *Go Digital*

COLLABORATE

What details can you see when you look closely at the grasshopper? What can you seen when you investigate nature? Write the details you observe in the chart.

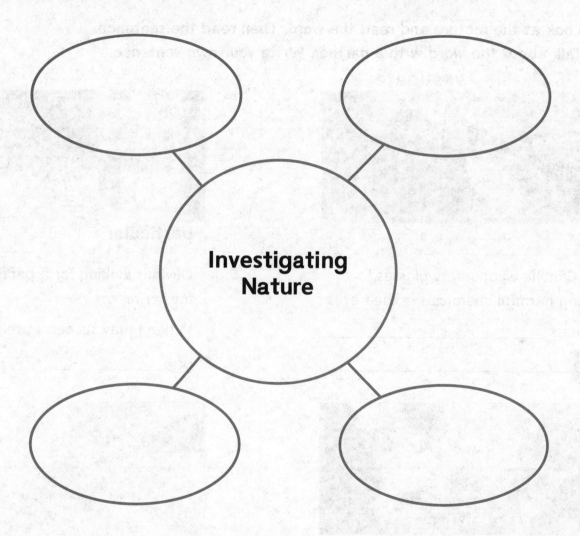

Investigating Nature

Discuss what you observe when you are investigating nature. Use words from the chart. You can say:

Looking closely, I can see _____.

When I investigate nature, I can observe _____.

More Vocabulary

COLLABORATE

Look at the picture and read the word. Then read the sentence. Talk about the word with a partner. Write your own sentence.

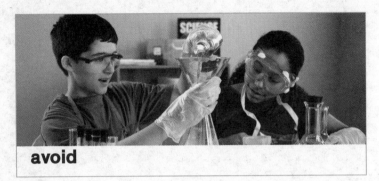

avoid

Justin and Camille wear safety glasses to **avoid** getting harmful chemicals in their eyes.

A cyclist wears _____

to *avoid* _____.

particular

Olivia is looking for a **particular** book to use for her report.

When I play soccer, I use a *particular* type

of _____.

interact

The players **interact** with the coach during the game.

I *interact* with my partner when we _____

_____.

prevent

We wash our hands to **prevent** the spread of germs.

Another word for *prevent* is _____

_____.

threatened

The animals are **threatened** by the large and hungry lion.

Small animals are *threatened* by larger animals because _____.

wondered

Amy **wondered** how the jet could fly with the space shuttle on it.

When I looked at the sky, I *wondered* _____

_____.

Words and Phrases
Transition Words

as well = also or too
Peter went to soccer practice and played in a game of basketball <u>as well</u>.

still = continue to be
Jan turned on all the lights in the house because she was <u>still</u> afraid of the dark.

Read the sentences below. Write the word or phrase that means the same as the underlined words.

Although Jasmine slept well, she <u>continued to be</u> tired.

Although Jasmine slept well, she was _____ tired.

Ethan read a story and wrote an essay <u>too</u>.

Ethan read a story and wrote an essay_____.

>> *Go Digital* Add *as well* and *was still* to your New Words notebook. Write a sentence to show the meaning of each.

Growing in Place

The Story of
E. Lucy Braun

iris

1 Talk About It

Look at the illustrations. Read the title. Talk about what you see. Write your ideas.

What does the title tell you?

_____

_____

_____

Based on the illustrations, what did Lucy Braun study? Justify your answer.

_____

_____

_____

Take notes as you read the text.

Essential Question

? How do we investigate questions about nature?

Read about how Lucy Braun's classification of plants continues to help scientists today.

Taking Root

How could two different things have the same name? Emma Lucy Braun might have **wondered** that as a child. Born in Cincinnati, Ohio, in 1889, Emma shared her first name with her mother. To **avoid** confusion, she used her middle name, Lucy. Naming things correctly became the basis for her life's work on plants.

Even as a child, Lucy was interested in plants. She often joined her older sister Annette and their parents on energetic walks through the nearby woods. Lucy enjoyed all the plants and wildflowers. Some seemed to shout at her with their wild colors. Others hid behind rocks and logs.

Lucy asked her mother how to tell all the plants apart. Lucy's mother taught her to develop her powers of observation. She pointed out the number and shape of leaves on a stem. Lucy kept a record of their observations. She also learned to draw what she saw. Then she could compare and contrast all sorts of plants.

Lucy and her mother gathered specimens for their herbarium, a collection of dried plants. They preserved leaves and flowers between sheets of paper. Lucy became more and more interested in botany, the study of plants. In high school, she started collecting and drying plants for her own herbarium. She continued adding plants all her life.

pink redstem filagrees

1 **Sentence Structure** Ⓐ Ⓒ Ⓣ

Reread the last sentence in the first paragraph. Circle the text that tells about Lucy's work. Why is naming things correctly important?

_____

2 **Specific Vocabulary** Ⓐ Ⓒ Ⓣ

Reread the first sentence in the last paragraph. Circle the text that tells what *herbarium* means. Write the definition in your own words.

Herbarium means _____

_____

3 **Comprehension**

Sequence

How did Lucy's interest in botany develop? Put a box around the events that helped Lucy develop her interest. Write about it.

_____

_____

1 Specific Vocabulary ACT

The word *fellow* means "someone who is in a similar situation as you." Underline the text that tells you why Lucy needed fellow ecologists.

2 Comprehension

Sequence

What events happened while Lucy attended university? Put a box around words that tell you. Write about the events.

_____

_____

_____

COLLABORATE

3 Talk About It

How did Lucy and her sister continue their scientific behaviors at home? Write your ideas.

At home, they _____

_____.

Lucy Braun's Snakeroot: This plant grows in Kentucky and Tennessee.

iris

robin's egg

nest

By making sketches, scientists learn to see details in natural objects.

Branching Out

Lucy and Annette attended the University of Cincinnati. Annette wanted to become an entomologist and study insects. Lucy took classes in geology, or the study of rocks and minerals. Her work with geologists transformed how she looked at the natural world. She continued her studies in botany, as well.

Lucy also became interested in ecology. Ecology looks at how living things **interact** with environments. Fellow ecologists helped her test an important theory. Lucy believed that plant life in some areas had been able to migrate over time. She mapped this movement back to when glaciers covered those regions with ice!

In Full Bloom

In 1917, Lucy began to teach botany at the University of Cincinnati. She and Annette lived in a house near the woods. Even at home the sisters continued their scientific behaviors. Lucy tended both indoor and outdoor gardens. Annette studied the moths that fluttered in a flurry of wings around lights outside. The sisters named part of their house "the science wing."

Lucy collected plants from all around the country. She photographed many of them, too. Color photography was still new at the time. Because of that, people enjoyed her lectures and slide shows a great deal.

The Fruits of Her Labor

Later in her life, Lucy wrote many field guides. Field guides are books that identify plants found in a **particular** area. In 1950, she published her most important guide. It describes the plants in the forests of the eastern United States. Ecologists still use it to study changes in the forests over time.

Today, Lucy has a few plants named after her. One of them, Lucy Braun's snakeroot, is currently **threatened**. Lucy's work in conservation, the protection of nature, may help scientists **prevent** its disappearance.

Lucy Braun lived to be 81 years old. In her years as a botanist, Lucy collected nearly 12,000 plants! Today her herbarium is part of the Smithsonian Institution in Washington, D.C. Visitors can study the plants she collected all her life.

(bkgd) RoseAnn Hayes;
(inset) J.S. Peterson/USDA

Plant Identification

Become a budding botanist! Follow these steps to identify plants in your area.

Materials: a magnifying glass and a reliable field guide

1. Identify the state or region and habitat where the plant grows.
2. Identify whether the leaf is evergreen or broad leaf.
3. Draw or photograph the leaf to record its shape and other details.
4. Observe the arrangement of leaves on the stem. See if they are opposite each other or not.
5. Narrow the list of possible plants in the field guide. Then find an exact match.

Make Connections

Talk about how the advice of Lucy's mother was helpful to Lucy's study of nature. **ESSENTIAL QUESTION**

Tell about a collection that you have or might like to start. How could you organize your collection? **TEXT TO SELF**

Text Evidence

1 Sentence Structure A C T

Reread the second sentence. Underline the phrase about field guides. What do the verbs tell you?

The verbs _____

_____ tell that field guides

_____.

2 Specific Vocabulary A C T

The word *whether* tells you that there is a choice to make. Circle the choices.

The choices about the _____

_____ are _____

or _____.

3 Comprehension Sequence

Reread the page. Circle the signal words. What do they describe?

The signal words _____

_____ tell about when

_____.

107

Respond to the Text

Partner Discussion Work with a partner. Answer the questions. Discuss what you learned about "Growing in Place." Write the page numbers where you found text evidence.

How did Lucy Braun become interested in plants as a child?

Text Evidence

I read that Lucy's mother taught Lucy to _____

_____.

Page(s): _____

For their herbarium, Lucy and her mother_____

_____.

Page(s): _____

How did Lucy Braun study plants later in life?

Text Evidence

In college, Lucy tested a theory about _____

_____.

Page(s): _____

Lucy studied plants at home by _____

_____.

Page(s): _____

Later, Lucy wrote _____.

Page(s): _____

Group Discussion Present your answers to the group. Cite text evidence to justify your thinking. Listen to and discuss the group's opinions about your answers.

Write Review your notes about "Growing in Place." Then write your answer to the Essential Question. Use text evidence to support your answer. Use vocabulary words from this week's reading in your writing.

How did Lucy Braun investigate plants?

During her childhood, Lucy learned about _____

_____.

In college, Lucy developed her interest by _____

_____.

After college, Lucy continued to _____

_____.

Share Writing Present your writing to the class. Discuss their opinions. Think about what the class has to say. Did they justify their claims? Explain why you agree or disagree with their claims.

I agree with _____ because _____.

I disagree because _____.

Take Notes About the Text I took notes about the text on the chart to answer the question: *How does the Plant Identification sidebar support the information in the text?*

pages 104–107

Darius

Detail
Step 2 tells to identify plants using leaves. Lucy learned to examine the shape and number of the leaves.

Topic
The Plant Identification sidebar supports the information in the text.

Detail
Step 3 tells to draw or photograph the leaves and record details. Lucy learned to record observations and draw plants in Ohio.

Detail
Step 5 instructs to match the plants using a field guide. Lucy wrote field guides.

Write About the Text **I used notes from my chart to write about how the sidebar supports the information in the text.**

Student Model: *Informative Text*

The Plant Identification sidebar supports the information in the text because it explains the steps Lucy used to identify plants. For example, step 2 in the sidebar instructs to identify plants using the shape of the leaves. Lucy learned to use the shape and number of leaves to identify plants. Step 3 instructs drawing or photographing the leaves. Lucy wrote about and drew the plants in the woods in Ohio. Finally, step 5 instructs to match the plant in a field guide. Lucy wrote many field guides. The steps in the sidebar support the process Lucy used to identify plants.

TALK ABOUT IT
COLLABORATE

Text Evidence
Draw a box around a sentence that comes from the notes. How did Darius use this detail to show it supported text information?

Grammar
Circle an irregular plural noun. What makes the word an irregular plural noun?

Connect Ideas
Underline the sentences that describe a step from the sidebar and what Lucy did. How can you combine the sentences to connect the ideas?

Your Turn
COLLABORATE

What influenced Lucy to become a scientist? Use text evidence in your writing.

>> Go Digital
Write your response online. Use your editing checklist.

? Essential Question

When has a plan helped you accomplish a task?

>> *Go Digital*

What task is the man in the photograph doing? How does having a plan help people complete tasks? Describe how having plans helps people.

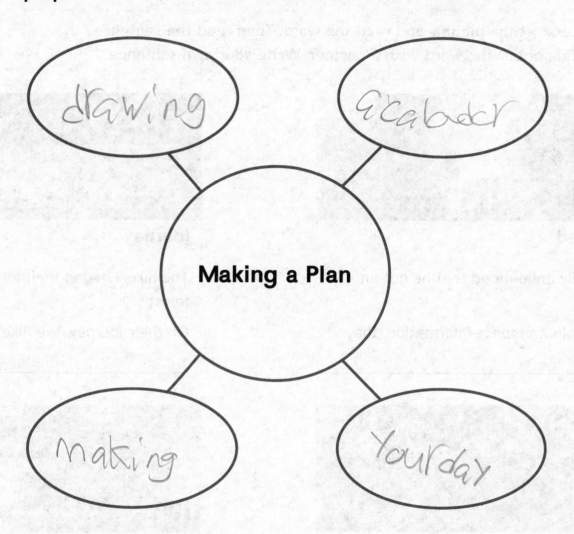

drawing

acabadr

Making a Plan

making

Yourday

Discuss how having a plan helps people do things. Use words from the chart. You can say:

Having a plan helps people to complete tasks by organized

_____.

More Vocabulary

Look at the picture and read the word. Then read the sentence. Talk about the word with a partner. Write your own sentence.

announced

Sean happily **announced** that he got an *A+* on the test.

When people *announce* information, they _tell other People_ .

brocade

The woven **brocade** included colorful flowers.

A *brocade* can be used for _Alecihen dres_ .

journey

The hikers began their long **journey** into the forest.

On their *journey*, the hikers saw _tres_ _grass Path_ .

lend

Mrs. Nelson **lends** a book to John until the end of the month.

I will *lend* _my soccer ball_ to _my Friend_ .

magnificent

The visitors enjoy the Grand Canyon's **magnificent** views of colorful rock layers.

I want to see the *magnificent* views of ___super car and a watr fall___.

weaving

The woman enjoys **weaving** yarn to make cloth.

In some parts of the world, *weaving* is an important ___to make blacket___.

regardless = **without effect**
It was cloudy outside, but the family went to the beach <u>*regardless*</u>.

soon afterward = **a short time after an event**
Caryn stopped at the library, and <u>*soon afterward*</u> *she went home.*

Read the sentences below. Write the word that completes each sentence.

Ivan will not win the race but he will run until the end of the race _____.

Brianna went to sleep and _____ was awakened by a noise.

The bird made a nest and _____ laid some eggs.

_____ of the rain, Tara will walk to school.

>> Go Digital Add the words *regardless* and *soon afterward* to your New Words notebook. Write a sentence to show the meaning of each.

Pixtal/age fotostock; Melvyn Longhurst China/Alamy

115

COLLABORATE

1 Talk About It

Read the title. Talk about what you see. Write your ideas.

What does the title tell you?

_____

_____

_____

_____

What kind of place do you see?

_____

_____

_____

_____

Take notes as you read the story.

The Magical Lost Brocade

Essential Question

? When has a plan helped you accomplish a task?

Read about how Ping follows a plan to find a lost brocade.

Long ago, in China, a poor woman and her son, Ping, lived in a tiny hut. The woman earned a living **weaving** beautiful **brocade** hangings, which her son sold. She wished she could give Ping a better home, but alas, that was impossible. So she decided to weave a brocade of a **magnificent** house with gardens. **At least** they could look at something lovely. It took three years to complete the brocade, and it was her finest work. However, soon afterward, a great wind swept into their hut and carried it away! The woman was grief-stricken. So Ping went off in pursuit of the brocade, assuring his mother he would bring it home.

Ping walked for three days and came to a stone house. A bearded man sat outside. "I'm searching for my mother's brocade," Ping said.

"A brocade flew by three days ago," said the man. "Now it's in a palace far away. I'll explain how you can get there and **lend** you my horse." Ping thanked the man and bowed deeply to express his gratitude.

"First, you must ride through Fire Valley," said the man. "You must cross over it regardless of the scorching heat, without uttering a word. If you utter even a single sound, you'll burn!" He continued, "After you've crossed Fire Valley, you'll arrive at Ice Ocean. You must ride through the icy waters without shivering. If you shiver even once, the outcome will be terrible! The sea will swallow you up!" The old man paused before concluding, "When you emerge from the sea, you'll be facing the Mountain of the Sun. The mountain is as steep as a straight line up to the sky! The palace sits on top of the mountain, and the brocade is in the palace."

Shawna Tenney

Text Evidence 🔍

1 Specific Vocabulary Ⓐ Ⓒ Ⓣ

The phrase *at least* means "even if something better is not true." Circle the text the sentence refers to. Underline the text that tells what the woman really wanted. Rewrite the sentence.

Although the woman didn't have

_____,

at least she had _____

_____.

2 Sentence Structure Ⓐ Ⓒ Ⓣ

Reread the last sentence in the first paragraph. Underline the text that tells why Ping left home. What did he tell his mother?

Ping told his mother that he will

_____.

3 Comprehension

Reread the last paragraph. Put a box around the text that tells what Ping must do to get the brocade. Then circle the text that tells what Ping must not do.

117

❶ Sentence Structure ACT

Reread the second sentence. Underline the text that tells about where Ping is going. Rewrite the sentence to describe the trip.

Ping arrived at _____

_____.

❷ Specific Vocabulary ACT

The word *grasping* means "holding something firmly." Circle the text that explains why Ping is grasping the reins.

Ping is grasping the reins because

_____.

COLLABORATE

❸ Talk About It

Discuss who or what helped Ping complete the journey to the palace. Justify your answer.

_____

_____

"It sounds like an extremely difficult **journey**," said Ping, "but I'll do my very best." He mounted the horse and traveled for three days, reaching the Fire Valley. As he crossed the valley, angry flames leaped out at him. The intense heat brought tears to Ping's eyes, but he said nothing.

When he reached the other side of the valley, he saw the Ice Ocean. With Ping's gentle guidance, the horse entered the frigid waters. The sea touched Ping with icy fingers, but he didn't shiver once. So horse and rider crossed the sea, emerging safely on the other side.

Next, Ping approached the Mountain of the Sun. He rode up the steep mountain, **grasping** the reins for dear life! Finally, he reached the top and dismounted at the palace door.

A lovely princess welcomed him. "I'm Princess Ling," she said. "I thought your mother's brocade was beautiful and wanted to copy it. So I sent a great wind to your home. I've now copied the brocade, so please take it home. Have a safe journey."

Shawna Tenney

"Thank you," said Ping, who stared at the beautiful princess. She was a perfect rose. He wondered if he could see her again and detected a **knowing** smile on her face as they said good-bye.

Ping mounted his horse, placing the brocade under his jacket. First, he rode down the steep Mountain of the Sun. Next, he rode back across Ice Ocean, without shivering once. Then he rode across Fire Valley, without making a sound. Finally, he arrived at the home of the bearded man, who sat outside just as he had the previous time. Ping thanked him, returned his horse, and began the long walk home.

Ping arrived home three days later. "Here is your brocade, Mother!" he **announced** as she cried tears of joy. Together, they unrolled it, and before their eyes, the brocade came to life! Suddenly their hut became a magnificent house with gardens. But that wasn't all—standing before them was Princess Ling! Ping and the princess got married, and a year later, Ping's mother became a loving grandmother. They all lived happily together in their beautiful home and gardens!

Make Connections

? Talk about how having a plan helped Ping accomplish his task. How did following the plan lead to his finding the lost brocade? ESSENTIAL QUESTION

When have you followed a plan in order to accomplish a task? Briefly describe the steps of the plan. TEXT TO SELF

Text Evidence 🔍

1 Specific Vocabulary Ⓐ Ⓒ Ⓣ

The word *knowing* tells that you know about something without saying anything about it. Circle the text in the last paragraph that tells you why Princess Ling had a knowing smile.

2 Sentence Structure Ⓐ Ⓒ Ⓣ

Read the fifth sentence in the second paragraph. Underline the text that tells you what the bearded man did the previous time.

The previous time, the bearded

man _____

_____.

3 Comprehension

Theme

Put a box around the text that tells you whether Ping kept his promise. How did a plan help Ping?

The plan helped Ping by _____

_____

_____.

Respond to the Text

Partner Discussion Work with a partner. Answer the questions. Discuss what you learned about "The Magical Lost Brocade." Write the page numbers where you found text evidence.

What plan must Ping follow to reach the palace?

First, Ping must _____.

Then, Ping must _____.

Finally, Ping must _____.

Text Evidence 🔍

Page(s): _____

Page(s): _____

Page(s): _____

How does the plan help Ping reach the palace?

At the top of the mountain, _____.

Princess Ling explains that _____.

When Ping returns home with the brocade, _____

_____.

Text Evidence 🔍

Page(s): _____

Page(s): _____

Page(s): _____

Group Discussion Present your answers to the group. Cite text evidence to justify your thinking. Listen to and discuss the group's opinions about your answers.

Write Review your notes about "The Magical Lost Brocade." Then write your answer to the Essential Question. Use text evidence to support your answer. Use vocabulary words from this week's reading in your writing.

How does a plan help Ping find the lost brocade?

Ping promises his mother_____.

On his journey, he meets the bearded man, who tells Ping _____

_____.

Ping follows the plan by _____

_____.

The plan helps Ping because _____

_____.

Share Writing Present your writing to the class. Discuss their opinions. Think about what the class has to say. Did they justify their claims? Explain why you agree or disagree with their claims.

I agree with _____ because _____.

I disagree because _____.

Write to Sources

Callie

Take Notes About the Text I took notes about the text on the chart to answer the question: *What event can you add to show how Princess Ling gets to Ping's house?*

pages 116–119

Text Clue	Conclusion
The princess lives in a palace. To get to the palace, Ping crossed Fire Valley, rode through Ice Ocean, and climbed the Mountain of the Sun.	The princess lives far away from Ping's home and it is difficult to get there.
Text Clue	**Conclusion**
The princess sent a great wind to get the brocade from Ping's house.	The princess has the power to use wind to get things for her.
Text Clue	**Conclusion**
Ping and his mother unrolled the brocade. The house from the brocade and Princess Ling appeared in front of them.	The princess traveled to Ping's house by wind. She got inside the brocade. She appeared when Ping and his mother unrolled the brocade.

Write About the Text I used notes from my chart to write a narrative that tells how Princess Ling gets to Ping's house.

Student Model: *Narrative Text*

Princess Ling lived in a palace on top of a mountain. The palace was far away from Ping's home. However, she had the power to use wind to help her reach Ping's house. First, she had the wind carry her to Ping's house over the Mountain of the Sun, the Ice Ocean, and Fire Valley. She thanked the wind for carrying her. Next, she waited until Ping arrived at his home. Then, she got inside the brocade. Finally, when Ping and his mother unrolled the brocade, Princess Ling appeared in front of them.

TALK ABOUT IT

COLLABORATE

Text Evidence

Draw a box around a sentence that comes from the notes. Is the information from a text clue or conclusion? How do you know?

Grammar

Circle a possessive pronoun and a possessive noun. How are they different?

Condense Ideas

Underline the sentences that tell about the palace. How can you combine them in one sentence?

Your Turn

COLLABORATE

Write about another place that Ping travels through before the Ice Ocean. Use text evidence in your writing.

≫ *Go Digital!*
Write your response online. Use your editing checklist.

TALK ABOUT IT

Weekly Concept Making It Happen

? **Essential Question**
What motivates you to accomplish a goal?

» *Go Digital*

124

What do the boy and girl in the photograph want to accomplish? What will they have to do? How do people accomplish their goals? Describe what they have to do in the chart.

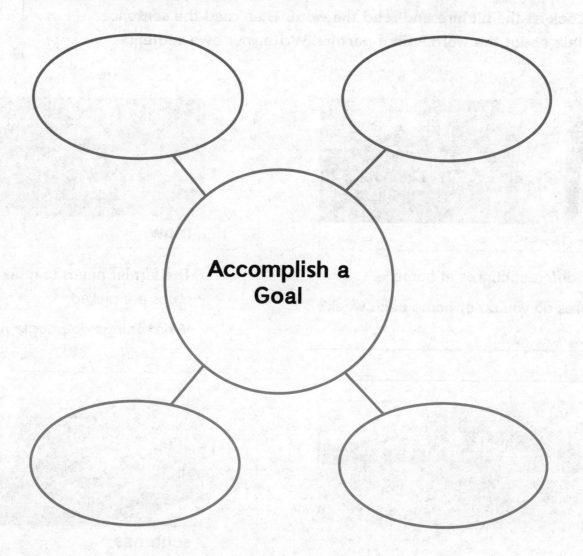

Accomplish a Goal

Discuss how people accomplish their goals. Use words from the chart. You can say:

To accomplish a goal, a person must _____

_____.

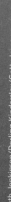

More Vocabulary

COLLABORATE

Look at the picture and read the word. Then read the sentence.
Talk about the word with a partner. Write your own sentence.

chores

Erika does different **chores** at home.

What chores do you do at home each week?

clean leaves cleanfor
take out the trash

glimpse

You can **glimpse** dolphins playing in the ocean.

What do you glimpse when you look out from a moving car? someone runing

_____

_____

mow

The farmer needs to **mow** the field after the crops are picked.

What things do people mow? grass
corn wheat carrot
potato

schemes

The pets have **schemes** for getting the food.

What schemes have you tried at home?

_____

_____

David Buffington/Blend Images/Getty Images; Jaroslaw Pawlak/iStock/360/Getty Images; Michael Pettigrew/iStock/360/Getty Images; Martin Ruegner/Getty Images

126

Poetry Terms

free verse

A **free verse** poem does not rhyme. It has no set line length.

I'm unhappy when dirty dishes are piled in the kitchen.

narrative

A **narrative** poem tells a story. It has characters and may have dialogue. It can rhyme.

My grandpa is a mountain,
Worrying, watching, tall.
I stand in his shadow, silent as a stone.

repetition

A poem has **repetition** when words or phrases repeat. Repetition helps to stress the meaning.

Training, training every day,

I train my pony my own way!

rhyme

Rhyme is the repetition of the same vowel sound.

I imagine us at the county fair
And think of all who'll see us there.

COLLABORATE

Work with a partner. Write words that rhyme. Use the words below. Underline words that repeat.

again   might

night   train

Every morning, and again at night

I train Little Red with all my _____.

Again, again, and yet again

I lead him around the pen to _____.

A Simple Plan

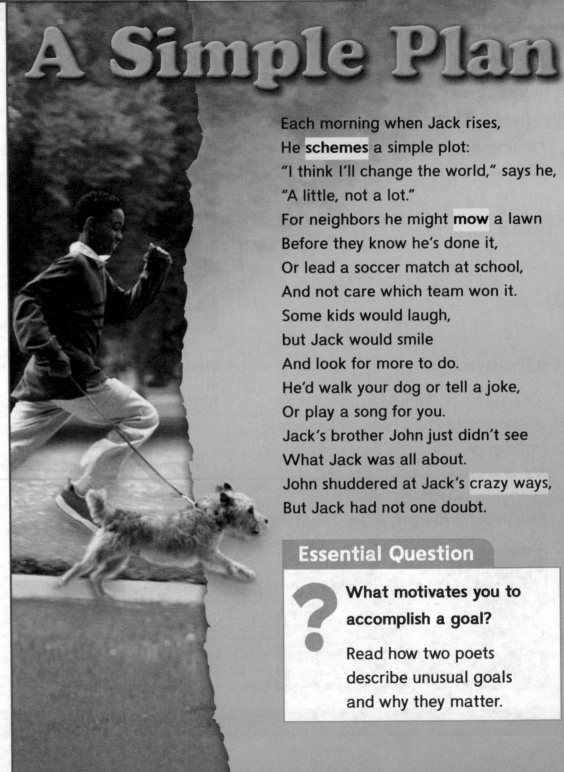

1 Literary Element
Rhyme

Reread lines 1–4. Circle the words that rhyme. Write the words.

_____

COLLABORATE

2 Talk About It

Reread lines 3–8. Underline the text that describes things Jack can do to "change the world." Why does he say "a little, not a lot"? Justify your answer.

Jack says "a little, not a lot"

because _____

_____.

3 Specific Vocabulary Ⓐ Ⓒ Ⓣ

The phrase *crazy ways* means "unusual ways". Underline the text that describes Jack's unusual ways. Why are his ways unusual?

Jack's ways are unusual because

_____.

Each morning when Jack rises,
He **schemes** a simple plot:
"I think I'll change the world," says he,
"A little, not a lot."
For neighbors he might **mow** a lawn
Before they know he's done it,
Or lead a soccer match at school,
And not care which team won it.
Some kids would laugh,
but Jack would smile
And look for more to do.
He'd walk your dog or tell a joke,
Or play a song for you.
Jack's brother John just didn't see
What Jack was all about.
John shuddered at Jack's **crazy ways**,
But Jack had not one doubt.

Essential Question

What motivates you to accomplish a goal?

Read how two poets describe unusual goals and why they matter.

"Who wants to do another's **chores**?"
John asked. "What does it mean,
'I'll change the world?' You're wasting time.
What changes have you seen?"
"Little brother," Jack explained,
"I used to think like you.
I thought, 'Why bother?' and 'Who cares?'
I see you do that, too.
I'd see some grass not mowed, or else
Kids not getting along,
And in the park no games to play—
I'd wonder what was wrong.
And then I had to ask myself,
What was I waiting for?
The change can start with me, you see,
That key is in my door.
I've memorized a thousand names,
And everyone knows me.
What do *you* do?" John had to think.
And he began to see.
Now each morning when Jack rises,
He hears his brother plan:
"I think I'll change the world," says John,
"If I can't, then who can?"

— Peter Collier

(l) Peter Zander/Workbook Stock/Getty Images; (r) Fancy/Alamy

❶ Specific Vocabulary 🅐🅒🅣

The phrase *wasting time* means "doing something pointless or useless." Circle the words that tell you why John thinks Jack is wasting time.

❷ Literary Element
Narrative

Reread lines 5–8. Underline the name of the character that is speaking.

COLLABORATE

❸ Talk About It

Discuss what John decides to do at the end of the poem. Describe what made him change his mind. Then write about it.

_____

_____

_____

_____

129

1 Talk About It

Reread lines 1–2. What kind of spill does the poem tell about? Discuss the text clues.

2 Literary Element
Repetition

Reread lines 2–5. Underline the repeated phrase. How does the author use the repeated phrase?

The author uses the repeated

phrase _____

to _____

_____.

3 Specific Vocabulary A**C**T

The word *sodden* means "very wet and heavy." Why are the sea birds sodden?

The sea birds are sodden because

_____

_____

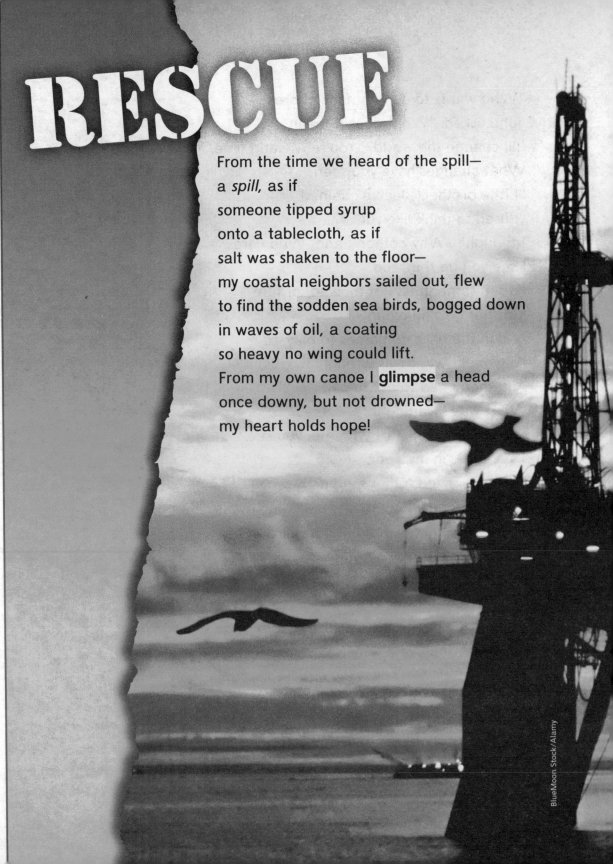

RESCUE

From the time we heard of the spill—
a *spill*, as if
someone tipped syrup
onto a tablecloth, as if
salt was shaken to the floor—
my coastal neighbors sailed out, flew
to find the sodden sea birds, bogged down
in waves of oil, a coating
so heavy no wing could lift.
From my own canoe I **glimpse** a head
once downy, but not drowned—
my heart holds hope!

BlueMoon Stock/Alamy

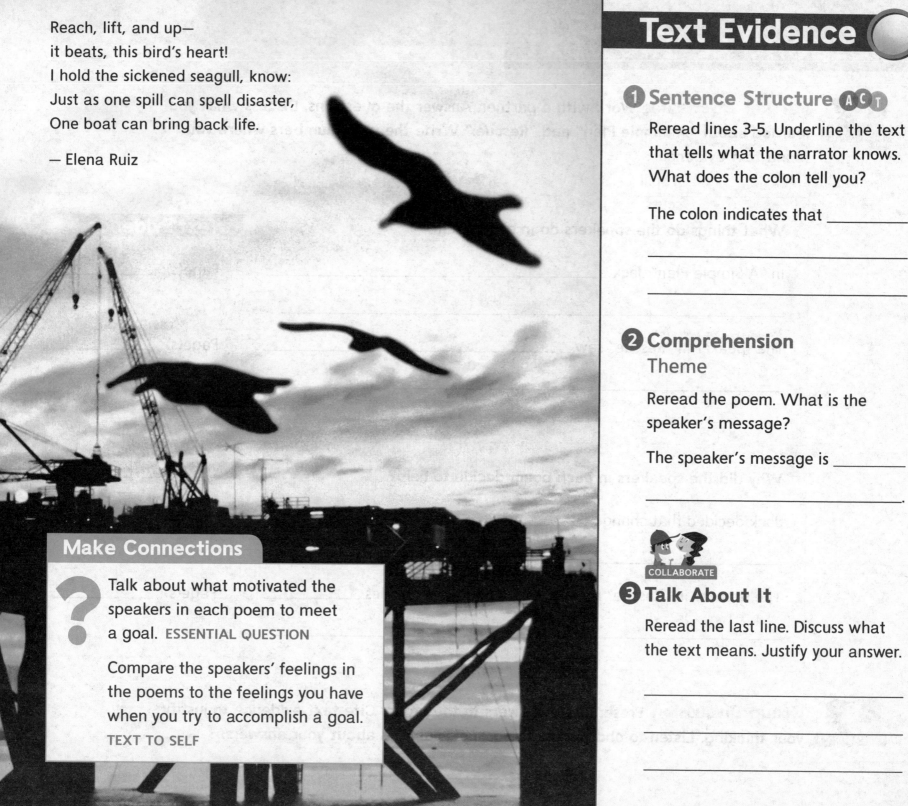

Reach, lift, and up—
it beats, this bird's heart!
I hold the sickened seagull, know:
Just as one spill can spell disaster,
One boat can bring back life.

— Elena Ruiz

Make Connections

? Talk about what motivated the speakers in each poem to meet a goal. ESSENTIAL QUESTION

Compare the speakers' feelings in the poems to the feelings you have when you try to accomplish a goal. TEXT TO SELF

Text Evidence 🔍

1 Sentence Structure Ⓐ Ⓒ Ⓣ

Reread lines 3–5. Underline the text that tells what the narrator knows. What does the colon tell you?

The colon indicates that _____

_____

_____

2 Comprehension
Theme

Reread the poem. What is the speaker's message?

The speaker's message is _____

_____.

COLLABORATE

3 Talk About It

Reread the last line. Discuss what the text means. Justify your answer.

_____

_____

_____

131

Partner Discussion Work with a partner. Answer the questions. Discuss what you learned about "A Simple Plan" and "Rescue." Write the page numbers where you found text evidence.

What things do the speakers do in each poem?

In "A Simple Plan" Jack _to change the world doing go things for people_.

Text Evidence
Page(s): _128_

The speaker in "Rescue" saw _a bird in water in oil_.

Page(s): _31_

Why did the speakers in each poem decide to help?

Jack decided that change _he want to change the world so he helped._

Text Evidence
Page(s): _128_

The speaker in "Rescue" holds a rescued bird and decides _bring it back to life_.

Page(s): _31_

Group Discussion Present your answers to the group. Cite text evidence to justify your thinking. Listen to and discuss the group's opinions about your answers.

Write Review your notes about "A Simple Plan" and "Rescue." Then write your answer to the Essential Question. Use text evidence to support your answer. Use vocabulary words from this week's reading in your writing.

What motivates the speakers in each poem to accomplish a goal?

Jack in "A Simple Plan" decided that change _____

because _____ .

The speaker in "Rescue" learns _____

from _____ .

The speakers in both poems saw a problem and decided _____

_____ .

Share Writing Present your writing to the class. Discuss their opinions. Think about what the class has to say. Did they justify their claims? Explain why you agree or disagree with their claims.

I agree with _____ because _____ .

I disagree because _____ .

Write to Sources

Pete

Take Notes About the Text I took notes about the text on the chart to answer the question: *In what ways is "A Simple Plan" a narrative poem?*

pages 128–129

Detail
The poem tells a story about Jack who makes a plan to change the world.

Topic
The poem "A Simple Plan" is a narrative poem.

Detail
The poem has two characters, Jack and his little brother John.

Detail
The poem has dialogue between Jack and John.

Write About the Text I used notes from my chart to explain why "A Simple Plan" is a narrative poem.

Student Model: *Informative Text*

"A Simple Plan" is a narrative poem because it tells a story and has characters and dialogue. First, the poem tells a story about two brothers John and Jack. They make a plan to change the world by helping others. Second, the poem describes the characters Jack and his little brother John. John helps his brother make a plan. Finally, the poem has a dialogue between the two characters. John explains to Jack why he has a plan. These three characteristics prove that "A Simple Plan" is a narrative poem.

TALK ABOUT IT

Text Evidence
Draw a box around the sentence that comes from the notes. Why did Pete use the information?

Grammar
Circle a prepositional phrase. What detail does the phrase tell?

Condense Ideas
Underline the two sentences about the characters John and Jack. How can you condense the sentences into one detailed sentence?

Turn box

Describe the use of rhyme in "A Simple Plan." Use text evidence in your writing.

>> Go Digital!
Write your response online. Use your editing checklist.

135

Unit 3
Getting from Here to There

The Big Idea

What kinds of experiences
can lead to new discoveries?

TALK ABOUT IT

Weekly Concept Cultural Exchange

? **Essential Question**
What can learning about different cultures teach us?

>> Go Digital

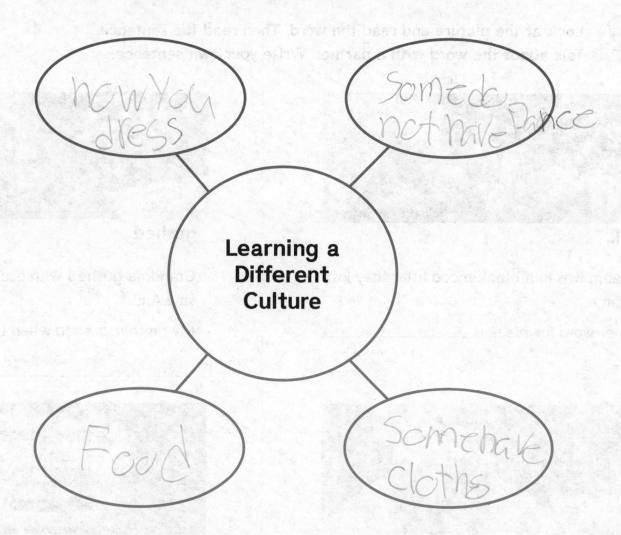

COLLABORATE What is the woman teaching her students? How can learning a dance teach you about a different culture? Describe what you can learn from a different culture in the chart.

how you dress

some do not have Dance

Learning a Different Culture

Food

Some have cloths

Discuss what you can learn from a different culture. Use words from the chart. Complete the sentence:

Learning about different cultures can teach me about storys that happend a long timeag in their place were Paple are from

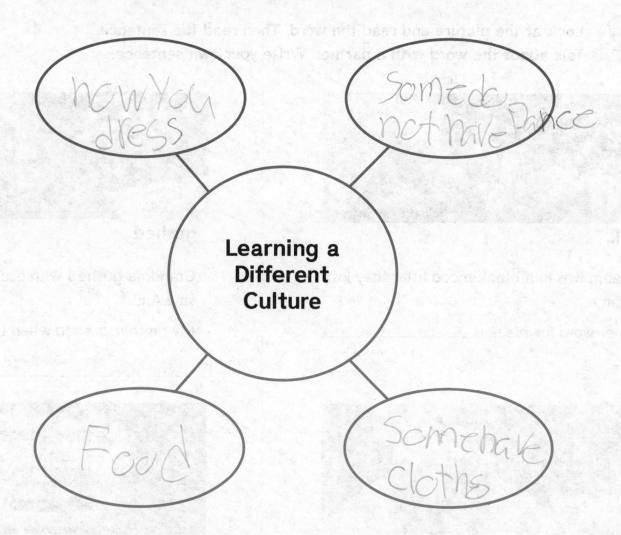

Michael Holahan/ZUMA Press/Corbis

More Vocabulary

Look at the picture and read the word. Then read the sentence. Talk about the word with a partner. Write your own sentence.

bleak

The team was in a **bleak** mood after they lost the game.

Another word for *bleak* is ___Sad___.

gushed

Grandma **gushed** with excitement when she saw Ana.

My mother *gushed* when I ___got a good grade___

flavors

Tania loves to taste the **flavors** of fresh fruit.

I taste sweet and sour *flavors* when I eat

___Kiwi___.

multilingual

People who know different languages can read a **multilingual** sign.

I can be *multilingual* if I learn ___Spanish___

___

rival

Max wants to beat his **rival** at the game.

You have a *rival* when you ___have a team___

_____.

surrounded

Liberty Island is **surrounded** by water on all sides.

In a forest, a hiker is *surrounded* by ___trees___

_____.

Words and Phrases
Adverb Phrase and Idiom

ever since = from the time when

Maria and Tina have been friends <u>ever since</u> they met on the bus.

on the other hand = however

Carl wants a dog for a pet. <u>On the other hand</u>, his sister wants a cat.

Read the sentences below. Write the phrase that completes each sentence.

Randy wants to go to the zoo. _____, Molly thinks it is too cold to be outside.

_____ Maria heard the song, she has been singing it.

_____ I started doing chores, my parents have given me an allowance.

Todd wants to play basketball after school today. _____, Todd's mom wants him to do his homework before dinner.

>> *Go Digital* Add the phrases *ever since* and *on the other hand* to your New Words notebook. Write a sentence to show the meaning of each.

141

COLLABORATE

1 Talk About It

Look at the photographs. Read the title. Talk about what you see. Write your ideas.

What does the title tell you?

_____

_____

_____

Why is a passport important for travel?

_____

_____

_____

What information does the map tell you?

_____

_____

_____

Take notes as you read the story.

A Reluctant
TRAVELER

PASSPORT

United States of America

Essential Question

? **What can learning about different cultures teach us?**

Read about what Paul discovers in Argentina and what he learns about himself.

"I think packing winter clothes in August is weird," Paul said, looking from his bedroom window onto West 90th Street. This wasn't going to be a fun vacation. He was sure of it.

His mom contradicted, "It's not weird, honey. Argentina's in the Southern hemisphere, and we're in the Northern hemisphere, so the seasons are opposite." To Paul, this was just another reason to want to stay in New York City. Paul wanted to spend the rest of his summer break hanging out with his friends, and not with Aunt Lila and Uncle Art in a faraway country.

Paul's parents, Mr. and Mrs. Gorski, were teachers, and this was a chance they couldn't pass up. Their apartment had been covered with travel guides full of cultural information ever since Mrs. Gorski's sister and her husband had relocated to Argentina six months ago. The Gorskis had big plans. Paul, on the other hand, wanted to sleep late and play soccer with his friends. They lived in a city already. Why were they going to Buenos Aires?

As their plane took off, Paul's dad said, "Look down there! That's the island of Manhattan. See? You can even see Central Park!" Paul never realized how completely **surrounded** by water New York was. Many hours later, as the plane was landing in Buenos Aires, Paul noticed similar outlines of a city on the water, and bright lights, just like home.

New York City

Buenos Aires

esla/Photodisc/Getty Images

MARINE & AVIATION

Text Evidence

1 Specific Vocabulary A C T

The phrase *hanging out* means "spending time with someone." Circle the words that tell you who Paul wanted to hang out with.

Paul wanted to hang out with _____

_____.

2 Sentence Structure A C T

Reread the first sentence of the last paragraph. Underline the two things that are happening at the same time.

What does Paul's dad see?

_____

_____

3 Comprehension

Reread the last paragraph. What does Paul realize about New York and Buenos Aires?

Paul realizes that _____

_____

_____.

143

Text Evidence

COLLABORATE

1 Talk About It

Reread the first paragraph. Why does Aunt Lila gush at the airport? Talk about it with a partner. Then write your ideas.

_____

_____

2 Specific Vocabulary ACT

The idiom *made a face* means "frowned or made an expression to show you dislike something." Why did Paul make a face?

Paul made a face because _____

_____

_____.

3 Sentence Structure ACT

Reread the last sentence in the last paragraph. Circle the text that justifies why Paul appreciates "people who move well."

"We have so much to show you!" Aunt Lila **gushed** when they met at the airport. They had a late dinner at a restaurant, just as they often did back home. But the smells coming from its kitchen were new. Uncle Art ordered in Spanish for everyone: *Empanadas* (small meat pies), followed by *parrillada* (grilled meat), *chimichurri* (spicy sauce), and *ensalada mixta* (lettuce, tomatoes, and onions).

Paul made a face. "Don't be critical, Paul," his mom said. "Just take a taste." Though some of the foods were new, the spices and **flavors** were familiar to Paul.

"Mom, I had something like this at César's house," Paul said, after biting into an empanada. "This is really good." As he was complimenting the food, Paul felt his **bleak** mood improving.

Their first full day in Buenos Aires brought a rush of new sights, sounds, and languages. Paul noticed that like New York, Buenos Aires had people from all over the world. His Aunt Lila remarked, "We speak Spanish, but I really need to be **multilingual**!"

On a plaza, Paul saw a group of people dancing to music he'd never heard. Paul had seen breakdancing on the street, but never dancing like this. "That's the tango," Uncle Art said. "It's the dance Argentina is famous for! Being a soccer player, Paul, I know you have an appreciation for people who move well."

"You know, that is pretty cool," Paul admitted.

Around noon, they piled back into the car and drove to the most unusual neighborhood Paul had seen yet. All the buildings were painted or decorated in yellow and blue. "Soccer season has started here," his Aunt Lila said.

"Huh?" Paul asked, wondering if there had been a misunderstanding. "Isn't it too cold for soccer?" he asked.

"It's nearly spring. And," his aunt added, "Boca and River are playing at La Bombonera, the famous stadium, this afternoon." She held out her hand, which held

five tickets to see these big teams play. Paul couldn't believe it.

"We're in the neighborhood of La Bombonera," Uncle Art said. "When Boca beats their **rival**, River, the people decorate their neighborhood in Boca colors!"

"Maybe I could paint my room in soccer team colors!" Paul blurted.

His mom smiled. "I congratulate you, Paul! You've turned out to be a really great traveler." Paul smiled, too.

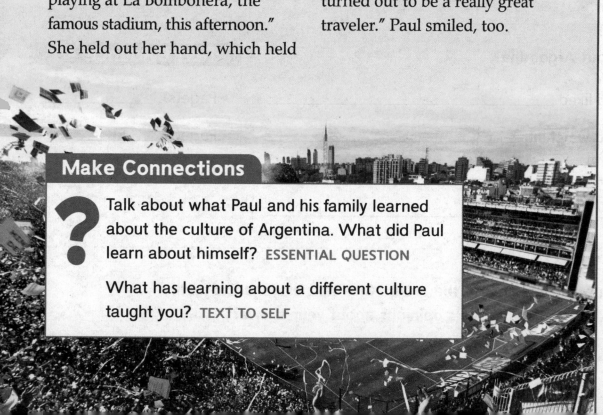

Make Connections

? Talk about what Paul and his family learned about the culture of Argentina. What did Paul learn about himself? ESSENTIAL QUESTION

What has learning about a different culture taught you? TEXT TO SELF

Text Evidence

1 **Specific Vocabulary** Ⓐ Ⓒ Ⓣ

The word *season* means "a period of time when an activity happens." For example, sports. Circle context clues that tell when soccer season happens.

COLLABORATE

2 **Talk About It**

Reread the fifth paragraph. Discuss why people decorate the neighborhood in Boca colors.

_____

_____

3 **Comprehension**
Theme

Read the last paragraph. Underline the sentence that tells the theme of the story. Why does his mom say this? Justify your answer.

_____

_____

Respond to the Text

Partner Discussion Work with a partner. Answer the questions. Discuss what you read in "A Reluctant Traveler." Write the page numbers where you found text evidence.

Why did Paul not want to go to Argentina?

I read that Paul thought the season in _____

because _____ .

Instead of traveling, Paul wanted to _____

_____ .

Text Evidence 🔍

Page(s): _____

Page(s): _____

What did Paul learn about Argentina?

I read that Paul tried and liked _____ .

In the plaza, Paul enjoyed watching _____ .

Paul visited _____

_____ .

Text Evidence 🔍

Page(s): _____

Page(s): _____

Page(s): _____

COLLABORATE

Group Discussion Present your answers to the group. Cite text evidence to justify your thinking. Listen to and discuss the group's opinions about your answers.

146

Write Review your notes about "A Reluctant Traveler." Then write your answer to the Essential Question. Use text evidence to support your answer. Use vocabulary words from this week's reading in your writing.

What did learning about Argentina teach Paul about himself?

Paul started to enjoy his trip to Argentina when he _____

_____.

Paul learned that Argentina is famous for _____

_____.

By traveling to Argentina, Paul learned _____

_____.

Share Writing Present your writing to the class. Discuss their opinions. Think about what the class has to say. Did they justify their claims? Explain why you agree or disagree with their claims.

I agree with _____ because _____

_____.

I disagree because _____

_____.

Write to Sources

Chen

Take Notes About the Text I took notes about the text on the idea web to answer the question: *What are some similarities between New York City and Buenos Aires?*

pages 142–145

Detail
Both cities are located near an ocean.

Detail
Both cities are bright with lights at night.

Main Idea
The cities have similarities.

Detail
People in both cities cook with some of the same spices and eat similar foods.

Detail
People from all over the world live there.

Yobro10/iStock/360/Getty Images

148

Write About the Text I used my notes from my idea web to write a dialogue about the similarities between New York and Buenos Aires.

Student Model: *Narrative Text*

After the trip, Paul told his mother, "I noticed similarities between New York and Buenos Aires."

"What did you notice?" his mother asked.

Paul said, "Well, both cities are located near an ocean. They are also bright at night."

His mother asked, "What else did you notice?"

"People in both cities cook with some of the same spices," he said. "They eat similar foods. And people from different places around the world live in both cities."

TALK ABOUT IT

COLLABORATE

Text Evidence

Underline a supporting detail that comes from the notes. How does the detail support the main idea?

Grammar

Circle a present-tense verb. Why did Chen use the present tense to tell about the cities?

Connect Ideas

Draw a box around the sentences that tell about the people in the cities. How can you combine the sentences into one sentence?

COLLABORATE

Your Turn

In the story, what is different about New York and Buenos Aires? Use text evidence in your writing.

>> Go Digital!
Write your response online. Use your editing checklist.

149

TALK ABOUT IT

? **Essential Question**
How can learning about
nature be useful?

>> *Go Digital*

150

COLLABORATE

How are the men harvesting the cranberries? Why is it useful to know about nature? Describe your ideas in the chart.

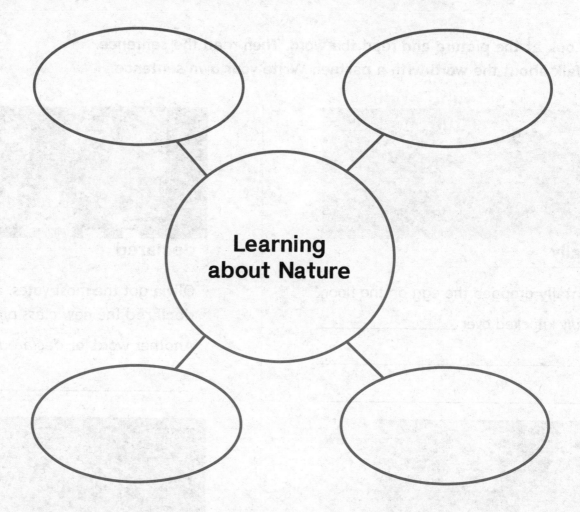

Learning about Nature

Discuss how learning from nature helped the men harvest cranberries. Use words from the chart. Complete the sentences.

The men harvest cranberries by _____.

It is useful to know about nature because _____

_____.

More Vocabulary

COLLABORATE

Look at the picture and read the word. Then read the sentence.
Talk about the word with a partner. Write your own sentence.

accidentally

Ela **accidentally** dropped the egg on the floor.

I *accidentally* knocked over _____

when I _____

_____.

daydreaming

Tyrell was **daydreaming** about the homerun
he scored during his baseball game.

Sometimes I find myself *daydreaming* about

_____.

declared

Olivia got the most votes, and she was
declared the new class president.

Another word for *declared* is _____

_____.

enormous

The giant tree is **enormous** compared to the
person.

A person is *enormous* compared to _____

_____.

hovering

The bee is **hovering** over a flower.

I have seen _____

hovering _____

_____.

managed

After many hours, the hikers **managed** to reach the top of the mountain.

The class _managed_ to collect _____

for _____.

Words and Phrases
Adverb Phrase and Verb

just then = at that moment

I sat down to eat. <u>Just then</u>, the puppy jumped onto the table.

kept = continued to be the same or do the same thing

Although we heard loud thunder, Ann <u>kept</u> sleeping.

Read the sentences below. Write the word or phrase that completes each sentence.

Mom called out that dinner was ready. _____, Emily ran into the room.

Although Ryan gave the puppy a toy, the puppy _____ chasing its tail.

Although it was getting dark, Dillon _____ hitting the ball against the wall.

Abby shook pepper onto her mashed potatoes. The pepper caused Abby to sneeze _____.

» _Go Digital_ Add _just then_ and _kept to_ your New Words notebook. Write a sentence to show the meaning of each.

Survivaland

COLLABORATE

1 Talk About It

Look at the picture. Read the title. Talk about what you see. Write your ideas.

What is on the computer screen?

_____

_____

What are the characters doing?

_____

_____

_____

What is the story about?

_____

_____

_____

Take notes as you read the story.

Essential Question

How can learning about nature be useful?

Read how four friends use their knowledge of nature to survive.

"I'm going to win *Survivaland*!" Raul **declared** as he started the computer game. His immobile character suddenly sprang into action on screen. He raced across the desert island pursued by a sandstorm.

"Not today," Latrice warned while moving her character on the screen. "I'll be the last player standing on the island!"

Juanita stomped her feet. "No way," she insisted, "I always devise a winning game plan."

Jackson frowned. "*Survivaland* is too complex," he complained. "You have to know all about nature to win, but in real life, knowing about nature is just not that important."

"You are *so* wrong!" Juanita cried.

A loud *crackle* sounded, and the entire room went dark. When the lights returned seconds later, the four players were very confused. Instead of controlling their characters on the computer screen, they were on the island themselves!

"I can't believe it—we're inside the game!" Raul exclaimed. "And this sandstorm is blinding me! What should we do?" Suddenly, a large sign in the sky flashed a message: RUN WEST TO ESCAPE THE STORM.

"Which way is west?" Jackson called.

"I know," Latrice exclaimed, pointing. "The sun is rising over there, and since the sun ascends in the east and sets in the west, west must be in the opposite direction."

Maryn Roos

1 Specific Vocabulary Ⓐ Ⓒ Ⓣ

The phrase *the last player standing* means "the winning player." Rewrite the sentence using different words and phrases.

_____

_____

2 Comprehension

Reread the fourth paragraph. Why does Jackson think the game is too complex? Underline your answer. What does he think about nature in real life?

Jackson thinks that _____

_____.

3 Sentence Structure Ⓐ Ⓒ Ⓣ

Reread the last sentence. Circle the text that tells a conclusion. What clues did Latrice use for the conclusion? Justify your answer.

Latrice knows that _____

_____.

Text Evidence

1 Specific Vocabulary ACT

The phrase *that was close* means "we almost didn't escape." Underline the text that tells why Raul said the phrase.

2 Comprehension

Reread paragraphs 3–5. Circle the text that tells what Raul knew about butterflies. Retell in your own words why Raul told the players to rub an onion over themselves.

Raul knew that _____

_____

_____.

3 Sentence Structure ACT

Reread the second sentence in the last paragraph. Put a box around the two nouns that the pronoun *them* refers to.

The pronoun _____

refers to _____

_____.

The four players ran until the sandstorm was safely behind them. "Whew, that was close!" Raul gasped with a shortage of breath.

Suddenly Juanita shouted, "No time to relax—there's new trouble overhead!" The group looked up and saw a gigantic butterfly **hovering** above them. Juanita feared the monster insect might fly down and land on her head.

Just then, Raul spotted onions growing nearby. He quickly pulled one up and smashed it with a stick. He pulled it apart, fashioned four onion pieces, and said, "Rub this all over yourselves. NOW!"

The giant butterfly floated down and rested its feet on Juanita, just as she had feared. She shrieked in fright, and the gigantic insect flew away. "I think my screaming scared it off," Juanita sighed.

"No, actually, the onion did," Raul explained. "Because butterflies taste with their feet, I knew that the onion's bitterness would drive the insect away."

Jackson looked perplexed. "Huh? Butterflies taste with their feet?" he exclaimed, confused.

"Yes," Raul replied, "don't you remember learning that last year in science class?"

"I guess I was **daydreaming** that day," Jackson admitted, adding, "Raul, you're a resourceful friend!"

Then, without warning, an **enormous** crow flew down and announced, "I'm hungry!" When the huge bird walked close to Jackson, Juanita tore off the silver bracelet and ring she was wearing and threw them as far as she could. The crow raced after the jewelry, and the friends ran the other way.

Even after the bird was out of sight, they kept running, and Jackson called to Juanita, "Why did you throw away your jewelry?"

Juanita explained, "I read in a nature book that crows are attracted to shiny objects, so I knew the giant bird would go after the jewelry instead of me!"

"You see?" Raul said, looking at Jackson. "Knowing about nature has saved us again from our tormentors."

Finally, the four friends stopped running—but not by choice. They **accidentally** tripped over a tree log and landed in gooey mud that covered their faces, making it impossible for them to see. They heard another loud *crackle*. When the four wiped the mud away and opened their eyes, they were back in Raul's game room, in front of the computer screen! All the mud was gone, and the electric blue sky had become four white walls.

"We're off the island!" Latrice cried. "We survived *Survivaland*, and all of us returned to a normal civilization!"

"So who won the game?" Raul wondered.

Jackson declared, "I think we all did—but I feel like the biggest winner, because I've **managed** to cultivate a new **appreciation** for nature."

"Agreed!" the friends cried, as they wondered what game they might like to play next.

Maryn Roos

Make Connections

? Talk about how the four friends used their knowledge of nature to get out of dangerous situations. **ESSENTIAL QUESTION**

How might you use information about nature to stay safe and healthy? **TEXT TO SELF**

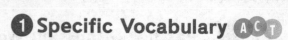
157

Respond to the Text

Partner Discussion Work with a partner. Answer the questions. Discuss what you read in "Survivaland." Write the page numbers where you found text evidence.

What problems did Raul, Latrice, Juanita, and Jackson have when they were in the computer game?

Text Evidence 🔍

The first problem was _____.　　Page(s): _____

Then, _____.　　Page(s): _____

The last problem was_____　　Page(s): _____

_____.

How did their knowledge of nature help them solve their problems?

Text Evidence 🔍

Latrice figured out how to _____.　　Page(s): _____

Raul helped the players escape _____　　Page(s): _____

_____.

Juanita knew that _____.　　Page(s): _____

Group Discussion Present your answers to the group. Cite text evidence to justify your thinking. Listen to and discuss the group's opinions about your answers.

Write Review your notes about "Survivaland." Then write your answer to the Essential Question. Use text evidence to support your answer. Use vocabulary words from this week's reading in your writing.

How did knowing about nature help Raul, Latrice, Juanita, and Jackson?

The players' problem was that _____

_____.

While in the computer game, the players solved the problems by _____

_____

_____.

At the end of the story, Jackson declared _____

_____.

The players realized that _____

_____.

Share Writing Present your writing to the class. Discuss their opinions. Think about what the class has to say. Did they justify their claims? Explain why you agree or disagree with their claims.

I agree with _____ because _____.

I do not agree because _____.

Write to Sources

Take Notes About the Text **I took notes about the text on the chart to answer the question:** *In your opinion, what is the most important lesson Jackson learned? Why do you think that?*

pages 154–157

Miguel

Text Clue	**Text Clue**	**Text Clue**
Latrice knew the directions for sunset and sunrise. She used the information to figure out the direction for west.	Raul knew that butterflies taste with their feet and don't like bitterness. He used the information to escape from the giant butterfly.	Juanita knew that crows are attracted to shiny objects. She used the information to escape from the hungry crow.

Opinion

Jackson learned that having knowledge of nature is useful.

Write About the Text I used notes from my chart to write
an opinion about the most important lesson Jackson learned.

Student Model: *Opinion*

     In my opinion, the most important lesson
Jackson learned was that it is useful to have
knowledge about nature. He learned this from
his friends. His friends saved them from danger.

     First, Latrice used the directions of sunset
and sunrise to figure out the direction of west.
Then, Raul knew that butterflies taste with
their feet and had the butterfly taste onion to
drive it away. Lastly, Juanita used jewelry to
make the crow go away, since she knew crows
like shiny objects.

     Jackson's friends taught him an important
lesson. Now he appreciates nature.

TALK ABOUT IT

Text Evidence

Underline a clue that comes from the notes.
How does the clue support Miguel's opinion?

Grammar

Draw a box around a possessive pronoun. What
information does the pronoun tell you?

Condense Ideas

Circle the sentences about friends. How can you
condense the clauses to create a more detailed
sentence?

Your Turn

In your opinion, which of Jackson's
friends had the best idea for survival?
Provide reasons for your response.

>> Go Digital!
Write your response online. Use your editing checklist.

COLLABORATE

What patterns do you see in the salt marsh? Where can you see patterns in nature? Write the information in the chart.

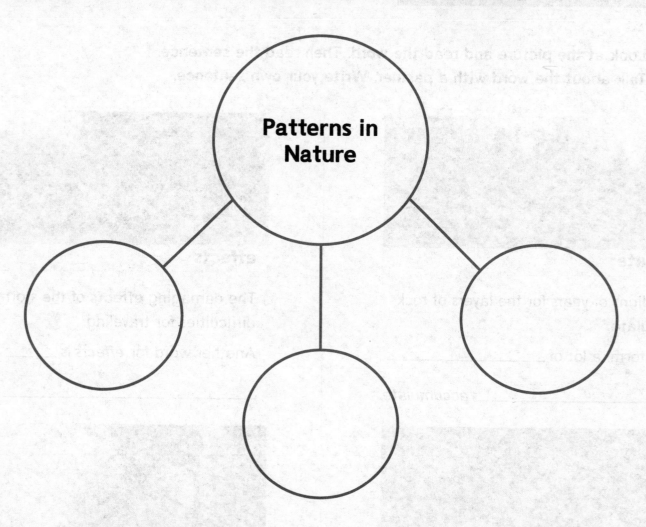

Patterns in Nature

Discuss the patterns you see in the salt marsh. Use words from the chart. You can say:

The salt marsh has patterns of _____.

They make a pattern because they _____

_____.

More Vocabulary

Look at the picture and read the word. Then read the sentence. Talk about the word with a partner. Write your own sentence.

accumulate

It took millions of years for the layers of rock to **accumulate**.

During a storm, a lot of _____

_____ *accumulate*.

depositing

The river is **depositing** water into the sea.

As water flows in rivers, it carries small pieces of rock and *deposits* them _____

_____.

effects

The damaging **effects** of the storm caused difficulties for traveling.

Another word for *effects* is _____

_____.

forces

The **forces** of a hurricane cause the tops of trees to blow sideways.

The *forces* of wind and water can cause _____

_____.

patterns

The tile has **patterns** of triangles and squares.

To find a *pattern* you need to look for _____

_____

_____.

substance

Rock is a **substance** that is hard and solid.

Water is a *substance* that is _____

_____.

Words and Phrases
Connecting and Preposition Words

moreover = **in addition**

Jack's idea may work. <u>Moreover,</u> it may be fun to try it.

upon = **on**

Mary's house sits <u>upon</u> a mountain.

Read the sentences below. Write the word or phrase that completes each sentence.

Alan piled one book _____ another book.

Soccer is fun to play. _____, soccer helps people stay healthy.

Apples are sweet and delicious. _____, apples are healthful.

The queen sat _____ a gold throne.

>> *Go Digital* Add the words *moreover* and *upon* to your New Words notebook. Write a sentence to show the meaning of each.

COLLABORATE

1 Talk About It

Look at the photograph. Read the title. Talk about what you see. Write your ideas.

What do the rocks look like?

_____

_____

_____

What kinds of patterns do you see?

_____

_____

_____

_____

What does the title tell you?

_____

_____

_____

Take notes as you read the text.

Patterns of Change

Essential Question

? **Where can you find patterns in nature?**

Read about patterns you can find in rocks and rock formations.

Rock Solid

"Solid as a rock" is a saying often used to describe something that's reliable, that doesn't change. But, in fact, rocks do change. The **effects** of water, wind, and temperature over long periods of time slowly transform one type of rock into another type of rock. These same **forces** also shape awe-inspiring landscapes and sketch designs on rock. Nature's **patterns** are visible in some rocks as small as pebbles and in wonders as vast as the Grand Canyon.

The photograph across these pages shows one example of nature's art. This structure of rock, known as the Wave formation, is made of sandstone. It is sand turned to rock over a long period of time.

Igneous Rocks

Igneous rocks are one type of rock. They are formed from hot, liquid rock called magma. Magma exists far below the Earth's surface, but it sometimes escapes to the surface through cracks, such as the mouths of volcanoes. Then, we call it lava.

This molten rock, or lava, is composed of minerals. As the minerals slowly cool, they form crystals. Eventually, the once fiery liquid hardens into a solid **substance**.

There are many kinds of igneous rock. Their textures and colors come from their crystallized minerals. You may be familiar with granite, which feels rough and comes in many colors. Another variety of igneous rock is obsidian, which is smooth and often black.

Granite

Obsidian

Text Evidence

1 Specific Vocabulary Ⓐ Ⓒ Ⓣ

The word *transform* means "to change form or shape." Circle the text that tells what transforms. Put a box around a synonym of transform.

_____ transforms

into _____.

2 Sentence Structure Ⓐ Ⓒ Ⓣ

Reread the second paragraph. Underline the name of the rock structure. What does the phrase *This structure of rock* refer to?

The rock structure is _____

_____.

3 Comprehension

Reread the fifth paragraph. What are some types of igneous rock? Underline two details. Write to retell the details.

_____

_____

1 Sentence Structure **ACT**

Reread the second sentence. Circle the text that *them* refers to. Then underline the text that explains what happens after wind and water erode them. Write about it.

After water and wind erode _____

_____

_____.

2 Specific Vocabulary **ACT**

The phrase *Just as* means "in the same way or equally" and can be used to compare. Underline the text that tells what things are being compared.

COLLABORATE

3 Talk About It

Reread the fifth paragraph. Discuss why the oldest layers of rock are at the bottom. Write about it.

_____

_____.

Sedimentary Rocks

Igneous rocks do not stay the same forever. Water and wind erode them, carrying away particles of broken rock and **depositing** them elsewhere. These particles may be left on a beach or riverbank, in a desert or the sea.

Gradually, the particles collect in layers. The contact between the particles and the weight of the layers squeeze out any pockets of moisture or air. Pressed together, the particles form a new material called sedimentary rock. It is formed from many different sorts of sediment. It can include rocks and sand, as well as biological matter, such as plants, bones, and shells.

Limestone

Just as there are different kinds of igneous rock, there are different kinds of sedimentary rock. Sandstone is formed from sand. Limestone is composed of bones and shells.

Rock Formations

Over time, a layer can be created entirely of one kind of sedimentary rock. Geologists who study rocks call a layer made of the same material and at about the same time a *stratum*. Another stratum of a different kind can be deposited on top of the first one. The plural for stratum is strata.

Marble

Sandstone

Many strata of different kinds of rock can **accumulate**. Each one will press down on those that came before it. Scientists learn a lot by studying the chronology of layers. The oldest layer will be at the bottom, the youngest at the top.

These layers of sedimentary rock can create dazzling patterns. Each layer will have its own texture and colors. Moreover, water and wind will continue to do their work.

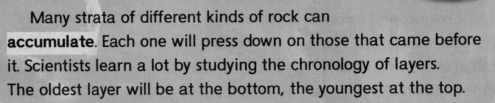

The Rock Cycle

Still, rocks continue to change. There is a third type of rock below the earth's surface, called metamorphic rock. These rocks are pressed down upon by the layers of rock above them. At the same time, they are heated by the magma beneath them. Eventually, the heat will cause some metamorphic rock to melt and become magma.

As the magma slowly cools, it will turn back into igneous rock. The repetition of this process is called the rock cycle. The rock cycle is a pattern—a pattern of change that repeats and continues. It transforms liquid rock into a solid substance. It builds cliffs from sand and bones. And it returns rock to liquid form.

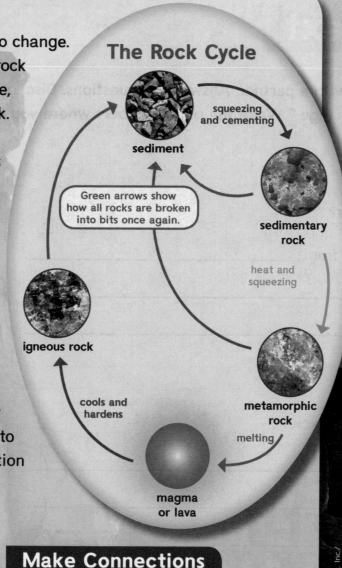

The Rock Cycle

squeezing and cementing

sediment

Green arrows show how all rocks are broken into bits once again.

sedimentary rock

heat and squeezing

igneous rock

metamorphic rock

cools and hardens

melting

magma or lava

(t to b) Steve Nagy/DesignPics; McGraw-Hill Companies, Inc./ Bob Coyle, photographer; Doug Sherman/Geofile; Doug Sherman/Geofile

Make Connections

? Talk about the patterns you can find in sedimentary rocks. Where do you see these patterns? **ESSENTIAL QUESTION**

Compare the patterns of change in rocks with other patterns you have seen. **TEXT TO SELF**

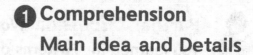

Text Evidence

❶ Comprehension
Main Idea and Details

Reread the first paragraph. Underline two details about metamorphic rock. Write about it.

_____

_____

_____

❷ Sentence Structure Ⓐ🄲🅣

Reread the first sentence in the last paragraph. Circle the text that tells what happens while the magma cools. How do you know the events happen at the same time?

I know because _____

_____.

❸ Specific Vocabulary Ⓐ🄲🅣

The word *cycle* means "related events that happen again and again." Put a box around text clues that help you figure out the meaning of *cycle*.

169

Partner Discussion Work with a partner. Answer the questions. Discuss what you learned in "Patterns of Change." Write the page numbers where you found text evidence.

What patterns are in rocks?

I learned that rocks change from _____. Page(s): _____

Strata are created by _____. Page(s): _____

Layers form patterns by _____. Page(s): _____

Text Evidence 🔍

What pattern is in the rock cycle?

First, _____. Page(s): _____

Then, _____. Page(s): _____

Finally, _____. Page(s): _____

The rock cycle is a pattern because _____

_____. Page(s): _____

Text Evidence 🔍

Group Discussion Present your answers to the group. Cite text evidence to justify your thinking. Listen to and discuss the group's opinions about your answers.

Write Review your notes about "Patterns of Change." Then write your answer to the Essential Question. Use text evidence to support your answer. Use vocabulary words from this week's reading in your writing.

What kinds of patterns can you find in rocks?

Strata are _____.

Examples of strata include _____.

Strata is one kind of pattern because _____

_____.

A rock cycle is a process of _____

_____.

A rock cycle is another kind of pattern because _____

_____.

Share Writing Present your writing to the class. Discuss their opinions. Think about what the class has to say. Did they justify their claims? Explain why you agree or disagree with their claims.

I agree with _____ because _____.

I do not agree because _____.

Write to Sources

Samantha

Take Notes About the Text I took notes on the idea web to answer the question: *How can you use the flow chart of the rock cycle to explain the text?*

pages 166–169

Topic
The flow chart of the rock cycle shows the information in the text.

Detail
The topic of both the text section and the flow chart is the rock cycle.

Detail
The text explains and the flow chart shows how rocks change in the cycle.

Detail
The text explains and the flow chart shows that the cycle repeats.

Write About the Text I used notes from my idea web to help me write an informative text about the flow chart.

Student Model: *Informative Text*

The pictures, arrows, and text in the flow chart show the information in the text. First, the topic of both the flow chart and the text is the rock cycle. Then, the flow chart shows with short text, pictures, and arrows how rock changes from one form to another. The text explains the same information. For example, squeezing and cementing changes sediment into sedimentary rock. Finally, the flow chart shows arrows to explain that the cycle repeats. The text explains that the cycle is a repeating pattern.

TALK ABOUT IT

Text Evidence
Draw a box around the topic sentence, which clearly states the main idea of the response. Why is a strong opening important?

Grammar
Circle the words *flow chart*. What prepositional phrase can Samantha add to give more detail about the flow chart?

Condense Ideas
Underline the two sentences about the cycle. How can you combine the sentences to create a more precise sentence?

Your Turn

Why are the green arrows in the flow chart important? Use text evidence in your writing.

>> *Go Digital!*
Write your response online. Use your editing checklist.

TALK ABOUT IT

Weekly Concept Teamwork

? **Essential Question**
What benefits come from people working as a group?

>> *Go Digital*

174

COLLABORATE

What are the artists doing? How does working as a group benefit the artists? Write the benefits in the chart.

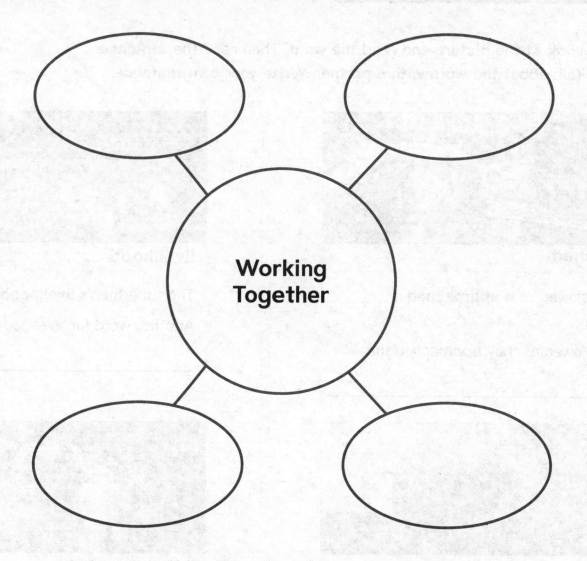

Working Together

Discuss how working together helps the group of artists. Use words from the chart. Complete the sentences:

By working together, the artists can _____.

Groups benefit because _____.

Look at the picture and read the word. Then read the sentence. Talk about the word with a partner. Write your own sentence.

COLLABORATE

approached

The train slowed as it **approached** the station.

The cars slowed as they *approached* the

_____.

livelihood

The fishermen's **livelihood** is catching fish.

Another word for *livelihood* is _____

_____.

efforts

The firefighters' **efforts** eventually put out the fire.

My *efforts* to _____
helped me do well in my class.

officials

Park rangers are **officials** who help and instruct visitors and campers in a park.

The *officials* at my school help _____

_____.

grandriver/Getty Images; Glow Images; Jacom Stephens/E+/Getty Images; Pixtal/age fotostock

platform

People work on a **platform** of an oil rig to get oil from underwater.

Workers drill for _____ from the *platform*.

tracked

A computer **tracked** the path of the storm.

A meteorologists *tracks* the storm to _____

_____.

Words and Phrases
Adverbs

meanwhile = at the same time

Teresa makes the sandwiches, <u>meanwhile</u> Rich gets the drinks.

quite = very

The tiny baby cried <u>quite</u> loudly.

Read the sentences below. Write the word that completes each sentence.

Tad was _____ brave when he rescued the kitten from the tree.

Carmen will make the poster, _____ I will type the report.

Our coach is _____ happy when our team works hard.

Robert's mother cooked dinner. _____, Robert set the table.

>> *Go Digital* Add the words *meanwhile* and *quite* to your New Words notebook. Write a sentence to show the meaning of each.

COLLABORATE

1 Talk About It

Look at the photograph. Read the title. Talk about what you see. Write your ideas.

What does the title tell you?

_____

_____

_____

What are the people in the photograph doing?

_____

_____

_____

Take notes as you read the text.

Gulf Spill Superheroes

Essential Question

?

What benefits come from people working as a group?

Read about how a variety of people worked together after the Deepwater Horizon oil spill in the Gulf of Mexico.

Fans of comic books know that sometimes it takes a team of superheroes to save the day. Each one uses his or her special powers to fight an enemy or solve a problem. On April 20, 2010, the Deepwater Horizon drilling **platform** exploded in the Gulf of Mexico. Massive fires raged above the waters. Down below, gallons and gallons of oil spewed from a broken pipeline. Such a huge disaster would require the skills and abilities of many heroes working together.

Fire boats at work at the off shore oil rig Deepwater Horizon.

Responders in the Water

Immediately after the explosion, firefighters worked with the U.S. Coast Guard to battle the blaze. Boats and aircraft transported survivors from the platform to safety before the rig sank.

Meanwhile, scientists raced to understand what was happening underwater. Each type of scientist had a specific function. Oceanographers mapped out the ocean floor and charted water currents in the area. Biologists looked for ways to protect animals in the region from the spreading oil.

What was most important, engineers discussed techniques to fix the broken well. The leak was more than a mile below the Gulf's surface. That was too deep for human divers to work effectively. For that reason, experts relied on robots with artificial arms and special tools to stop the spill. Many of their first **efforts** failed.

After nearly three months, workers finally plugged up the damaged well. It would take many more months to clean up the mess left behind.

◀ Workers move absorbent material to capture some spilled crude oil at Fourchon Beach, Louisiana.

Text Evidence

❶ Specific Vocabulary Ⓐ Ⓒ Ⓣ

The word *spewed* means "leaked." Underline the text that provides context clues to the meaning of the word.

❷ Comprehension
Main Idea and Details

Reread the first paragraph. Why is it important to work in teams? Circle two details. What do the details have in common?

The details show that _____

_____.

❸ Sentence Structure Ⓐ Ⓒ Ⓣ

Reread the first sentence of the fourth paragraph. Circle the subject and underline the predicate of the sentence. What does the phrase *What was most important* refer to?

_____

_____

① Talk About It

Reread paragraphs 1–2. Discuss why the section is titled "Watchers from the Sky." Justify your answer.

_____

_____

② Specific Vocabulary Ⓐ Ⓒ Ⓣ

The expression *leapt into action* means "acted immediately." Circle the text that tells why the responders leapt into action.

They leapt into action because ____

_____.

③ Comprehension
Main Idea and Details

Reread the third paragraph. Underline two details. Put a box around the main idea.

The main idea is _____

_____

Watchers from the Sky

From the water, it was hard to see where the oil was spreading. Responders had to collaborate with other agencies, such as the NASA space program. Satellites in the sky sent information to scientists on the ground. Meteorologists **tracked** storms that might pose an obstacle to the response teams. Photographs helped team leaders decide how to assign their workers.

Pilots and their crews flew over the Gulf region in helicopters and planes. Some studied how the oil slick moved from place to place. Others directed the placement of floating barriers to protect sensitive areas. Some crews transferred needed supplies back and forth between land and sea.

Heroes on Land

As the oil **approached** land, new responders leapt into action. Veterinarians dedicated their efforts to helping out marine animals, such as pelicans and turtles. They would capture and treat affected animals before returning them to the wild. Naturalists and ecologists cleaned up the animals' habitats. Quite often, these groups' efforts overlapped and they helped one another. Volunteers also helped out on many tasks.

Biologists catch an oil-soaked brown pelican to clean and return to the wild.

Local fishermen also needed help. They relied on crabs, shrimp, and other seafood for their **livelihood**. Government **officials** monitored fishing areas to decide which were safe. Bankers and insurance companies also reached out to the fishermen. They helped find ways to make up for the lost income from seafood sales.

(bkgd) Photodisc/Getty Images; (inset) Saul Loeb/AFP/Getty Images

In Florida, experts worked together in a "think tank." They needed to trap floating globs of oil before they ruined area beaches. They created the SWORD, or Shallow-water Weathered Oil Recovery Device. The SWORD was a catamaran with mesh bags hung between its two pontoons. The small craft would mimic a pool skimmer and scoop up oil as it moved. Because of its size and speed, the SWORD could be quite flexible responding to spills.

Workers place absorbent materials to catch oil in Orange Beach, Alabama.

As we have seen, the Deepwater Horizon accident required heroic efforts of all kinds. In some cases, workers' jobs were quite distinct. In others, their goals and efforts were similar. The success of such a huge mission depended on how well these heroes worked together. The lessons learned will be quite valuable if and when another disaster happens.

Make Connections

How did people from other locations work together with those responders at the site of the Gulf oil spill? ESSENTIAL QUESTION

How have others helped you achieve a goal? Explain how you all worked together to meet the challenge. TEXT TO SELF

Text Evidence

1 Specific Vocabulary A C T

The phrase *think tank* means "a group of people who work together to solve problems." Circle the text that tells why experts needed a think tank. What was the solution?

The solution was _____

_____.

2 Comprehension

Main Idea and Details

Reread the first paragraph. How did the SWORD help solve the problem? Underline two details.

The details describe how _____

_____

_____

COLLABORATE

3 Talk About It

Discuss how everyone worked together to solve the problems of the oil spill. Support your answer with text evidence.

Respond to the Text

COLLABORATE **Partner Discussion** Work with a partner. Answer the questions. Discuss what you learned about "Gulf Spill Superheroes." Write the page numbers where you found text evidence.

	Text Evidence
What did you learn about the Deepwater Horizon oil spill?	
I read that _____.	Page(s): _____
After the explosion, responders worked to _____	Page(s): _____
_____	
_____	

	Text Evidence
How did people work together to find solutions for the oil spill?	
Responders needed to _____.	Page(s): _____
They collaborated with _____	Page(s): _____
_____	
_____	

COLLABORATE **Group Discussion** Present your answers to the group. Cite text evidence to justify your thinking. Listen to and discuss the group's opinions about your answers.

Write Review your notes about "Gulf Spill Superheroes." Then write your answer to the Essential Question. Use text evidence to support your answer. Use vocabulary words from this week's reading in your writing.

What benefits came from people working together after the spill?

The responders needed to colloborate with other groups of people because _____

_____.

Workers helped stop the leak and clean up the spill by _____

_____.

Some benefits of groups working together include _____

_____

_____.

Share Writing Present your writing to the class. Discuss their opinions. Think about what the class has to say. Did they justify their claims? Explain why you agree or disagree with their claims.

I agree with _____ because _____.

I disagree because _____.

Write to Sources

Yolanda

Take Notes About the Text I took notes about the text on the chart to answer the question: *What do you think was the biggest problem of the oil spill? Explain your response.*

pages 178–181

Opinion	Text Evidence
I believe the biggest problem was cleaning up the oil spill.	It was difficult to see where oil was spreading. Teams had to work together.
	Veterinarians, naturalists, and ecologists had to clean the animals and the habitats.
	Local fisherman could not catch and sell fish because they were not safe.

Write About the Text I used notes from my chart to write an opinion about the biggest problem of the spill.

Student Model: *Opinion*

In my opinion, the biggest problem was cleaning up the oil spill. The responders had a lot to solve. One problem was that it was difficult to see where oil was spreading. Teams had to work together to figure it out. Another problem was that veterinarians, naturalists, and ecologists had to catch and clean animals, such as pelicans and turtles. They also needed to clean up the habitats before they returned the animals to the wild. In addition, local fisherman could not catch and sell fish because they were not safe.

TALK ABOUT IT

Weekly Concept Into the Past

? Essential Question

How do we explain what happened in the past?

>> *Go Digital*

186

What is the woman doing? How can the woman learn what happened in the past by examining artifacts? Write ways you can learn about the past in the chart.

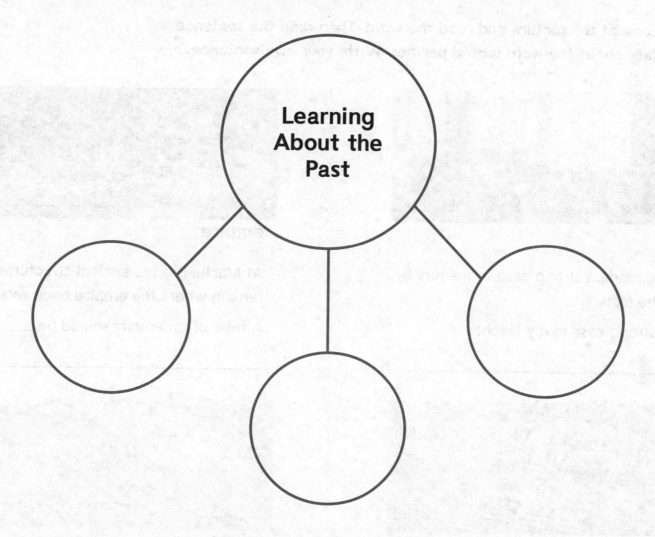

Learning About the Past

Discuss how people can learn about and explain the past. Use words from the chart. You can say:

People can learn about and explain the past by _____

_____.

More Vocabulary

Look at the picture and read the word. Then read the sentence.
Talk about the word with a partner. Write your own sentence.

COLLABORATE

case

The lawyer made a strong **case** to the jury by showing the facts.

I made a strong *case* to my teacher

when I _____.

code

This **code** uses a combination of dots and dashes to represent numbers.

Sam and Mary use a *code* to _____

_____.

empire

At Machu Picchu, ancient structures still remain where the **empire** once was.

A ruler of an *empire* should be _____

_____.

proof

The tracks are **proof** that animals were here.

Scientists use *proof* to _____

_____.

188

series

The street has a **series** of houses.

A *series* has _____

_____.

statistics

The census shows **statistics** about the population.

Another word for *statistics* is _____

_____.

Words and Phrases
Connecting Words

even though = although or "despite the fact"

Josh stayed outside <u>even though</u> it was starting to rain.

likely = probably

Although it was warm today, it is <u>likely</u> that it will snow tomorrow.

Read the sentences below. Write the word or phrase that completes each sentence.

Nate decides to eat a banana _____ apples are his favorite fruit.

_____ the team lost, they were proud of themselves.

The students will _____ use flashcards to practice fractions.

Maria did not study for the test, so it is _____ she did not do well on the test.

>> *Go Digital* **Add the phrase *even though* and the word *likely* to your New Words notebook. Write a sentence to show the meaning of each.**

COLLABORATE

1 Talk About It

Look at the photograph. Read the title and captions. Discuss what you see. Write your ideas.

What does the title tell you?

_____

_____

_____

What does the photograph show?

_____

_____

_____

Who lived in the buildings?

_____

_____

Take notes as you read the text.

Essential Question

? **How do we explain what happened in the past?**

Read two different views about the uses of a mysterious object.

The Inca Empire was centered in what is now Peru. It was taken by Spanish conquest in the middle of the 16th century.

Nigel Smith/SuperStock/Corbis

What Was the Purpose of the Inca's STRANGE STRINGS?

String Theory

Was the quipu an ancient mathematical calculator?

Most of us do not do math problems without an electronic calculator. It would be even tougher without paper and pencil. Now imagine adding numbers with a device that looks like a mop! The quipu (pronounced KWEE-poo) was an invention of the Incas, an ancient civilization in South America. Most quipus were not preserved, but about 600 of them still remain intact.

Quipus are made of cotton and wool strings, sometimes hundreds of them, attached to a thicker horizontal cord. Both the archaeologist and the historian have tried to figure out how the

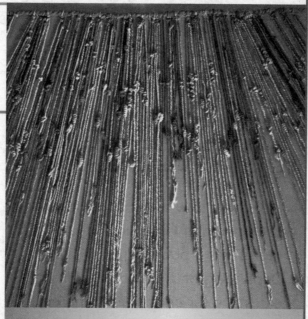

The quipu is an object that has baffled archaeologists for many years.

quipu works. Here is their solution: Knots were tied to the dangling strings to represent numbers.

The quipus were likely used by Inca officials to record and keep track of data, including **statistics** on anything from the number of crops produced by a village to the number of people living in a house.

1 Sentence Structure Ⓐ Ⓒ Ⓣ

Reread the last sentence of the second paragraph. Underline the text that tells whose solution the sentence describes. What was the problem?

The problem was _____

_____.

2 Specific Vocabulary Ⓐ Ⓒ Ⓣ

The word *data* means "information or facts." Put a box around text that has a similar meaning as data. What data did officials record?

_____

_____

3 Comprehension

Reread the last paragraph. Circle the text that tells how the Incas probably used the quipus.

The officials used the quipus to ____

_____

Text Evidence

❶ Sentence Structure Ⓐ ❸ Ⓣ

Reread the third sentence in the first paragraph. Underline the text that tells how the value of the knots change. Write about it.

The value of the knots changes by

_____.

❷ Specific Vocabulary Ⓐ ❸ Ⓣ

The phrase *add it all up* means "to put information together." Underline what information the text puts together.

The author uses the phrase to _____

_____.

❸ Comprehension

Author's Point of View

Reread the second paragraph. Put a box around the text that tells the author's point of view of the quipu.

The author's point of view is that

_____.

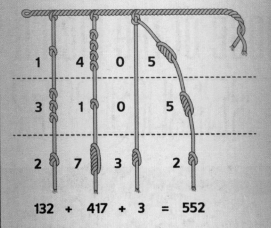

1   4   0   5

3   1   0   5

2   7   3   2

$$132 + 417 + 3 = 552$$

Top Knots = 100s
Middle Knots = 10s
Bottom Knots = 1s

Follow the illustration to understand how to count with a quipu.

Here is how a quipu would work: Each group of knots on a string represents a power of 10. Depending on their position, knots can stand for ones, tens, hundreds, and thousands. Clusters of knots increase in value the higher they are on the string. As a result, Incas with special training could add up the knots on a string to get the sum. They could also add up the total of many strings or even many quipus.

The patterns of the knots show repeating numbers. When you add it all up, it seems clear that the quipu was nothing less than an amazing low-tech calculator.

 ## Spinning a Yarn

The Incas had a 3-D language written in thread!

Mystery surrounds the Inca civilization. In its peak era—the middle of the 1400s—the Incas built thousands of miles of roads over mountains, and yet they had no knowledge of the wheel. They made houses of stone blocks that fit together perfectly without mortar, a bonding material. The biggest mystery may be how the Incas kept their **empire** together without a written language.

The solution to the last mystery might be an odd-looking object called a quipu. Only a few hundred of these remnants of the Inca culture still exist.

Researchers discuss a quipu.

Quipus are made of wool strings that hang from a thick cord. On the strings are groups of knots. Many researchers believe the knots stand for numbers—even though no evidence supports this. But others make a strong **case** that the knots of the quipu were really language symbols, or a form of language.

Researchers found an identical three-knot pattern in the strings of seven different quipus. They think the order of the knots is **code** for the name of an Incan city. They hope to reconstruct the quipu code based on this and other repeating patterns of knots.

More conclusive **proof** that the quipu is a language comes from an old manuscript, a **series** of handwritten pages from the 17th century. It was found in a box holding fragments of a quipu. The author of the manuscript says the quipus were woven symbols. The manuscript even matches up the symbols to a list of words.

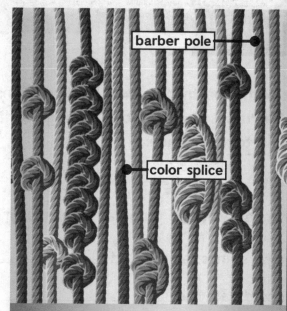

barber pole

color splice

Some experts now believe that the quipu's knots, colors, and patterns made it more than just a counting device. Decoding the quipu may reveal historical records.

The Inca empire covered nearly 3,000 miles. Perhaps the strings of the quipu helped hold it together.

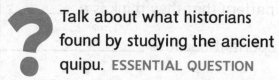

Make Connections

? Talk about what historians found by studying the ancient quipu. ESSENTIAL QUESTION

Think about an object that confused you the first time you saw it. How did you find out what it was for? TEXT TO SELF

Text Evidence

❶ Specific Vocabulary Ⓐ Ⓒ Ⓣ

The word *evidence* means "facts that show something is true." What does the author mean by *even though no evidence supports this?*

_____

_____

COLLABORATE

❷ Talk About It

Reread the third paragraph. Explain why the manuscript is important. Justify your response.

_____

_____

❸ Comprehension
Author's Point of View

Reread the last paragraph. Circle the sentence that tells the author's opinion. Write about it.

_____

_____

193

Respond to the Text

Partner Discussion Work with a partner. Answer the questions. Discuss what you learned about "What Was the Purpose of the Inca's Strange Strings?" Write the page numbers where you found text evidence.

Why do people think the Incas used the quipu as a calculator?

I read that knots on the quipu strings represented _____.

The quipus were used to record data like _____

_____.

Each knot had value based on _____.

Text Evidence 🔍

Page(s): _____

Page(s): _____

Page(s): _____

Why do people think the Incas used the quipu for language?

It is a mystery that the Incas had an empire without a written _____

_____.

Researchers found a three-knot pattern that they think is a _____.

The 17th century manuscript is important because _____

_____.

Text Evidence 🔍

Page(s): _____

Page(s): _____

Page(s): _____

COLLABORATE

Group Discussion Present your answers to the group. Cite text evidence to justify your thinking. Listen to and discuss the group's opinions about your answers.

COLLABORATE

Write Review your notes about "What Was the Purpose of the Inca's Strange Strings?" Then write your answer to the Essential Question. Use text evidence to support your answer. Use vocabulary words from this week's reading in your writing.

How do we explain what happened in the past?

Many people think the Incas used the quipu to _____

_____

_____

Others think that the quipu was a form of _____

_____

_____

There are still many mysteries about the quipu, including _____

_____

COLLABORATE

Share Writing Present your writing to the class. Discuss their opinions. Think about what the class has to say. Did they justify their claims? Explain why you agree or disagree with their claims.

I agree with _____ because _____.

I disagree because _____.

Write to Sources

pages 190–193

Take Notes About the Text I took notes about the text on the chart to answer the question: *Why do some researchers think that quipus were a form of language?*

Marta

Text Clue
Researchers found identical patterns on many quipus. Researchers think the patterns could be code for an Incan city name.

Text Clue
A 17th century manuscript stated that quipus were symbols and matched up the symbols with words.

Conclusion
Quipus were a form of written language.

Write About the Text I used notes from my chart to write an informative text that explains why some researchers believe quipus were a form of written language.

Student Model: *Informative Text*

Some researchers claim that quipus were a form of written language. Two discoveries help support that claim. In the first discovery, researchers found an identical knot pattern on different quipus. They believe the pattern could be code for an Incan city name. In the second discovery, researchers found a manuscript from the 17th century. In the manuscript, the author stated that quipus were symbols. The author also matched up the symbols to words. These discoveries explain why some researchers think quipus were a form of written language.

TALK ABOUT IT

COLLABORATE

Text Evidence
Circle evidence that comes from the notes. How does the evidence support the conclusion?

Grammar
Underline a present-tense verb. Circle a past-tense verb Why did Marta use two verb tenses?

Connect Ideas
Draw a box around sentences that tell about the manuscript. How can you combine the sentences to connect the ideas?

Your Turn

COLLABORATE

What do other researchers believe the quipus were used for? Use text evidence to support your answer.

>> *Go Digital!*
Write your response online. Use your editing checklist.

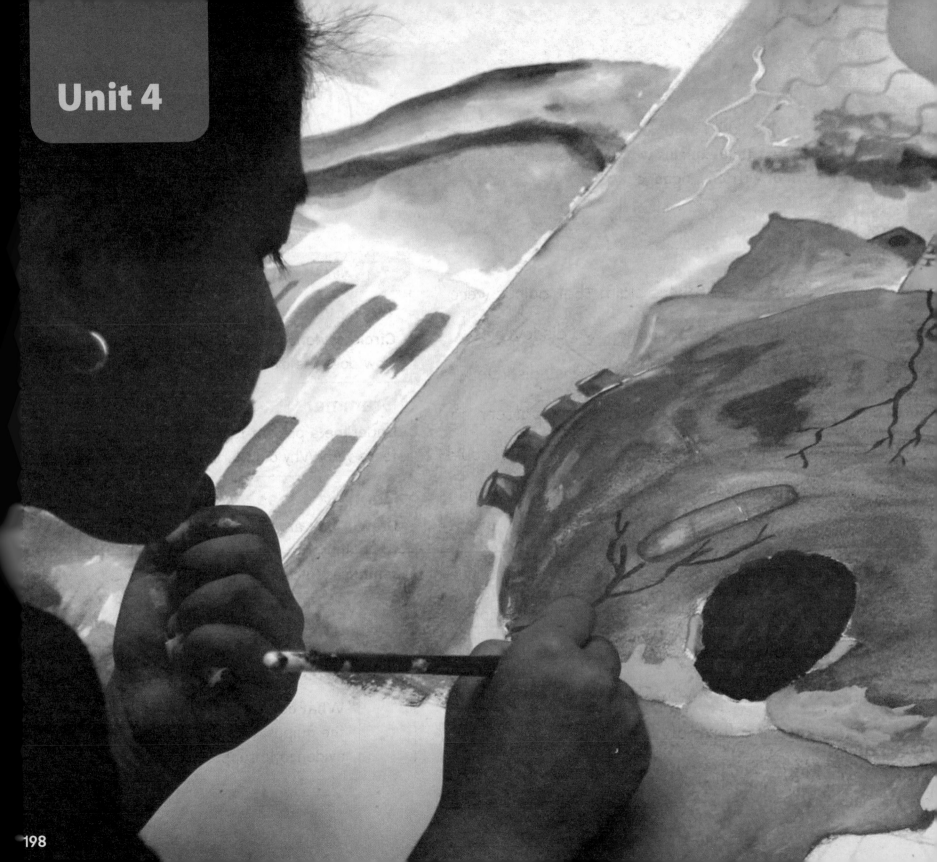

IT'S UP TO YOU

THE BIG IDEA

How do we decide what's important?

TALK ABOUT IT

? **Essential Question**
What kinds of stories do we tell? Why do we tell them?

>> Go Digital

200

How does the boy tell a story? Write the different ways people tell stories in the chart.

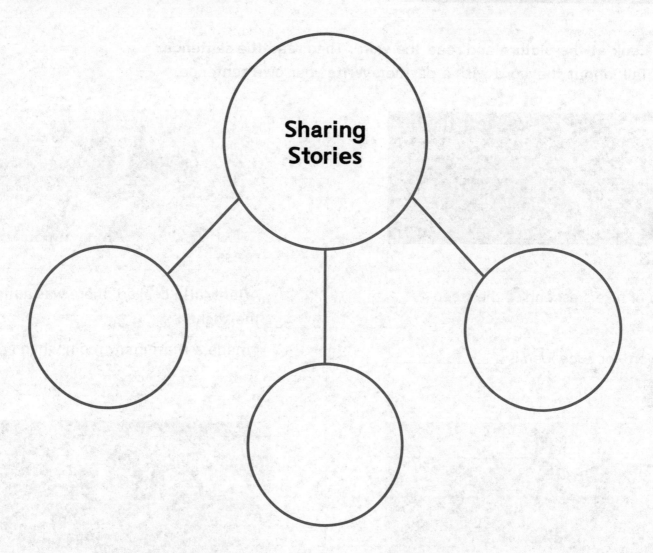

Sharing Stories

Discuss what we can learn from sharing stories. Use words from the chart. You can say:

People tell stories by _____. Learning about stories

teaches us _____.

More Vocabulary

COLLABORATE

Look at the picture and read the word. Then read the sentence. Talk about the word with a partner. Write your own sentence.

ascended

The group of hikers **ascended** the steep mountain.

Another word for *ascended* is _____.

mess

After Marla cooked, there was a **mess** in the kitchen.

I made a *mess* in my room when I _____.

bare

The family ran on the beach with **bare** feet.

During winter, I put on gloves to _____ my *bare* _____.

proved

Max **proved** to the crowd that he could finish the race.

I have *proved* to _____ how

good I am at _____.

202

Alex Treadway/Media Bakery; gemenacom/iStock/Getty Images Plus; Aaron Roeth Photography; Robert Michael/Corbis

shriveled

Raisins are made from grapes that dried and **shriveled** from the sun.

I see *shriveled* _____ on the ground in the fall.

ROADS MAY BE ICY

warnings

Road signs give **warnings** for drivers when the weather is bad.

We have fire drills to practice _____ when we hear **warnings**.

Words and Phrases
on account of and *about to*

on account of = because of
The baseball game started late <u>on account of</u> bad weather.

about to = almost ready
Ethan was <u>about to</u> cut the grass when it started to rain.

Read the sentences below. Write the phrase that means the same as the underlined words.

Julio was late to school <u>because of</u> a broken alarm clock.

Julio was late to school _____ a broken alarm clock.

Jana was <u>almost ready to</u> sit down for dinner when the phone rang.

Jana was _____ sit down for dinner when the phone rang.

>> *Go Digital* Add the phrases *about to* and *on account of* to your New Words notebook. Write a sentence to show the meaning of each.

1 Talk About It

Look at the picture. Read the title. Talk about what you see. Write your ideas.

What does the title tell you?

_____

_____

_____

_____

What is the girl doing?

_____

_____

_____

_____

Take notes as you read the story.

How **Mighty Kate** Stopped the Train

Essential Question

? What kinds of stories do we tell? Why do we tell them?

Read a tall tale about a heroic young girl who saves the day.

Jimmy Holder

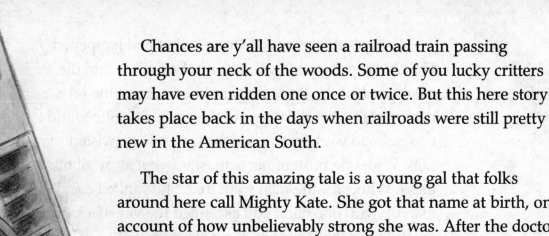

Chances are y'all have seen a railroad train passing through your neck of the woods. Some of you lucky critters may have even ridden one once or twice. But this here story takes place back in the days when railroads were still pretty new in the American South.

The star of this amazing tale is a young gal that folks around here call Mighty Kate. She got that name at birth, on account of how unbelievably strong she was. After the doctor weighed her on a scale, the tiny babe picked up the doc to see how much he weighed! Deeds like that **proved** just how mighty Kate was, and her nickname stuck like paper to glue.

Growing up, Mighty Kate continued to impress her family and neighbors with her great strength. When she went walking through the woods, if a boulder was in her path, she never stepped around it. She just picked up that rock, tossed it aside, and sauntered along her way! Once, her pappy's horse and buggy got stuck in a ditch. Mighty Kate stepped in and pulled them both out—with just one hand!

But let's not get "off track" from the amazing railroad story you really should hear now.

One night, when Mighty Kate was right near 15 years old, a powerful storm struck outside her home. The wind and rain raged so hard that homes shook in fear, and trees ran for their lives! From her window, Mighty Kate saw a work train crossing Creek Bridge. Suddenly, there was a thunderous crash. The loud noise caused the weeping willows to weep so hard that their tears flooded the entire area!

Text Evidence

1 Sentence Structure A C T

Reread the second sentence of the third paragraph. Underline the word the pronoun *it* refers to. Underline the two dependent clauses. What do they tell about?

The clauses tell _____

_____.

2 Specific Vocabulary A C T

The expression *off track* means "to go in a different direction." Circle the text that tells why the narrator doesn't want to get off track.

The narrator wants to _____

_____.

3 Comprehension
Point of View

Reread the last paragraph. Circle the text that describes things like people. Why does the narrator do this? Justify your answer.

The narrator _____

_____.

205

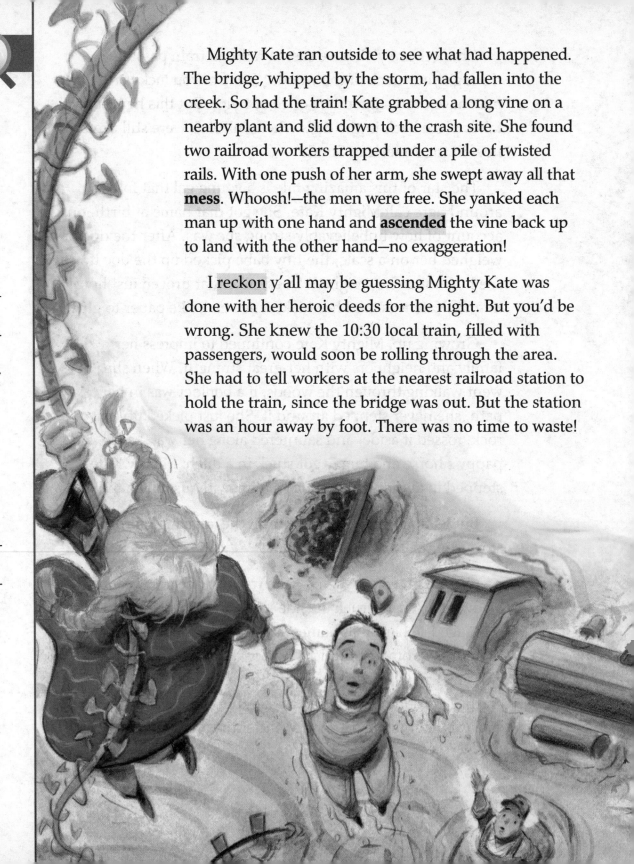

Mighty Kate ran outside to see what had happened. The bridge, whipped by the storm, had fallen into the creek. So had the train! Kate grabbed a long vine on a nearby plant and slid down to the crash site. She found two railroad workers trapped under a pile of twisted rails. With one push of her arm, she swept away all that **mess**. Whoosh!—the men were free. She yanked each man up with one hand and **ascended** the vine back up to land with the other hand—no exaggeration!

I reckon y'all may be guessing Mighty Kate was done with her heroic deeds for the night. But you'd be wrong. She knew the 10:30 local train, filled with passengers, would soon be rolling through the area. She had to tell workers at the nearest railroad station to hold the train, since the bridge was out. But the station was an hour away by foot. There was no time to waste!

1 Sentence Structure Ⓐ Ⓒ Ⓣ

Reread the last sentence of the first paragraph. Underline the text that tells how Kate used her arms. Why does the sentence end with "no exaggeration!"?

The end of the sentence tells _____

_____

_____.

2 Specific Vocabulary Ⓐ Ⓒ Ⓣ

The word *reckon* means "to think or suppose." Circle a synonym. What does the narrator reckon?

_____

_____

COLLABORATE

Talk About It

3 Discuss why the narrator says "There was no time to waste!"

206

With the wind and rain attacking her, Mighty Kate set out for the train station. Soon she came to River Bridge, which had somehow managed to stay up in the storm. Kate commenced to cross the bridge. Floodwaters rushed just beneath her feet. Suddenly, she spotted a huge log floating in the river. It was headed straight for the bridge—and for Kate!

Mighty Kate leaned over the railing. She stood still, as if posed for a photograph. As the log was about to strike, Kate grabbed it. She began to wring the wood with her **bare** hands. Pretty soon, that fat, wet log was nothing but a **shriveled** twig!

After crossing the bridge, Mighty Kate ran straight to the station. When she got there, the passenger train had already left. Kate raced after it along the tracks but couldn't catch up. Then she got an idea. She whistled loudly—so loudly that the engineer heard it and stopped the train.

Kate ran up and told him how Creek Bridge was out. The engineer hugged and thanked the brave young girl who had saved the day.

And because of Mighty Kate's mighty good idea, today we have whistles on trains to give **warnings** along the track!

Jimmy Holder

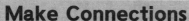

Make Connections

Discuss the way the author told the story of Mighty Kate. Why do you think she told it this way? ESSENTIAL QUESTION

What stories do you most like to tell to people? How do you tell them? TEXT TO SELF

Text Evidence

❶ Sentence Structure A C T

Reread the second sentence. Underline the text that describes River Bridge. What happened to the bridge during the storm?

The bridge _____

_____.

COLLABORATE

❷ Talk About It

Reread the fourth paragraph. Discuss how Kate saved the day. Justify your answer. Write about it.

_____

_____

_____

❸ Comprehension
Point of View

Reread the last paragraph. Put a box around the text that tells the narrator's point of view.

Respond to the Text

Partner Discussion Work with a partner. Answer the questions. Discuss what you learned about "How Mighty Kate Stopped the Train." Write the page numbers where you found text evidence.

What was special about Kate as a child?

I read that people called her Mighty Kate because _____

When Kate was born, she lifted _____.

Kate saved a horse and buggy by _____

_____.

Text Evidence

Page(s): _____

Page(s): _____

Page(s): _____

How did Kate stop the train?

Kate saved two men by _____.

Then Kate ran to _____.

Kate had an idea to _____.

The story is a tall tale because _____

_____.

Text Evidence

Page(s): _____

Page(s): _____

Page(s): _____

Page(s): _____

Group Discussion Present your answers to the group. Cite text evidence to justify your thinking. Listen to and discuss the group's opinions about your answers.

Write Review your notes about "How Mighty Kate Stopped the Train." Then write your answer to the Essential Question. Use text evidence to support your answer. Use vocabulary words from this week's reading in your writing.

How is "How Mighty Kate Stopped the Train" a tall tale?

"How Mighty Kate Stopped the Train" is a tall tale because _____

_____

I know this because details about Kate _____

_____.

The narrator exaggerates details by _____

_____.

The narrator tells the tall tale to _____

_____.

Share Writing Present your writing to the class. Discuss their opinions. Think about what the class has to say. Did they justify their claims? Explain why you agree or disagree with their claims.

I agree with _____ because _____.

I disagree because _____.

Write to Sources

pages 204–207

Karim

Take Notes About the Text I took notes about the text on my idea web to answer the question: *How does Mighty Kate's strength compare to other people?*

Clue
As a baby, Kate lifted a doctor to see how much he weighed. Other babies can't do this.

Conclusion
Mighty Kate is stronger than a regular person.

Clue
She picked up boulders and threw them out of her way. A regular person isn't strong enough to do this.

Clue
She pulled a horse and buggy out of a ditch with just one hand. Regular people aren't strong enough to do this.

Write About the Text I used the notes from my idea web to write a paragraph about Mighty Kate.

Student Model: *Narrative Text*

Mighty Kate is much stronger than most people. As a baby, she picked up her doctor to see how much he weighed, but other babies can't do this. Mighty Kate picked up boulders and threw them, unlike other people. Most people are not strong enough to pick up a boulder and throw it. Mighty Kate pulled a horse and buggy out of a ditch with just one hand. It would take many people to do the same thing. People called her Mighty Kate because she is stronger than other people.

TALK ABOUT IT

COLLABORATE

Text Evidence
Draw a box around a sentence that comes from the notes. How does Karim use this information as a clue?

Grammar
Circle a sentence with the pronoun *this*. What does the pronoun refer to?

Condense Ideas
Underline the sentences that tell about lifting and throwing a boulder. How can you condense the sentences to create a more precise sentence?

Your Turn

COLLABORATE

Write a paragraph to describe other actions that compare Mighty Kate's strength to your strength.

>> *Go Digital!*
Write your response online. Use your editing checklist.

TALK ABOUT IT

Weekly Concept Discoveries

? **Essential Question**
What can you discover when you give things a second look?

>> *Go Digital*

212

COLLABORATE

What do you see in the photograph? What discoveries do you make from giving a second look? Write in the chart what you can discover from taking a second look.

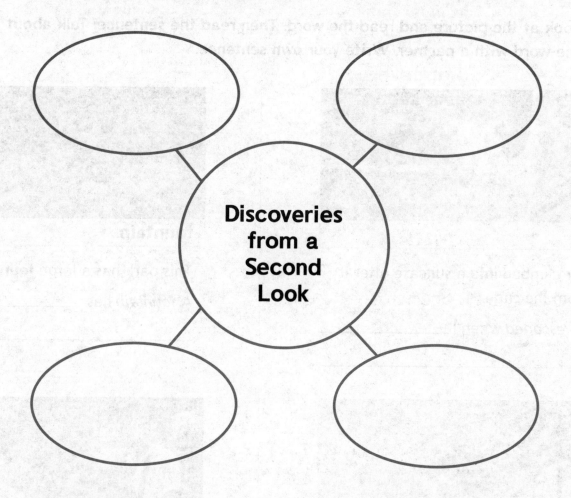

Discoveries from a Second Look

Discuss what discoveries you can make from giving a second look at something. Use words from the chart. Complete the sentences.

At first I saw a _____. Then from giving a second look, I

discovered _____

_____.

213

More Vocabulary

Look at the picture and read the word. Then read the sentence. Talk about the word with a partner. Write your own sentence.

escaped

The hamster climbed into a suitcase after it **escaped** from the cage.

My pet bird *escaped* when I _____

_____ .

fountain

This park has a large **fountain** in the garden.

A *fountain* has _____

_____ .

exhibit

My family learned about dinosaurs at the **exhibit** in the natural history museum.

I saw an *exhibit* about _____

when I went to _____ .

lobby

At some movie theaters, people can buy tickets in the **lobby**.

A *lobby* is a place where people can _____

_____ .

personalities

Sadie has an outgoing **personality** and volunteers to answer the teacher's question.

Another word for *personality* is _____

_____.

prefer

Some children **prefer** to eat green apples.

When I have a choice of _____,

I *prefer* _____.

Words and Phrases
Idiom and *Pronoun*

The idiom *better late than never* means "doing something late is better than not doing it at all."

Jake's homework is late, but <u>better late than never</u>.

The pronoun *whoever* means "any person who." You can use the word when you do not know the person.

<u>Whoever</u> crosses the line first is the winner.

Read the sentences below. Write a word or phrase that means the same as the underlined words.

Jake scored a goal at the end of the game, but <u>better late than never</u>.

Jake scored a goal at the end of the game, but

_____.

<u>Whoever</u> sees Dan should tell him to go home.

_____ sees Dan should tell him to go home.

>> Go Digital Add the idiom *better late than never* and the pronoun *whoever* to your New Words notebook. Write a sentence to show the meaning of each.

Monashee Frantz/age fotostock; Steve Debenport/E+/Getty Images

1 Talk About It

Look at the picture. Read the title. Talk about what you see. Write your ideas.

What does the title tell you?

_____

_____

_____

What does the illustration show?

_____

_____

_____

How is a play different from a fiction story?

_____

_____

_____

Take notes as you read the play.

216

Where's Brownie?

CAST

SAM and **ALEX JENSEN:** Twin sisters with different **personalities.** SAM is athletic and outgoing. ALEX is quiet and studious.

NARRATOR: One of the sisters, ten years later.

EVAN: A classmate.

NICK: The building superintendent.

NICKY: Nick's young son.

Essential Question

? **What can you discover when you give things a second look?**

Read about kids who piece together clues to find a missing pet.

Elizabeth Buttler

Scene One

Setting: A two-person bedroom in an apartment. SAM sits at a messy desk, creating a poster. EVAN works at a clean desk. Nearby are an empty terrarium and a paper bag that is wet and torn at the bottom.

Narrator: Whoever claimed that "two heads are better than one" never met my twin sister. Half the time, she makes problems worse rather than better. Like when we lost Brownie, our pet chameleon . . .

(ALEX enters. SAM and EVAN quickly cover up their work.)

Alex: How was the science fair? Did everyone like Brownie?

Sam: They did. Mr. Rollins was astounded that my **exhibit** was so good. *(SAM tries to hide the empty terrarium from ALEX.)*

Alex: So where's Brownie? And why is Evan here?

(EVAN and SAM begin texting on hand-held devices.)

Alex: How should I interpret this silence? You're making me feel suspicious. And where's Brownie?

Sam: Um, Brownie's missing. But look! Evan and I made these.

(SAM pulls out a poster she had concealed on her desk.)

Sam: We'll put them up at school tomorrow.

Alex: What makes you think Brownie's back at school?

Sam: Because that's the last place I saw him. In that bag.

Alex: Hey, the bottom of the bag is all wet.

Sam: Maybe it got wet in the lobby. Little Nicky was playing in the fountain with his foldy-paper boat thingies.

Alex: That's *origami*, to be precise. Hey! The bag has a rip.

Sam: Rip? I didn't see a rip. Oh, at the bottom.

Alex: Follow me. I think I know where Brownie is!

Narrator: We raced to the lobby. Brownie had been missing for over an hour, but better late than never!

❶ Specific Vocabulary Ⓐ Ⓒ Ⓣ

The phrase *rather than* means "instead of." Circle the text that tells what the twin sister does *not* do.

The twin sister does not _____

_____.

❷ Sentence Structure Ⓐ Ⓒ Ⓣ

Reread the last sentence of the Narrator's first dialogue. Underline the text that describes the topic of the sentence. What does the ellipsis at the end tell you?

The ellipsis tells me that _____

_____.

❸ Comprehension
Point of View

Reread the Narrator's dialogue. Which sister do you think is the narrator? Justify your answer.

The narrator is _____

_____.

217

Text Evidence

① Specific Vocabulary ⒶⒸⓉ

The phrase *as to* means "about or concerning." Circle the text that describes what *as to* refers to. Rewrite the sentence.

_____

_____

② Sentence Structure ⒶⒸⓉ

Reread Evan's first dialogue. Underline the text that tells what the phrase *It says here* refers to. What did he learn?

Evan learned that _____

_____.

COLLABORATE

③ Talk About It

What did Evan learn about chameleons? How do you know chameleons are a type of lizard? Justify your answer.

Scene Two

Setting: The lobby of the apartment building. A tall, green, potted plant stands next to a small fountain, where NICKY is playing. ALEX, SAM, and EVAN talk to NICK near a bulletin board.

Nick: So these posters are about your lizard, Brownie. I'm still perplexed as to why you think he's down here.

Sam: Because we already checked upstairs.

Alex: Brownie's a chameleon. We think he **escaped** when Sam set the bag down near the fountain.

Nick: Hey, Nicky! Any brown lizards in the lobby?

Nicky: Nope.

Nick: Maybe you should reconsider this and try searching your apartment again.

Evan: Wait a minute. *(checks his device)* It says here that chameleons climb trees.

Nick: Nicky! Any brown lizards in that tree?

Nicky: Nope.

Evan: It also says that chameleons **prefer** running water, like that fountain.

Nick: Nicky! Any brown lizards in the fountain?

Nicky: Nope.

Elizabeth Buttler

218

Nick: What else does that thing say?

Sam: Yeah, inquisitive minds want to know.

Alex: *(to SAM)* Don't you want to find Brownie, or are you thinking "out of sight, out of mind"?

Sam: He's just a lizard, Alex. I mean chameleon. It's not exactly "absence makes the heart grow fonder."

Evan: Listen to this! Chameleons change color to match their environments when they're confused or afraid.

Alex: Of course! Nicky, any GREEN lizards over there?

Nicky: *(points into the tree)* There's just that one.

Alex: It's Brownie!

Sam: *(confused)* Brownie has always been brown.

Alex: That's because we put only brown things in his cage, like branches and wood chips.

Evan: Maybe you should buy him a green plant.

Sam: And a little fountain.

Nicky: And boats to go sailing!

Narrator: Well, that's how we found our beloved Brownie, and all was well with the world once more!

Make Connections

How do Alex's and Evan's observations help them find Brownie? **ESSENTIAL QUESTION**

Think about a time in your life when you had to take a second look at someone or something. What changed between your first and second observations? **TEXT TO SELF**

1 Sentence Structure Ⓐ Ⓒ Ⓣ

Reread Nick's dialogue. What does *that thing* refer to? Underline the text in the previous page that tells you. What does Nick ask?

Nick asks about _____

_____.

COLLABORATE

2 Talk About It

Reread Sam's second dialogue. Discuss the meaning of the saying *absence makes the heart grow fonder.* Circle the reason Sam gives.

The saying means _____

_____.

3 Comprehension

Point of View

Read the last dialogue. What is Narrator's point of view about Brownie? Underline context clues that tell you.

Respond to the Text

COLLABORATE

Partner Discussion Work with a partner. Answer the questions. Discuss what you learned about "Where's Brownie?" Write the page numbers where you found text evidence.

What does Alex learn about Brownie and what does she figure out?

First, Alex gets suspicious because _____.

Then, Alex notices that the paper bag _____.

Finally, Alex figures out that Brownie is in _____

because _____.

Text Evidence 🔍

Page(s): _____

Page(s): _____

Page(s): _____

How does the information Evan learns help the twins find Brownie?

Evan learns that chameleons _____

_____.

The children find Brownie by using _____

_____.

Text Evidence 🔍

Page(s): _____

Page(s): _____

COLLABORATE

Group Discussion Present your answers to the group. Cite text evidence to justify your thinking. Listen to and discuss the group's opinions about your answers.

Write Review your notes about "Where's Brownie?" Then write your answer to the Essential Question. Use text evidence to support your answer. Use vocabulary words from this week's reading in your writing.

How did Alex and Evan figure out where to find Brownie?

Alex figured out that Brownie is probably _____

because _____.

Evan learned that chameleons _____

_____.

The information helped the children find Brownie by _____

_____.

Share Writing Present your writing to the class. Discuss their opinions. Think about what the class has to say. Did they justify their claims? Explain why you agree or disagree with their claims.

I agree with _____ because _____.

I disagree because _____.

Write to Sources

Reggie

Take Notes About the Text I took notes on the chart to respond to the prompt: *Add a dialogue between Sam and Alex in Scene One. Have them discuss their exhibit in detail.*

pages 216–219

Text Clues	Conclusion	New Dialogue
Alex: How was the science fair? Did everyone like Brownie? **Sam:** They did. Mr. Rollins was astounded that my exhibit was so good.	Alex is interested and wants to know details about the exhibit. Sam responds to Alex's questions and tells Alex about how Mr. Rollins responded.	**Alex:** Alex asks Sam to describe the terrarium. **Sam:** Sam tells Alex what he put in the terrarium. **Alex:** Alex asks how Mr. Rollins reacted. **Sam:** Sam tells Alex about Mr. Rollins's response to the exhibit. **Alex:** Alex asks Sam how he got the idea. **Sam:** Sam thought about what a chameleon wants to have in a terrarium. **Alex:** Alex thinks Sam's idea is clever.

Write About the Text I used my notes from my chart to write new dialogue between Sam and Alex about the exhibit to add to Scene One.

Student Model: *Narrative Text*

Alex: What did you have in the terrarium?

Sam: I put a tiny waterfall, plants, rocks, and moss.

Alex: What did Mr. Rollins like about your exhibit?

Sam: He liked that I had a waterfall, plants, rocks, and moss.

Alex: How did you get the idea for them?

Sam: I asked myself if I were a chameleon, what would I want in my terrarium?

Alex: That's very clever, Sam.

TALK ABOUT IT

Text Evidence
Draw a box around a line of dialogue that comes from the notes. What text clues did Reggie use to write the new dialogue?

Grammar
Circle the pronoun *them*. Who does the pronoun *he* refer to and how do you know?

Condense Ideas
Underline the text that repeats in Sam's dialogues. How can you condense the sentences?

Your Turn

Write a new dialogue for Scene Three. Have Sam and Alex discuss their plan to find Brownie if he goes missing again. Use details from Scene Two.

>> Go Digital!
Write your response online. Use your editing checklist.

TALK ABOUT IT

? Essential Question
What can people do to bring about a positive change?

>> Go Digital

MR. PRESIDENT HOW LONG MUST WOMEN WAIT FOR LIBERTY

COLLABORATE

What actions are the women taking? What do the women want to change? Write words in the chart about what people do to make positive changes.

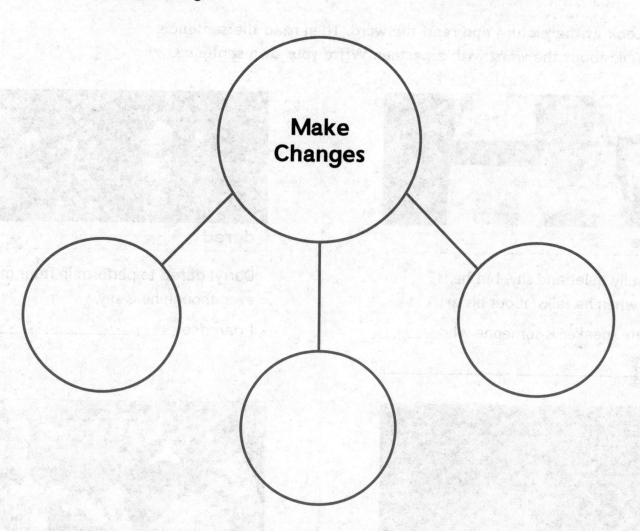

Make Changes

Discuss ways people take action to make positive changes. Use words from the chart. You can say:

The women took action to _____.

To make positive changes, people take action by _____.

More Vocabulary

COLLABORATE

Look at the picture and read the word. Then read the sentence.
Talk about the word with a partner. Write your own sentence.

articulate

Sean is usually quiet and shy, but he is **articulate** when he talks about his art.

An *articulate* speaker is someone who _____

_____.

courage

Firefighters show great **courage** when they put out dangerous fires.

A firefighter shows *courage* because _____

_____.

dared

Darryl **dared** to perform in front of a crowd even though he is shy.

I *dared* to _____.

devoured

The kids **devoured** every fantasy book they could find.

When I wanted to learn more about _____,

I *devoured* every _____.

inspired

Mrs. Green made art fun and **inspired** the children to create colorful pictures.

_____ *inspired* me to _____.

spontaneous

The girls were surprised by the rain, so their reaction to run was **spontaneous**.

When I get scared, my *spontaneous* reaction is to _____.

Words and Phrases
Suffixes -*ly* and -*er*

The word *hesitantly* has the suffix -*ly,* which means "in a way or like."

hesitantly = in an unsure or hesitant way
Chen walked <u>hesitantly</u> into the principal's office.

The word *lecturer* has the suffix -*er,* which means "a person who does something."

lecturer = a person who lectures or gives a speech
The class had a guest <u>lecturer</u> today.

Read the sentences below. Write the word that completes each sentence.

Krysta looked _____ at the judges.

Brent is a good _____ because he likes speaking to crowds.

Many people heard the _____ who spoke about the city's history.

Anna _____ raised her hand to answer the difficult question.

>> Go Digital Add the words *hesitantly* and *lecturer* to your New Words notebook. Write a sentence to show the meaning of each.

1 Talk About It

Look at the images. Read the title. Talk about what you see. Write your ideas.

What does the title tell you about Frederick Douglass?

_____

_____

_____

_____

How can a person be a voice for something?

_____

_____

_____

_____

Take notes as you read the text.

FREDERICK DOUGLASS

Freedom's Voice

Essential Question

What can people do to bring about a positive change?

Read about what Frederick Douglass did to bring about positive change for African Americans.

Bettmann/Corbis

Growing Up with Slavery

When Frederick Douglass was growing up in Maryland, he never could have imagined that he would become a great civil rights leader. Born Frederick Bailey, he was enslaved, or living in slavery, until the age of twenty. Frederick's life was difficult. He never knew his father and was separated from his mother at a young age. If he **dared** to defy his "master" in any way, he was punished. One of the few bright spots of his youth was being taught to read by the wife of a slave holder. Perhaps it was his love of words, along with his **courage**, that **inspired** Frederick to reach for the kind of life he was entitled to have.

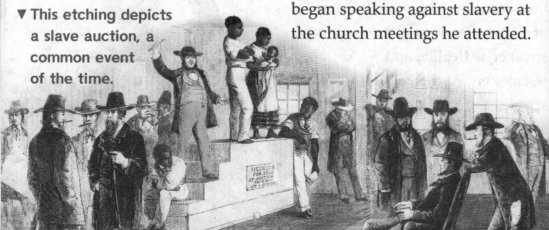

▼ This etching depicts a slave auction, a common event of the time.

Bettmann/Corbis

A Life-Changing Speech

In 1838 Frederick sought his freedom by escaping to the North. In New York City, he married Anna Murray. Then he and Anna moved to New Bedford, Massachusetts.

In New Bedford, Frederick changed his last name to Douglass to protect himself against slave catchers. That was just the first of many changes. He also discovered a group of people—abolitionists— who shared his hope of ending slavery. He had read about the abolition movement in William Lloyd Garrison's newspaper, *The Liberator*. Frederick **devoured** every issue because the ideas inspired him so much. Soon he began speaking against slavery at the church meetings he attended.

Text Evidence

1 Sentence Structure ACT

Reread the first sentence of the second paragraph. Circle the word that tells who or what was trembling with fright.

2 Specific Vocabulary ACT

The word *neutral* means "not supporting any side of an argument or cause." Underline the reason that the audience wouldn't be neutral. What did Frederick argue in his speeches?

Frederick argued for _____

_____

_____.

3 Comprehension

Author's Point of View

Reread the last paragraph. Put a box around the words that describe Frederick's speeches. What is the author's point of view of Frederick?

The author's point of view is _____

_____

_____.

New Opportunities

In 1841, The Massachusetts Anti-Slavery Society held a meeting in Nantucket. Frederick was eager to hear the abolitionist speakers and traveled to the meeting with anticipation. However, when he arrived, something totally unexpected happened. An abolitionist who had heard Frederick speak at a church meeting asked him to speak to this large gathering!

Frederick went to the front of the meeting hall, trembling with fright. At first, he spoke quietly and hesitantly. He felt anxious standing in front of so many people—especially white people! However, once he got started, his fear evaporated. He spoke from his heart, describing the horrors of slavery. Frederick was a stirring speaker, **articulate** and outspoken. At the end of his speech, the audience's reaction was **spontaneous**— suddenly everyone stood up and cheered! Among those cheering was none other than William Lloyd Garrison.

After the meeting, Garrison congratulated Frederick and offered him a job as a speaker for the Society. Frederick agreed and was hired as a full-time lecturer. He felt he had found a purpose for his life.

Frederick traveled through New England and the Midwest, giving passionate speeches that captivated audiences. It was impossible to listen to his powerful words and remain **neutral**. Frederick had a commanding presence and spoke with eloquence and dignity. He was making a name for himself.

Making His Mark

In addition to giving speeches, Frederick had time reserved for his writing. In 1845 he wrote an autobiography, *Narrative of the Life of Frederick Douglass, an American Slave*. The book became a huge success, making him even more famous.

In his autobiography, Frederick revealed that he was a fugitive. For his safety, friends suggested that he go on a speaking tour in Great Britain. Frederick was very popular there, and people lined up to hear him speak.

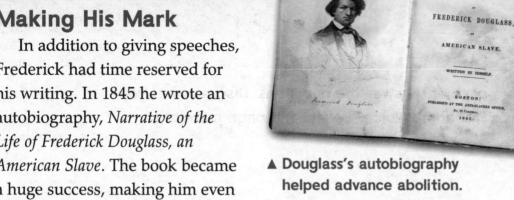

▲ Douglass's autobiography helped advance abolition.

▲ *The North Star* was the newspaper published by Frederick Douglass and his wife.

In 1847 Frederick returned to the United States. By now, he had a family and missed them terribly. Upon his return, they moved to Rochester, New York, where Frederick started his own abolitionist newspaper. *The North Star* was an unusual newspaper. It published articles not only about the antislavery cause, but also about the unequal status of women. Frederick also worked tirelessly to end segregation in Rochester's schools.

Make Connections

? Talk about what Frederick Douglass did to bring about positive change for African Americans. **ESSENTIAL QUESTION**

When have you worked to bring about positive change? What was the result? **TEXT TO SELF**

(t) Aurora Photos/Alamy. (b) Everett Collection Inc./Alamy

Text Evidence

1 Sentence Structure Ⓐ Ⓒ Ⓣ

Reread the first sentence. Circle the text that tells what else Frederick was doing. Rewrite the sentence.

While _____

_____

2 Specific Vocabulary Ⓐ Ⓒ Ⓣ

The word *tour* means "a planned trip." Underline the text that tells what Frederick did during the tour.

During the tour, Frederick _____

_____.

COLLABORATE

3 Talk About It

Compare the *The North Star* with another newspaper. Discuss why it was an unusual newspaper.

The North Star was unusual

because _____

_____.

Respond to the Text

Partner Discussion Work with a partner. Answer the questions. Discuss what you learned about "Frederick Douglass: Freedom's Voice." Write the page numbers where you found text evidence.

What inspired Frederick Douglass to end slavery?

Frederick read _____.

Soon he began _____.

In 1841, Frederick spoke at _____.

Text Evidence 🔍

Page(s): _____

Page(s): _____

Page(s): _____

What did Frederick Douglass do to speak out against slavery?

Frederick worked for _____.

Frederick wrote _____.

In Rochester, New York, Frederick _____

_____.

Text Evidence 🔍

Page(s): _____

Page(s): _____

Page(s): _____

Group Discussion Present your answers to the group. Cite text evidence to justify your thinking. Listen to and discuss the group's opinions about your answers.

Write Review your notes about "Frederick Douglass: Freedom's Voice." Then write your answer to the Essential Question. Use text evidence to support your answer. Use vocabulary words from this week's reading in your writing.

What did Frederick Douglass do to bring about positive change?

Frederick worked to end _____.

In addition to giving speeches, Frederick Douglass wrote a book about _____

_____.

Frederick's newspaper _____

_____.

Frederick Douglass brought about positive change by _____

_____.

Share Writing Present your writing to the class. Discuss their opinions. Think about what the class has to say. Did they justify their claims? Explain why you agree or disagree with their claims.

I agree with _____ because _____.

I disagree because _____.

Write to Sources

Brandon

pages 228–231

pages 228–231

Take Notes About the Text I took notes about the text on the chart to answer the question: *Why does the author use sequence to organize the text about Frederick Douglass?*

First

Frederick Douglass was born into slavery. He was separated from family.

↓

Next

As a young boy, the wife of a slave holder taught him to read.

↓

Then

He escaped to the North in 1838. He started to speak against slavery.

↓

Last

In 1841, he became a speaker and worked with abolitionists. In 1847, he started a newspaper about the antislavery cause and unequal status of women.

Robert Daly/OJO Images/Alamy

Write About the Text I used notes from my chart to write an informative paragraph about why the author uses sequence to organize the text.

Student Model: *Informative Text*

The author uses sequence to show how Frederick Douglass's life changed. Frederick was born into slavery and separated from his family. However, when he was a young boy, the wife of a slave holder taught him to read. Then Frederick escaped to the North in 1838 to find freedom. He began to speak out against slavery. In 1841, he became a speaker and worked with other abolitionists. Finally, in 1847, he started an abolitionist newspaper. The author uses sequence to show how Frederick Douglass's life changed from living in slavery as a child to living in freedom as an adult.

TALK ABOUT IT

Text Evidence
Draw a box around a sentence that comes from the notes. How does this information support the main idea?

Grammar
Circle the verbs in the first and last sentences. Why did Brandon use present-tense verbs?

Connect Ideas
Underline the two sentences that tell about what happened in 1838. How can you combine these sentences to connect the ideas?

Your Turn

How did Frederick Douglass's childhood affect his life as an adult? Use text evidence in your writing.

>> Go Digital!
Write your response online. Use your editing checklist.

TALK ABOUT IT

Weekly Concept Consider Our Resources

? Essential Question

Why are natural resources valuable?

>> *Go Digital*

236

COLLABORATE

How do people use salt? Why are natural resources, such as salt, important? Write words in the chart to describe why natural resources are important.

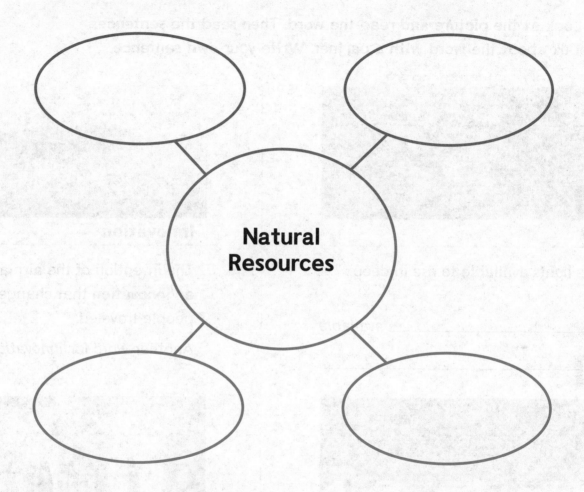

Natural Resources

Discuss reasons why natural resources are important. Use words from the chart. Complete the sentences.

People use natural resources to _____.

Natural resources are important because _____

_____.

More Vocabulary

COLLABORATE

Look at the picture and read the word. Then read the sentence.
Talk about the word with a partner. Write your own sentence.

available

Divers have lights **available** to use in deep water.

I have _____ *available*

to use for _____.

innovation

The invention of the airplane was an **innovation** that changed the way people traveled.

Another word for *innovation* is _____.

extracted

The workers **extracted** salt from the sea.

The dentist *extracted* _____

from _____.

limited

The boys will run out of paint soon because they have a **limited** amount of paint.

I have a *limited* amount of _____.

I have only _____.

provide

The trees in the forest **provide** a home for animals such as squirrels.

Helmets *provide* _____

when _____.

sources

The sun and wind are natural **sources** of energy.

Some *sources* of heat are _____

_____.

along with = in addition to
Mai packed her swimsuit <u>along with</u> a beach towel.

nonetheless = however

The hike was difficult. <u>Nonetheless</u>, it was fun.

Read the sentences below. Write the word or phrase that best completes the sentence.

Kara put her lunch in her backpack, _____ her books.

The school band lost the competition. _____, they played well.

Joe missed the first bus in the morning. _____, he got to school on time.

I went to the water park with my family, _____ my best friend.

>> *Go Digital* Add the phrase *along with* and the word *nonetheless* to your New Words notebook. Write a sentence to show the meaning of each.

COLLABORATE

1 Talk About It

Look at the photograph. Read the title. Talk about what you see. Write your ideas.

What does the title tell you?

_____

_____

_____

_____

_____

What does the photograph show?

_____

_____

_____

_____

_____

_____

Take notes as you read the text.

Power from NATURE

Wind turbines are placed in open areas.

Essential Question

? **Why are natural resources valuable?**

Read about the ways natural resources provide energy.

240

Renewable and Nonrenewable Energy

Click! You just turned on a lamp. A faraway power plant most likely supplied the electricity for that lamp by burning coal. Coal, which has to be **extracted** from deep within the earth, is a natural resource.

Natural resources are nature's gifts, the riches that exist in the natural world. They include metals and minerals, along with vegetation, soil, and animals in the wild. They include the things that are a necessity for all life—water, air, and sunlight.

One important use for natural resources is to **provide** energy. Energy makes things work. It runs our cars, computers, heating and cooling systems, kitchen appliances, telephones, televisions, and industrial machinery. Where do we get all this energy? Natural resources serve as energy **sources**.

Energy sources are divided into two categories. Renewable energy sources—such as sunlight and wind—can be renewed, or continuously refilled. They do not run out. In contrast, nonrenewable energy sources can be depleted, or used up. Coal, natural gas, and oil—also called petroleum—fall into this category. Only a **limited** amount of these substances, called fossil fuels, exists. Nuclear energy is also nonrenewable because it requires uranium. Amounts of uranium are finite, or limited.

Cooling towers at a nuclear facility

A natural gas pipeline

Text Evidence

1 Sentence Structure (A)(C)(T)

Reread the last sentence in the first paragraph. Circle the clause that gives more information about coal. What do you need to do with coal?

_____

_____

2 Comprehension

Author's Point of View

Reread the first sentence in the second paragraph. Underline the author's point of view about natural resources. Put a box around the text evidence.

Natural resources are gifts because

_____

_____

3 Specific Vocabulary (A)(C)(T)

The meaning of the word *depleted* appears in the sentence. Underline the definition. Circle a word that has an opposite meaning.

241

Text Evidence

❶ Specific Vocabulary

The word *scale* means "size or level of something." Circle the text in the third paragraph that tells an example of a huge scale.

❷ Sentence Structure ⒶⒸⓉ

Reread the first sentence in the third paragraph. Put a box around the text that the pronoun *them* refers to. What can create problems?

_____

_____.

❸ Comprehension
Author's Point of View

Reread the third paragraph. Underline the text that describes the author's point of view.

The author's point of view is _____

_____

_____.

From the start of human history, people used renewable energy. For example, sails captured wind to move ships, and wood was burned to cook food. Then, about 150 years ago, human energy needs exploded. New machines required more energy. New ways to harness, or control, energy for use had to be developed. From the 19th century on, most energy has come from nonrenewable sources.

Challenges and Problems

Nonrenewable energy has filled our needs on a huge **scale**. However, satisfying our energy hunger has been challenging. Supplies of coal, natural gas, oil, and uranium are buried underground. They must be discovered and extracted. Also, human technology is needed to transform natural resources into usable forms of energy. For example, gasoline has to be manufactured from oil and then delivered to customers.

Although nonrenewable energy sources have filled our needs, continuing to use them poses problems. They not only can run out but also can pollute the environment. Burning coal produces gases that can poison the air. Some scientists argue that these gases have heated up our atmosphere. They say global warming will affect our climate so dramatically that glaciers will melt and sea levels will rise.

In addition, it is not just our atmosphere that can be polluted. Oil from spills often seeps into the ocean. Extracting natural gas can pollute a site's surroundings. Nuclear energy creates dangerous waste.

U.S. Energy Use from 1949–2010

Types of Energy, Percentage of Energy Used by Year (approximate)

SOURCE OF ENERGY	1949	1969	1989	2010
Fossil Fuels	91%	93%	86%	83%
Nuclear Power	0%	1%	6%	9%
Renewable Energy	9%	6%	8%	8%

What are solutions to our energy challenges? We must find some answers. One possibility is a return to renewable energy, which generally causes less pollution than fossil fuels. However, renewable energy is currently expensive and complex to harness on a large scale

Solutions for the Future

Solar power, or power from the sun, shows promise. Solar panels on houses can absorb the sun's energy to provide heat. Nonetheless, because Earth rotates on its axis and circulates in a yearly cycle around the sun, the sun's energy is less **available** at certain times and seasons and in different places. It will take **innovation** and investment to maximize our use of solar power and other renewable energy.

We also can learn to use nonrenewable energy more wisely. Government and private industry have a role to play in protecting our natural resources and in reducing pollution. Moreover, individuals can try to conserve energy. We can remember to turn off lights, TVs, computers, and other devices when we are not using them. Small personal efforts can add up to big changes in our energy future.

Oil rigs for drilling oil are often found offshore.

Make Connections

Talk about some of the ways natural resources are valuable. **ESSENTIAL QUESTION**

What ways does the text suggest that individuals can save energy? What are some other things you can do personally to save energy? **TEXT TO SELF**

Text Evidence

1 Specific Vocabulary Ⓐ Ⓒ Ⓣ

The word *promise* means "sign that something good will happen." Circle the text that tells why solar power shows promise. What problem can solar power solve?

_____

_____

2 Comprehension

Author's Point of View

Reread the second paragraph. Underline the text that tells the author's point of view of renewable energy. Justify your answer.

The author's point of view is _____

_____

_____

COLLABORATE

3 Talk About It

Discuss some ways people can use energy more wisely.

Respond to the Text

COLLABORATE

Partner Discussion Work with a partner. Answer the questions. Discuss what you learned about "Power from Nature." Write the page numbers where you found text evidence.

What are natural resources?	**Text Evidence** 🔍
According to the author, natural resources are _____.	Page(s): _____
The two categories of natural resources are _____.	Page(s): _____
We need natural resources because _____.	Page(s): _____

What challenges do we have in using natural resources?	**Text Evidence** 🔍
Challenges of using nonrenewable energy are _____ _____.	Page(s): _____
Challenges of using renewable energy are _____ _____.	Page(s): _____
We need to use energy wisely because _____.	Page(s): _____

COLLABORATE

Group Discussion Present your answers to the group. Cite text evidence to justify your thinking. Listen to and discuss the group's opinions about your answers.

COLLABORATE

Write Review your notes about "Power from Nature." Then write your answer to the Essential Question. Use text evidence to support your answer. Use vocabulary words from this week's reading in your writing.

Why are natural resources valuable?

Natural resources are valuable because _____.

The two categories of natural resources are _____.

Using nonrenewable energy requires _____

_____.

Using renewable energy requires _____

_____.

We need to use the resources wisely because _____

_____.

COLLABORATE

Share Writing Present your writing to the class. Discuss their opinions. Think about what the class has to say. Did they justify their claims? Explain why you agree or disagree with their claims.

I agree with _____ because _____.

I disagree because _____.

Write to Sources

Natalie

Take Notes About the Text I took notes on the idea web to answer the question: *Is nonrenewable energy a good solution for our energy needs? Write about your opinion.*

pages 240–243

Detail
People can run out of nonrenewable energy sources.

Detail
There is dangerous waste from nuclear energy.

Detail
Natural gas and coal cause pollution.

Topic
There are problems with nonrenewable energy sources.

Detail
Oil can spill into the ocean.

Detail
Coal can poison the air with gases that heat up the atmosphere. This causes glaciers to melt and sea levels to rise.

Write About the Text I used notes from my idea web to write about my opinion on using nonrenewable energy sources.

Student Model: *Opinion*

People use nonrenewable energy sources to get their energy. However, I do not think people should keep using these sources. One reason is because the sources might run out. These sources also cause pollution. Coal can poison the air with gases that heat up the atmosphere. This causes glaciers to melt. It also causes sea levels to rise. Oil can spill in the ocean. Waste from nuclear energy is dangerous. For these reasons, people should try to stop using nonrenewable energy sources.

TALK ABOUT IT

COLLABORATE

Text Evidence

Draw a box around a sentence that comes from the notes. How does this detail support Natalie's opinion?

Grammar

Circle the text that the second sentence refers to. What is the purpose of this sentence?

Connect Ideas

Underline the sentences that tell what happens when the atmosphere heats up. How can you combine the sentences to connect the ideas?

Your Turn

COLLABORATE

In your opinion, did the author justify why renewable energy sources are a good solution for our energy needs? Use text evidence in your writing.

>> *Go Digital!*
Write your response online. Use your editing checklist.

TALK ABOUT IT

? **Essential Question**
How do you express something that is important to you?

>> *Go Digital*

How is the man in the photograph expressing what is important to him? How do you express yourself? Write words in the chart to tell how people express themselves.

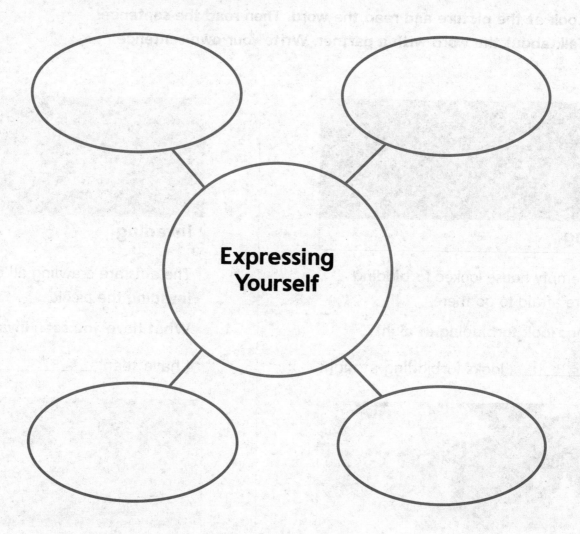

Expressing Yourself

Discuss different ways people express themselves. Use words from the chart. You can say:

People express what is important to them by _____

_____.

More Vocabulary

Look at the picture and read the word. Then read the sentence.
Talk about the word with a partner. Write your own sentence.

forbidding

The dark, empty house looked **forbidding**.
People were afraid to go there.

What things look forbidding at night?

_____ looks forbidding at night.

greedy

The **greedy** puppies did not leave any food
for the other dogs.

What does a greedy child do?

A greedy child _____.

invading

The ants are crawling all over the food and
invading the picnic.

What have you seen invading a picnic?

I have seen _____ invading a picnic.

veil

A **veil** of thick fog hid our view of the bridge.

When have you seen a veil of dark clouds?

I've seen a veil of dark clouds _____.

Poetry Terms

alliteration

Alliteration is when two or more words begin with the same consonant sound.

Becky **b**aked **b**anana **b**read.

simile

A **simile** compares two different things. It uses *like* or *as*.

The **horse** is <u>as</u> white <u>as</u> snow.

The **horse** is white <u>like</u> snow.

metaphor

A **metaphor** compares two things.

The **lake** is a **mirror**.

stanza

A **stanza** is a group of lines in a poem. The poem "We Have a Little Garden" by Beatrix Potter has two stanzas:

We have a little garden,
    A garden of our own,
And every day we water there
    The seeds that we have sown.

We love our little garden,
    And tend it with such care,
You will not find a faded leaf
    Or blighted blossom there.

Plattform/Getty Images; Comstock/PictureQuest; JFCreative/Getty Images*

1 Talk About It

Read the title. What does the author want to do? Discuss your ideas with a partner. Then write about it.

_____

_____

2 Comprehension
Theme

Reread lines 3–4. Underline what the speaker is asking summer to do.

The speaker wants to _____

_____.

3 Literary Element
Simile

Reread the second stanza. Circle the two things the poet compares in a simile.

The poet compares _____

_____.

How Do I Hold the Summer?

The sun is setting sooner now,
My swimsuit's packed away.
How do I hold the summer fast,
Or ask it, please, to stay?

The lake like cold, **forbidding** glass—
The last sailboat has crossed.
Green leaves, gone gold, fall, float away—
Here's winter's **veil** of frost

Essential Question

? How do you express something that is important to you?

Read three ways that poets express what matters to them.

I thought of ice and barren limbs—
    Last winter's snow so deep!
I know I cannot **ball up** light,
    And green grass just won't keep,

So I'll search for signs of summer,
    Hold memories of each—
Soft plumes of brown pressed in a book,
    The pit of one ripe peach,

Each instance of a cricket's chirp,
    And every bird's sweet call,
And store them up in a poem to read
    When snow begins to fall.

— Maya Jones

(l) Peter Zander/Workbook Stock/Getty Images; (r) Fancy/Alamy

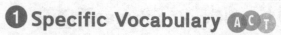

Text Evidence

1 Specific Vocabulary A C T

Read the third line. The phrase *ball up* means "to roll something into a ball." Circle the thing that the speaker wants to ball up. Why can't the author ball up light?

_____

_____

2 Literary Element
Stanza

Reread the second stanza. Underline the key idea of the stanza. Write about it.

The key idea is _____

_____.

COLLABORATE

3 Talk About It

Reread the last stanza. Discuss what the speaker plans to do with her memories of summer.

The speaker plans to _____

_____.

253

Text Evidence

❶ Specific Vocabulary ⒶⒸⓉ

The word *uninvited* is used as a verb. Circle the text that tells where it was uninvited. What does uninvited mean?

Uninvited means _____

_____.

❷ Literary Element
Simile

Reread the fourth stanza. Circle the simile. What two things does the speaker compare?

_____

_____

❸ Comprehension
Theme

Reread the last stanza. Underline what the speaker does with the fly. Write about it.

_____

_____

It lighted, uninvited
upon the china plate
next to the peas.

No hand I raised
nor finger flicked
but rather found a lens

framed, focused,
zoomed in, held
the hands, still—

the appearance of hands,
like two fine threads, caught
plotting, planning—

greedy goggle eyes, webbed wings
like me, **invading**—
but no time to pause, he'd go—

and right at the last
instead of a swat,
I snapped!

— Ken Kines

(t) Perry Hanson Concepts/Alamy; (bl) Stockbyte/Getty Images;
(br) Noam Armonn/Alamy

WHEN I DANCE

Always wanna break out,
   use my arms and legs
      to shout!

On any dark day
   that doesn't go
      exactly my way—

I bust a move,
   get a groove,
      feet feel the ground—

That slap's
   the only sound
      slap, pound

my body needs to charge,
   I play my tracks,
      I make it large

to take myself away!
Nothing else
      I need to say.

— T. C. Arcaro

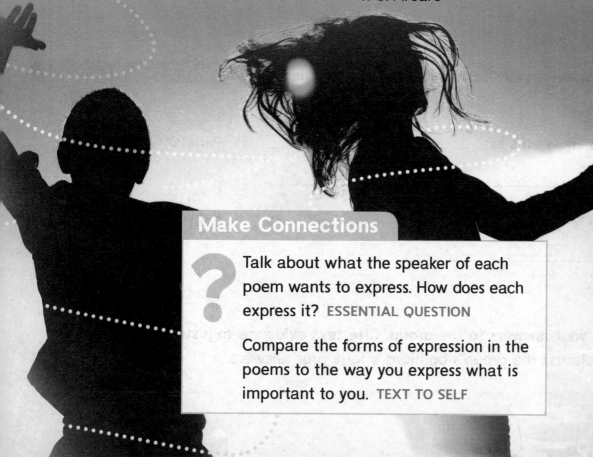

Make Connections

? Talk about what the speaker of each poem wants to express. How does each express it? **ESSENTIAL QUESTION**

Compare the forms of expression in the poems to the way you express what is important to you. **TEXT TO SELF**

---

❶ Literary Element
Alliteration

Reread the fourth stanza. Underline the alliteration. What effect does this alliteration give the poem?

_____

_____

❷ Comprehension
Theme

Reread the fifth stanza. Underline the words that tell you why the speaker needs to dance.

The speaker dances because _____

_____

COLLABORATE

❸ Talk About It

Discuss how dancing makes the speaker feel. Then write about it.

_____

_____

255

Respond to the Text

Partner Discussion Work with a partner. Answer the questions. Discuss what you learned about "How Do I Hold the Summer?" "Catching a Fly," and "When I Dance." Write the page numbers where you found text evidence.

What is important to the speaker of "How Do I Hold the Summer?"

Text Evidence 🔍

The speaker wants to _____.   Page(s): _____

Instead, the speaker decides to _____.   Page(s): _____

The speaker will write _____.   Page(s): _____

What is important to the speakers of "Catching a Fly" and "When I Dance"?

Text Evidence 🔍

The speaker of "Catching a Fly" wants to _____   Page(s): _____

_____.

"When I Dance" is about a kid that _____   Page(s): _____

_____.

Group Discussion Present your answers to the group. Cite text evidence to justify your thinking. Listen to and discuss the group's opinions about your answers.

COLLABORATE

Write Review your notes about "How Do I Hold the Summer?", "Catching a Fly," and "When I Dance." Then write your answer to the Essential Question. Use text evidence to support your answer. Use vocabulary words from this week's reading in your writing.

> **How do the speakers of each poem express what is important to them?**
>
> The speaker of "How Do I Hold the Summer?" writes a _____
>
> _____.
>
> The speaker of "Catching a Fly" uses a camera to _____
>
> _____.
>
> The speaker of "When I Dance" likes to _____
>
> _____.

COLLABORATE

Share Writing Present your writing to the class. Discuss their opinions. Think about what the class has to say. Did they justify their claims? Explain why you agree or disagree with their claims.

I agree with _____ because _____.

I disagree because _____.

Write to Sources

pages 252–255

Take Notes About the Text I took notes about the text on the chart to answer the question: *What similes does the poet use? What do the similes mean?*

Esther

Text Clue

"The lake like cold, forbidding glass" from "How Do I Hold the Summer?"

Text Clue

A simile uses "like" or "as" to compare two unlike things. So, the phrase is a simile.

Conclusion

The poet uses a simile to compare the lake to cold, forbidding glass. In fall, the lake is too cold to swim in.

Write About the Text I used notes from my chart to write an informative paragraph about a simile in a poem.

Student Model: *Informative Text*

In the poem "How Do I Hold the Summer?" the poet describes the lake in the fall. The poet writes, "the lake is like cold, forbidding glass." This comparison is a simile because the poet uses the word "like" in it. The poet compares the lake to glass, and I know glass is very hard. The poet also uses the words "cold" and "forbidding." I know that something forbidding is not welcoming. The water would be cold in fall. You would not want to swim in the cold water. You would not feel welcome in it. The poet describes the water in fall and uses the simile to tell what the lake is like in fall.

TALK ABOUT IT

COLLABORATE

Text Evidence

Draw a box around a sentence that comes from a text clue in the notes. How does this information support that the poet uses a simile?

Grammar

Circle the pronoun *it* in the third sentence What does this pronoun refer to?

Condense Ideas

Underline the two sentences that tell about water in fall. How can you combine the sentences to condense the ideas?

Your Turn
COLLABORATE

Identify and explain a metaphor in a poem. Use text evidence in your writing.

>> *Go Digital!*
Write your response online. Use your editing checklist.

259

What's Next?

The Big Idea

In what ways can things change?

TALK ABOUT IT

Weekly Concept New Perspectives

? **Essential Question**

What experiences can change
the way you see yourself and
the world around you?

» *Go Digital*

COLLABORATE

What can the people see from the top of a skyscraper that they can't see from the ground? Write in the chart what happens when you see things from a new perspective.

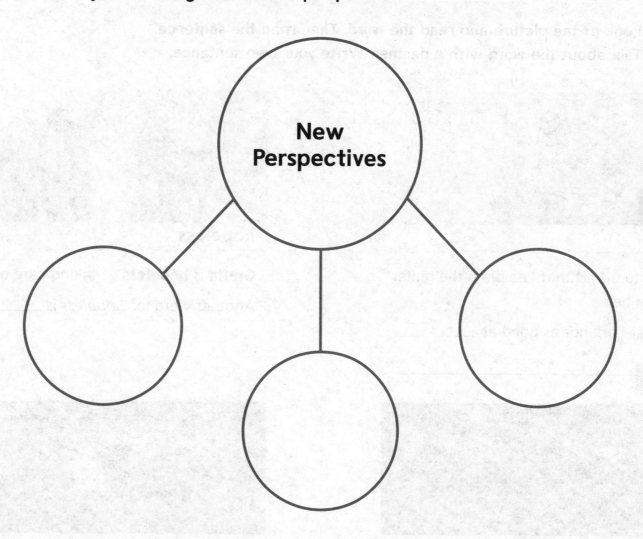

New Perspectives

Discuss how a new perspective helps you to see the world differently. Use words from the chart. Complete the sentence.

Looking from a new perspective helps people see _____

because _____.

More Vocabulary

Look at the picture and read the word. Then read the sentence. Talk about the word with a partner. Write your own sentence.

admit

Jamie has to **admit** that Lee plays the guitar better than her.

I *admit* that I am not as good at _____

as I am at _____.

hopeless

Gretta is **hopeless** at taking care of plants.

Another word for *hopeless* is _____.

clever

The **clever** man figured out the way to get out of the difficult maze.

A *clever* person can solve _____

_____.

session

The band had a practice **session** before the concert.

My friends and I have a study *session* to _____

_____.

situated

The children's tree house is **situated** in the backyard of the house.

The school playground is *situated* _____

_____.

suppose

The children **suppose** they will find the solution if they work together.

Another word for *suppose* is _____.

Words and Phrases
Adverb Phrase and Adverb

You can use the phrase *at least* to correct or change something that you just said.

Jesse loves peas, or <u>at least</u> she eats them.

The word *even* shows that something is surprising or unlikely.

The cat <u>even</u> opens the door with her paws.

Read the sentence. Write the word or phrase that best fits each sentence.

Pat's favorite color is red. He wears red a lot.

Pat's favorite color is red, or _____ he wears red a lot.

My little brother knows a lot about U.S. presidents. He recites each name in order.

My little brother knows a lot about U.S. presidents. He

_____ recites each name in order.

>> Go Digital Add the phrase *at least* and the word *even* to your New Words notebook. Write a sentence to show the meaning of each.

Luc Beziat/Getty Images; Blend Images - KidStock/Brand X Pictures/Getty Images

COLLABORATE

1 Talk About It

Read the title. Talk about what you see. Write your ideas.

What does the title tell you?

_____

_____

_____

_____

In what kinds of things can Miguel be "in the middle"?

_____

_____

_____

_____

Take notes as you read the story.

Miguel in the Middle

Essential Question

? What experiences can change the way you see yourself and the world around you?

Read about what causes the title character to change his view of himself.

Rogerio Soud

For as long as I can remember, I've always been in the middle. I'm the middle child in my family. I've always sat in the middle of the classroom in school. Even my first and last names, Miguel Martinez, start with an M—the middle letter of the alphabet.

Luckily, I'm also in the middle of a large circle of friends. Most of them are classmates in school—well, at least they were until now. You see, I started middle school in September, and the transition from elementary school caused some painful changes for me. All of my closest friends go to a different middle school in the area, because of the way our school district is mapped out. The only classmate I know from my old school is Jake, who's a genius in math, but since it's not my favorite subject, we never became friends.

Another big change is that I'm no longer **situated** in the middle of the classroom. My seat is now in the front row. Also, my new teachers shovel tons more homework at us (especially in math) than we used to get. So you can imagine why my heart wasn't exactly dancing when middle school began.

TONIGHT'S MATH HOMEWORK

Text Evidence

❶ Sentence Structure Ⓐ Ⓒ Ⓣ

Reread the last sentence of the second paragraph. Circle the text that describes Jake. Why are Miguel and Jake not friends?

They are not friends because _____

_____.

❷ Comprehension
Compare and Contrast

Reread the last paragraph. Underline the text that contrasts the new school with the old school.

One difference is _____

_____.

❸ Specific Vocabulary Ⓐ Ⓒ Ⓣ

The phrase *shovel tons more homework at us* helps to describe how Miguel feels. Underline the text that tells his feelings about middle school. How does he feel?

_____

_____

267

1 Specific Vocabulary Ⓐ Ⓒ Ⓣ

The phrase *may as well* is used to suggest doing something. Put a box around the text that describes what Miguel suggests. Why does he say this?

He says it because _____

_____.

2 Comprehension

Reread the fourth paragraph. Underline the text that tells what Miguel thought about Jake. How is it different from what happened?

Miguel thought _____

_____.

3 Sentence Structure Ⓐ Ⓒ Ⓣ

Reread the last sentence of the fifth paragraph. Circle the text that tells why Jake used slices of a pizza. What did Miguel learn?

_____

_____

By the end of October, Jake and I had become good friends. It happened because I was so **hopeless** trying to do my math homework. I have a disdain for math—especially fractions. To me, fractions are a foreign language—I may as well be trying to learn Greek or Latin. So one day, I approached Jake after school.

"Hey, Jake," I began, "I was wondering if you could—"

"Help you with the math homework, right?" he said, completing my sentence. "Sure, I'd be happy to help you, Miguel."

I was stunned because, to be truthful, I wasn't sure until that moment if Jake even knew my name. And yet here he was, happy to save me from drowning in my sea of math problems.

That night, Jake and I had a study **session**, and it was time well spent. I must **admit** that Jake's a superb math teacher. He used slices of a pizza pie to explain the idea of eighths and sixteenths, and by the end of the night, I finally understood why eight-sixteenths is the same as one-half!

The next day in class, I was even able to answer one of the math problems our teacher put on the chalkboard. She was surprised when I raised my hand, and guess what—so was I!

Rogerio Soud

They say time flies when you're having fun, and I guess it's really true. I can't believe winter vacation is almost here! The school days have been flying by like a jet plane. I **suppose** it's because I'm a much more focused student—especially in math—than I ever was before. Until this year, I always looked forward to the prospect of a school break. Now, I actually feel sad that I'll be away from middle school for two weeks.

The other day, the most amazing thing happened when our teacher gave us a math brainteaser. She asked, "If you wrote all the numbers from one to one hundred, how many times would you write a nine?" The question was harder than it seemed.

Most of the students said ten, although some **clever** kids said eleven, because they realized that ninety-nine has two nines, not just one. But Jake and I were the only students with the correct answer—twenty! Everyone else forgot to count all the nineties.

Jake and I plan to hang out together during winter break. He promised to show me the Math Museum downtown. It won't just be us, however, since all my new friends from middle school will come, too. You see, even though I now have a completely different perspective on math, some things haven't changed. I'm still in the middle of a large circle of friends!

Make Connections

? Discuss the ways that Miguel changed after entering middle school. What caused him to change? ESSENTIAL QUESTION

When has a new place changed the way you see yourself or the world around you? TEXT TO SELF

Text Evidence

1 Talk About It

Reread the first paragraph. Discuss what Miguel means when he says the *school days have been flying by like a jet plane.* Write your ideas.

_____

_____

2 Specific Vocabulary A C T

The phrase *looked forward to* means "waited excitedly for something." Circle what Miguel looked forward to. What context clue in the sentence tells you that he does not look forward to it this year?

I know because _____

_____.

3 Comprehension

Reread the last two sentences. Circle what has changed. Underline what hasn't changed.

Respond to the Text

Partner Discussion Work with a partner. Answer the questions. Discuss what you learned about "Miguel in the Middle." Write the page numbers where you found text evidence.

How did Miguel feel about going to middle school at the beginning of the story?

Text Evidence 🔍

Miguel had to go to a new school because _____.   Page(s): _____

Miguel felt hopeless at math because _____.   Page(s): _____

Miguel was not friends with Jake because _____

_____

How did Miguel change by the end of the story?

Text Evidence 🔍

Jake taught Miguel about _____.   Page(s): _____

Miguel learned to like math because _____   Page(s): _____

_____

Group Discussion Present your answers to the group. Cite text evidence to justify your thinking. Listen to and discuss the group's opinions about your answers.

COLLABORATE

Write Review your notes about "Miguel in the Middle." Then write your answer to the Essential Question. Use text evidence to support your answer. Use vocabulary words from this week's reading in your writing.

What experiences changed the way Miguel saw himself in middle school?

Miguel was unhappy at his new middle school because _____

_____.

Jake helped Miguel with _____.

Miguel learned to enjoy math because _____.

With Jake's help Miguel's attitude about math and school changed because _____

_____.

By winter, Miguel was _____.

COLLABORATE

Share Writing Present your writing to the class. Discuss their opinions. Think about what the class has to say. Did they justify their claims? Explain why you agree or disagree with their claims.

I agree with _____ because _____.

I disagree because _____.

Write to Sources

Gilbert

Take Notes About the Text I took notes about the text on the chart to answer the question: *In your opinion, was Miguel happy to attend middle school?*

pages 266–269

Text Clue	Opinion
Miguel has a group of friends, but they go to a different middle school.	Miguel does not have friends in middle school. He is lonely in middle school.
Miguel says the transition from elementary to middle school caused painful changes.	Miguel is not happy about going to middle school.
Teachers give students a lot more homework.	Miguel is not happy about having a lot of homework.
Miguel becomes friends with Jake and learns to like math. He feels sad about the school break.	Miguel likes middle school because things have improved at school.

Ana Abejon/iStock/360/Getty Images

Write About the Text I used notes from my chart to write an opinion about whether Miguel was happy to attend middle school.

Student Model: *Opinion*

At the beginning of the school year, Miguel was not happy to attend middle school. Now, he is happy because things got better. Miguel's friends were his classmates in elementary school, but in middle school he did not know anyone. I think he felt lonely. Miguel said that middle school was painful. Also, he said that he had a lot more homework. This tells me that he was not happy in middle school. Then things improved and his feelings changed. He made friends with Jake and learned to like math. He was even sad about the school break.

TALK ABOUT IT

COLLABORATE

Text Evidence

Draw a box around a sentence that comes from the notes. How does this clue support Gilbert's opinion?

Grammar

Circle words that tell sequence in the first two sentences. Why do verbs in the sentences match sequence?

Condense Ideas

Underline the two sentences give reasons why Miguel was unhappy. How can you condense the ideas into one sentence?

Your Turn

COLLABORATE

Do you think Miguel will continue to do well in middle school? Write your opinion. Use text evidence in your writing.

>> Go Digital!
Write your response online. Use your editing checklist.

COLLABORATE

What are the people in the photograph doing? Why is it better to share an experience with others? How can sharing experiences help you to adapt to change? Write your answers in the chart.

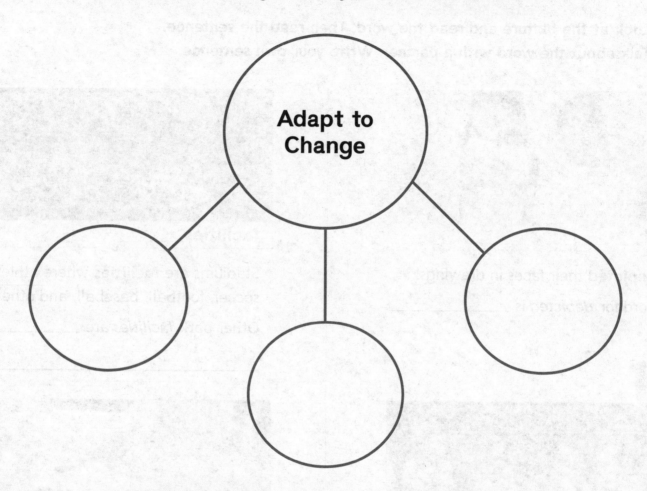

Adapt to Change

Discuss how sharing experiences helps people adapt to change. Use words from the chart. Complete the sentences.

By sharing experiences, people can support _____.

Then, people can adapt to change because _____

_____

More Vocabulary

Look at the picture and read the word. Then read the sentence.
Talk about the word with a partner. Write your own sentence.

COLLABORATE

depicted

The girls **depicted** their faces in drawings.

Another word for *depicted* is _____.

facilities

Stadiums are **facilities** where athletes play soccer, football, baseball, and other sports.

Other park *facilities* are _____

_____.

employment

Last summer my older sister had **employment** as a camp counselor.

I want to work as a _____

_____ for employment.

ingredients

Claire gathered many **ingredients** to bake bread.

You can buy the *ingredients* to make dinner

at a _____.

lay

The dog **lay** on the green lawn.

At the beach I *lay* on _____.

sullen

Amy did not get much sleep yesterday, so she looked tired and **sullen**.

I feel *sullen* when _____

_____.

Words and Phrases
Verbs

bear = to accept or put up with

Jack's new coat helps him <u>bear</u> the cold weather.

matter = to be important

I forgot my house key, but it didn't <u>matter</u> because Mom was home.

Read the sentences below. Write the word or phrase that means the same as the underlined words.

The type of book that Elly selected <u>was not important</u>.

The type of book that Elly selected did not _____.

Grandma will not <u>put up with</u> bad manners.

Grandma will not _____ bad manners.

» Go Digital Add the word *bear* and the phrase *matter* to your New Words notebook. Write a sentence to show the meaning of each.

1 Talk About It

Look at the picture. Read the title. Talk about what you see. Write your ideas.

What does the title tell you?

_____

_____

_____

What are the girls doing?

_____

_____

_____

How do you communicate with family members who are far away?

_____

_____

Take notes as you read the story.

The Day the Rollets

Got Their Moxie Back

Ron Mazellan

Essential Question

? **How do shared experiences help people adapt to change?**

Read about how a family comes together during a period of great hardship in the United States.

Sometimes, the thing that gets you through hard times comes like a bolt from the blue. That's what my older brother's letter was like, traveling across the country from a work camp in Wyoming. It was 1937, and Ricky was helping to build **facilities** for a new state park as part of President Roosevelt's **employment** program. Though the program created jobs for young men like Ricky, it hadn't helped our dad find work yet.

I imagined Ricky looking up at snow-capped mountains and sparkling skies, breathing in the smell of evergreens as his work crew turned trees into lumber and lumber into buildings. It almost made an 11-year-old weakling like me want to become a lumberjack.

Back in our New York City apartment, the air smelled like meatloaf and cabbage. Dad sat slant-wise in his chair by the window, obviously trying to catch the last rays of sunlight rather than turn on a light. My older sister Ruth and I **lay** on the floor comparing the letters Ricky had sent us. "Shirley, Ricky says they had a talent show, and he wore a grass skirt and did a hula dance while playing the ukulele!" Ruth reported with delight. "I'll bet he was the cat's pajamas!"

"It'd be swell to have our own talent show!" I replied.

"Should I start sewing grass skirts?" Mom asked from the kitchen, which was **just** the corner where someone had plopped down a stove next to a sink and an icebox. "Now come set the table. Dinner's almost ready."

1 **Sentence Structure** Ⓐ Ⓒ Ⓣ

Reread the last sentence in the first paragraph. Circle the clause that tells about the program. Why didn't it help Dad?

It didn't help Dad because _____

_____.

2 **Comprehension**

Compare and Contrast

Reread the third paragraph. Put a box around the text that tells what Dad and the girls are doing. How are their moods different?

_____

_____

3 **Specific Vocabulary** Ⓐ Ⓒ Ⓣ

The word *just* means "nothing more than." Underline the context clues that tell that the kitchen is just a corner. Describe the kitchen.

_____

_____

Text Evidence

❶ Specific Vocabulary ⒶⒸⓉ

The word *fidgeted* means "moved in a nervous way." Underline the text that tells why Ruth fidgeted. Rewrite the sentence replacing the word *fidgeted*.

_____

_____

❷ Sentence Structure ⒶⒸⓉ

Read the third sentence of the last paragraph. Circle the text that tells why Dad went to the soup kitchen. How did he feel about going to the soup kitchen?

_____

_____

_____

COLLABORATE

❸ Talk About It

Discuss how Dad feels. Why does he feel that way? Justify your answer. Write about it.

_____

_____

280

Dad stayed where he was, **sullen** and spent. "Any jobs in the paper?" Mom asked, her voice rich with sympathy. Dad shook his head no. He had worked as an artist in the theater for years, but most productions were still strapped for cash. Dad sketched posters for shows that did get the green light, just to keep his skills sharp. He even designed posters for "Rollet's Follies," with Ruth and me **depicted** in watercolor costumes.

For dinner, Mom served a baked loaf of whatever **ingredients** she had that worked well together. From the reddish color, I could assume that she had snuck in beets. "I guarantee you'll like these beets," she said, reading my frown. "It's beet loaf, the meatless meat loaf," she sang as she served up slices.

Ruth fidgeted in her seat, still excited about the talent show. Though calm on the outside, inside I was all atwitter, too.

Over the next week, Ruth and I practiced our Hawaiian dance routine. Our parents worried about heating bills as cold weather settled in. One Saturday, my father decided to grin and bear it, and grab some hot coffee at the local soup kitchen, where he hoped to hear about available jobs. Ruth and I begged to go along. Since the kitchen offered doughnuts and hot chocolate on weekends, he agreed.

Ron Mazellan

Most everyone in line was bundled up against the cold. Many of us had to rely on two or three threadbare layers. Like many other men, Dad bowed his head as if in shame.

The line moved slowly. Bored, Ruth began practicing her dance steps. I sang an upbeat tune to give her some music. Around us, downturned hats lifted to reveal frowns becoming smiles. Soon, folks began clapping along. Egged on by the supportive response, Ruth twirled and swayed like there was no tomorrow.

"Those girls sure have moxie!" someone shouted.

"They've got heart, all right!" offered another. "Why, they oughta be in pictures!"

"With performances like that, I'd nominate them for an Academy Award!" a woman called out.

"Those are my girls!" Dad declared, his head held high.

Everyone burst into applause. For those short moments, the past didn't matter, and the future blossomed ahead of us like a beautiful flower. I couldn't wait to write Ricky and tell him the news.

Make Connections

? Talk about ways that Ricky, Ruth, and Shirley helped each other adapt to the times. **ESSENTIAL QUESTION**

Think about a time when others helped you adapt to a new situation. How did your experience compare with the Rollet family's? **TEXT TO SELF**

Text Evidence

COLLABORATE

1 Talk About It

Reread the first paragraph. Discuss where the people are. Why are they in line? Use text evidence in your response. Write about it.

The paragraph describes _____

_____

_____

2 Specific Vocabulary ACT

The word *moxie* means "spirit or energy." Underline the text in the second paragraph that explains why the girls have moxie.

3 Comprehension

Compare and Contrast

Reread the last paragraph. Compare Dad's mood with how he felt at the beginning of the story.

_____

_____

COLLABORATE

Partner Discussion Work with a partner. Answer the questions. Discuss what you learned about "The Day the Rollets Got Their Moxie Back." Write the page numbers where you found text evidence.

What news did Ricky share? How did it affect his family?

Text Evidence 🔍

Ricky wrote to his family about _____.

Page(s): _____

After reading the letter, Shirley and Ruth decided to _____

Page(s): _____

_____.

What happened while the family waited in line for the soup kitchen?

Text Evidence 🔍

While waiting, Shirley and Ruth _____

Page(s): _____

_____.

Dad was proud because _____

Page(s): _____

_____.

COLLABORATE

Group Discussion Present your answers to the group. Cite text evidence to justify your thinking. Listen to and discuss the group's opinions about your answers.

COLLABORATE

Write Review your notes about "The Day the Rollets Got Their Moxie Back." Then write your answer to the Essential Question. Use text evidence to support your answer. Use vocabulary words from this week's reading in your writing.

How did the Rollet family help each other adapt to changes during hard times?

Ricky's letter was an unexpected _____, and it inspired Shirley and Ruth to _____

_____.

At the line for the soup kitchen, Shirley and Ruth _____

_____.

Shirely and Ruth helped Dad feel_____.

Dad was proud because _____

_____.

COLLABORATE

Share Writing Present your writing to the class. Discuss their opinions. Think about what the class has to say. Did they justify their claims? Explain why you agree or disagree with their claims.

I agree with _____ because _____.

I disagree because _____.

Write to Sources

pages 278–281

Take Notes About the Text I took notes about the text on the chart to respond to the prompt: *Write a new scene during dinner. Include a dialogue between Ruth and Shirley.*

Bree

Text Clues	New Scene
In Ricky's letter, he wrote about a talent show. He wore a grass skirt, did hula, and played a ukulele. Shirley and Ruth want to have their own talent show.	Ruth says she can't wait to put on a talent show. She asks Shirley to dance with her. Shirley tells Ruth that they need to get some music first. Ruth agrees and wants to start right away.
Dad was worried because there were no jobs in the newspaper.	Dad stayed silent during dinner. He just looked worried.
Mom made beet loaf for dinner.	Mom tells Ruth and Shirley that they need to finish dinner.

Write About the Text I used notes from my chart to write a new scene during dinner.

Student Model: *Narrative Text*

As we ate around the dinner table, Ruth said, "I can't wait to put on a talent show. I want to perform like Ricky. I can dance. Shirley, do you want to dance with me?"

I responded, "Before you start dancing, you need some music. Why don't we start with that?"

Ruth jumped up from the table as said, "OK. Let's get started right away."

Just then, Mom told Ruth and me, "You need to finish your dinner first. Sit down and eat, please."

Dad ate silently probably because he was worried.

TALK ABOUT IT

COLLABORATE

Text Evidence

Draw a box around a sentence that comes from the notes. How did Bree use this information to write a new scene?

Grammar

Circle the pronoun *I*. Who does the pronoun refer to? Who did Bree use as the narrator?

Connect Ideas

Underline Ruth's first dialogue. How can you combine the sentences and connect the ideas?

Your Turn

COLLABORATE

Add a scene to the end of the story. Write about Dad telling Mom what Shirley and Ruth did at the soup kitchen. Use details from the story.

≫ Go Digital!
Write your response online. Use your editing checklist.

TALK ABOUT IT

?

Essential Question

What changes in the environment affect living things?

≫ Go Digital

COLLABORATE

What do monarch butterflies do in winter? What do they do in spring? What happens to living things when there are changes in the environment? Write about changes in the chart.

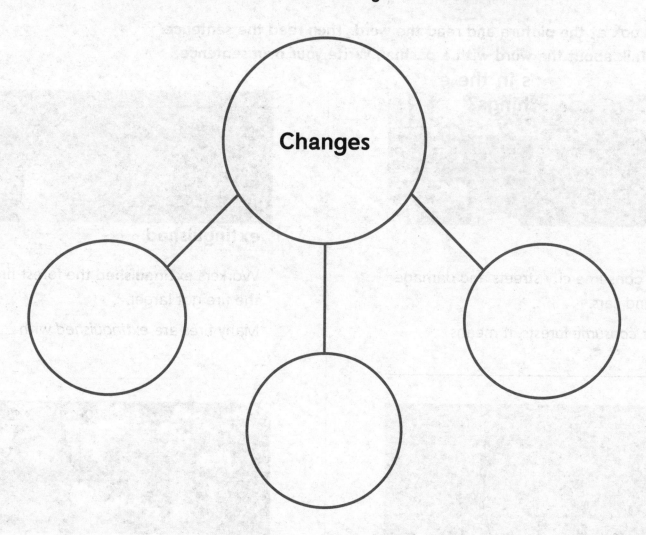

Changes

Discuss how changes in the environment affect living things. Use words from the chart. You can say:

In the winter, monarch butterflies _____.

When there are changes in the environment, living things _____.

Look at the picture and read the word. Then read the sentence. Talk about the word with a partner. Write your own sentence.

consume

Floods can **consume** city streets and damage buildings and cars.

When fires *consume* forests, it means

that _____.

encourages

The warm weather in spring **encourages** plants to grow.

Warm weather *encourages* me _____

_____.

extinguished

Workers **extinguished** the forest fire before the fire got larger.

Many fires are *extinguished* with _____.

flourish

When Jason takes care of his garden, plants and flowers **flourish**.

Plants *flourish* when they get _____

_____.

Words and Phrases
Phrasal Verb and Conjunction

occur

Tornadoes usually **occur** on land.

Snowstorms usually *occur* in _____

_____ .

suppress

Lindsey is trying to **suppress** her laugh.

I *suppress* a laugh when I _____

_____ .

take over = gain control of something
The new owner of the store will <u>take over</u> *the business.*

You can use the word *whether* to tell that something will or will not happen whatever the situation is.
<u>*Whether*</u> *we win or lose, we will try our best.*

Read the sentences below. Write the word or phrase that best fits the sentence.

You need to do your homework,_____
you like it or not.

In springtime, the flock of geese _____
the lake in the park.

When her favorite show is on TV, Krysta likes to

_____ the remote control.

_____ you are a player or coach, everyone must be at practice.

>> Go Digital Add *take over* and *whether* to your New Words notebook. Write a sentence to show the meaning of each.

COLLABORATE

1 Talk About It

Read the title. Discuss what you see. Write your ideas.

What does the title tell you?

_____

_____

_____

What happens during a forest fire?

_____

_____

_____

What can cause a forest fire?

_____

_____

_____

Take notes as you read the text.

Forests on Fire

Essential Question

? **What changes in the environment affect living things?**

Read about the effects of forest fires on plants, animals, and people.

A few years ago, several red squirrels—an endangered species—had a temporary home at the Phoenix Zoo. Rescued from a ravaging wildfire that had already destroyed thousands of acres of land, the squirrels were waiting for the fire to be **extinguished** before being returned to the wild. Forest fires are part of nature, so it is important for us to understand not only how to fight fires, but also why they **occur**.

Destructive and Productive

Like rainstorms, wildfires are a force of nature. However, unlike rainstorms, wildfires are almost always destructive. They **consume** everything in their way, including plants, trees, and animals. Sometimes, they take human lives and homes as well.

Like a big storm, the destructive power of wildfires is terrifying. On the other hand, naturally occurring wildfires are also productive forces. Whether their flames race through a forest, a prairie, or acres of brush, these fires produce necessary changes in their environment. Like rain, they can allow new life to **flourish**.

Benefits of Naturally Occurring Wildfires

A naturally occurring wildfire, sometimes called a forest fire, happens without any human cause. Three factors must be present for one to burn. These include fuel, such as dry grasses; oxygen, which is in our atmosphere; and a heat source to ignite the fuel. A lightning strike usually sparks a naturally occurring wildfire. The danger of fire is highest during a drought, when an area has experienced little rain.

Wildfires have happened throughout history, and they help to regenerate Earth and its species. When vegetation decays, wildfires clear it away so that new plant life can grow.

Rapsodia/Riser/Getty Images

❶ Comprehension

Compare and Contrast

Reread the second paragraph. Circle the text that tells how wildfires and rainstorms are different. Write about it.

_____

_____

❷ Sentence Structure Ⓐ Ⓒ Ⓣ

Reread the third sentence of the fourth paragraph. Underline what the pronoun *these* refers to. What do the semicolons do?

The semicolons _____

_____

❸ Specific Vocabulary Ⓐ Ⓒ Ⓣ

The word *ignite* means "to start burning." Underline a word in the next sentence with a similar meaning. What can ignite fuel?

_____

1 Specific Vocabulary ACT

The word *eliminating* means "getting rid of." Underline the text that tells the result of eliminating the canopies. How do fires eliminate canopies?

Fires eliminate canopies by _____

_____.

2 Comprehension

Compare and Contrast

Reread the second paragraph. Put a box around the text that compares new plant life with old. How is new plant life better than old plant life?

_____

_____

COLLABORATE

3 Talk About It

What are the benefits of wildfires? Explain your answer using text evidence.

_____

Open cone

New seedling

A young forest

The black spruce tree needs a fire's heat to cause its cones to open and scatter seeds. Eventually, seedlings sprout, and a new forest will grow.

Fire also releases nutrients back into the soil, making it more fertile. And by eliminating leafy canopies of mature trees, fire allows nourishing sunlight to reach a forest floor.

Often, this new plant life will be better adapted to fire than what existed before. Some species will have fire-resistant roots, leaves, or bark. Other species will actually depend on fire to reproduce and thrive.

Stability and Diversity

Among its benefits, fire promotes stability. By eliminating invasive species that can take over an area, fire **encourages** the healthy growth of a region's own vegetation.

At the same time, fire promotes diversity. It ensures that plant life will exist at different stages of development. For example, a forest recently struck by fire will have new seedlings. Not far away, in a forest struck by fire twenty years earlier, there may be small trees. And nearby, there may be a forest of mature trees, untouched by fire for years.

These variations in plant life provide food and habitats for different kinds of insects, birds, and mammals. Woodpeckers eat insects in burned-out trees. Sparrows depend on seeds for food. Predators such as foxes are drawn by small prey. Forests at different stages attract a diversity of animals to a region.

The Human Factor

Although wildfires have benefits, they also are feared and misunderstood. As a result, our government tried to **suppress** them completely throughout the 20th century. This policy had a negative impact on the environment. The gradual buildup of decayed vegetation provided more fuel to feed fires. Consequently, wildfires became noticeably fiercer.

More recently, the government has used two different strategies to manage wildfires. One is to try to limit fires before they burn out of control. The other is to set small "prescribed" fires to reduce the amount

Whether wildfires are small or large, firefighters are needed to help contain them.

of fuel in the environment. Hopefully, the danger of catastrophic fires is now receding.

Unfortunately, human carelessness, such as a campfire left to smolder, also can start a fire. While a natural or prescribed wildfire can be beneficial, this is not true of fires that result from malice or mistakes. These happen at times and places that may cause irreparable damage to plant, animal, and human life. Fires cannot control themselves, so humans will always have to figure out how best to handle them.

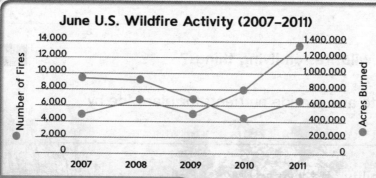

June U.S. Wildfire Activity (2007–2011)

Number of Fires — Acres Burned

Make Connections

Talk about how wildfires change the environment for plants. **ESSENTIAL QUESTION**

Why is it important for you to be careful around a fire of any kind, even in a home? **TEXT TO SELF**

Gene Blevins/LA Daily News/Corbis

Text Evidence

1 Sentence Structure Ⓐ Ⓒ Ⓣ

Reread the last two sentences in the first paragraph. Underline the two effects of buildup of decayed vegetation.

2 Specific Vocabulary Ⓐ Ⓒ Ⓣ

The word *carelessness* means "not being careful." Underline an example of carelessness. What are other examples of human carelessness?

_____

_____

COLLABORATE

3 Talk About It

Reread the last sentence. Discuss why it is important to figure out how to handle wildfires. Justify your answer. Write about it.

_____

_____

Respond to the Text

COLLABORATE

Partner Discussion Work with a partner. Answer the questions. Discuss what you learned about "Forests on Fire." Write the page numbers where you found text evidence.

What are the effects of wildfires on living things?

Wildfires are destructive when _____

_____.

Wildfires are helpful because _____

_____.

Text Evidence 🔍

Page(s): _____

Page(s): _____

What are the benefits of wildfires on living things?

Wildfires help to regenerate and provide nutrients for plant life by _____

_____.

Wildifires also provide stability and diversity by _____

_____.

Text Evidence 🔍

Page(s): _____

Page(s): _____

COLLABORATE

Group Discussion Present your answers to the group. Cite text evidence to justify your thinking. Listen to and discuss the group's opinions about your answers.

Write Review your notes about "Forests on Fire." Then write your answer to the Essential Question. Use text evidence to support your answer. Use vocabulary words from this week's reading in your writing.

> **How does a wildfire change the environment and affect living things?**
>
> Wildfires have destructive effects by _____
>
> _____.
>
> However, wildfires also have beneficial effects by _____
>
> _____.
>
> People realize that wildfires are both _____
>
> _____.

Share Writing Present your writing to the class. Discuss their opinions. Think about what the class has to say. Did they justify their claims? Explain why you agree or disagree with their claims.

I agree with _____ because _____.

I disagree because _____.

Write to Sources

Take Notes About the Text I took notes about the text on the chart to answer the question: *How are wildfires harmful and helpful to the environment?*

pages 290–293

Jane

Topic	Topic
Wildfires are harmful.	Wildfires are helpful.
Details	**Details**
Wildfires destroy plants and animals. Wildfires destroy human lives and homes.	Wildfires burn away decay. Wildfires make soil more fertile. Wildfires burn top leaves so sunlight can reach low-growing plants.

296

Write About the Text I used notes from my chart to write an informative paragraph about wildfires.

Student Model: *Informative Text*

Wildfires are harmful and helpful to the environment. Wildfires are destructive. They destroy plants, animals, and homes. However, wildfires can be beneficial. Fires burn away decay, allowing new plants to grow. Fires also help make soil more fertile and sunlight can reach the forest floor. Finally, wildfires get rid of nonnative plants so native plants can thrive. Wildfires can damage an environment, but they also renew a forest with new growth.

TALK ABOUT IT

COLLABORATE

Text Evidence

Draw a box around a sentence that comes from the notes. How does Jane use the information?

Grammar

Circle an adjective that describes the soil. Why does Jane use this adjective?

Connect Ideas

Underline the sentences that tell about how wildfires destroy. How can you combine the sentences and connect the ideas?

Your Turn

COLLABORATE

Write about how prescribed fires can be beneficial or harmful to a forest. Use text evidence in your writing.

>> *Go Digital!*
Write your response online. Use your editing checklist.

Weekly Concept Now We Know

Essential Question

How can scientific knowledge change over time?

>> *Go Digital*

What is the scientist doing? How do scientists get new information? How can new information change scientific knowledge? Write words in the chart.

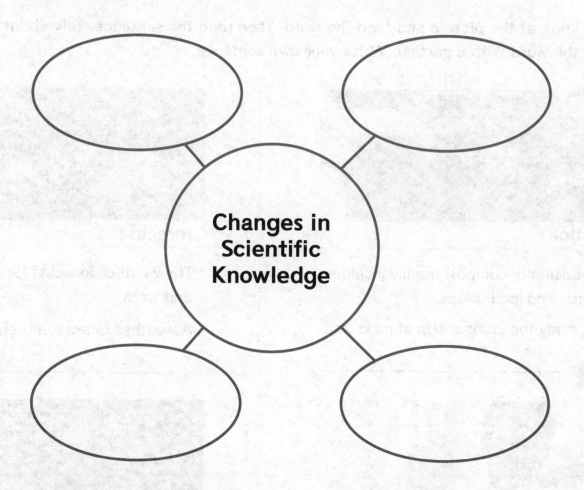

Changes in Scientific Knowledge

Discuss how new information causes changes in scientific knowledge. Use words from the chart. You can say:

Scientists get new information by _____.

New information can change scientific knowledge when _____

_____.

More Vocabulary

COLLABORATE

Look at the picture and read the word. Then read the sentence. Talk about the word with a partner. Write your own sentence.

composition

The **composition** of compost usually includes leaves, grass, and food scraps.

Geologists study the *composition* of rocks and

soil to _____.

confronting

Mario conducts tests to **confront** the results of his experiment.

To *confront* a hypothesis, you can _____.

| MON | TUES | WED | S | FRI |

forecast

The weather **forecast** for the week is sunny and warm.

A weather *forecast* is useful when _____

_____.

launched

The rocket **launched** into space.

After the students *launched* the model rocket,

it _____.

transport

The family used a moving truck to **transport** boxes and furniture to their new house.

When you *transport* something, you _____

_____.

venture

Scientists use vehicles to explore and **venture** onto the deep ocean floor.

To *venture* is to go somewhere that is

_____.

Words and Phrases
Adverb Phrases

at once = at the same time
Carla got many text messages <u>at once</u>.

in place = in one position without moving
Tom used tape to hold the photograph <u>in place</u>.

Read the sentences below. Write the phrase that means the same as the underlined words.

My dog stays <u>in one position</u> until I give her a signal to move.

My dog stays _____ until I give her a signal to move.

The room was loud because the children talked <u>at the same time</u>.

The room was loud because the children all talked

_____.

>> *Go Digital* **Add the phrases *at once* and *in place* to your New Words notebook. Write a sentence to show the meaning of each.**

COLLABORATE

1 Talk About It

Read the title. Talk about what you see. Write your ideas.

What does the title tell you?

_____

_____

_____

What does the photograph show?

_____

_____

_____

Where do you think the photograph was taken?

_____

_____

Take notes as you read the text.

CHANGING VIEWS OF EARTH

Essential Question

? **How can scientific knowledge change over time?**

Read about how our understanding of Earth has changed along with scientific developments over time.

On the Ground, Looking Around

No matter where on Earth you go, people like to talk about the weather. This weekend's **forecast** may provide the main criteria for planning outdoor activities. Where does all that information about the weather come from? The ability to predict storms and droughts required centuries of scientific innovation. We had to look up at the skies to learn more about life here on Earth.

Long ago, humans based their knowledge on what they experienced with their eyes and ears. If people could heighten their senses, they might not feel so mystified by the events **confronting** them daily. For example, something as simple as the rising sun perplexed people for centuries. They believed that the Earth stayed in place while the Sun moved around it. This was called the geocentric model.

In the early 1600s, an Italian named Galileo pointed a new tool called the telescope toward the night sky. As a result of his heightened vision, he could see stars, planets, and other celestial spheres with new clarity. Each observation and calculation led him to support a radical new model of the solar system. In the heliocentric version proposed by the scientist Copernicus, the Sun did not orbit the Earth. The Earth orbited the Sun.

Galileo's telescope helped prove that Copernicus's heliocentric view was correct. ▶

These diagrams show the geocentric (Earth in the center), and the heliocentric (Sun in the center) views of the solar system.

Hulton Archive/Getty Images

① **Sentence Structure** Ⓐ Ⓒ Ⓣ

Reread the second sentence in the second paragraph. Circle the cause. Underline the effect. What do the words *if* and *might* tell you?

The words tell me that _____

_____.

② **Specific Vocabulary** Ⓐ Ⓒ Ⓣ

The word *perplexed* means "to feel confused about something that is hard to understand." Underline a word in the paragraph that has a similar meaning. What perplexed people?

_____

_____

③ **Comprehension**

Cause and Effect

Reread the third paragraph. Underline the effect of using a telescope. Write about it.

_____

_____

Text Evidence

1 Sentence Structure A C T

Reread the last sentence of the second paragraph. Underline the text that tells about the text between the dashes. What happened to the scientists?

_____

_____

2 Comprehension
Cause and Effect

Reread the last paragraph. Put a box around the causes for using aircraft.

The causes for using aircraft were

_____

_____

COLLABORATE

3 Talk About It

Based on the chart, discuss which layers scientists studied using hot-air balloons and aircraft.

_____

In the Sky, Looking Down

New technology allowed scientists to evaluate theories better than ever. Measuring devices such as the thermometer and barometer offered new insights into weather patterns. However, people were still limited to ground-based learning. What if they could travel into the sky, where the weather actually happened?

In the mid-1700s, some scientists sent measurement devices higher

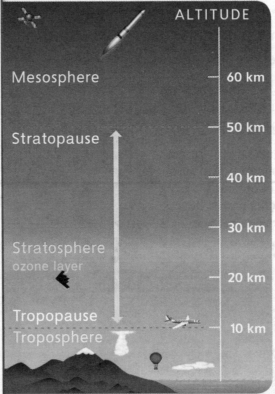

As humans reached higher, we learned more and more about Earth's atmosphere.

and higher. At first they used kites. Before long, hot-air balloons offered new ways to **transport** the tools—and sometimes scientists themselves—into the sky.

However, scientists were not satisfied studying the lower layers of Earth's atmosphere. The more they learned, the higher they wanted to go. They also wanted to obtain information more quickly and accurately. Kites and balloons were hard to control. As a result, they occasionally veered off course or got lost, taking their data with them.

The development of aircraft in the early 1900s promised safer ways to observe Earth's surface and the atmosphere above it. Kites and balloons could reach altitudes of approximately three kilometers. By comparison, airplanes lifted scientists to a height of five kilometers and more. Radio technology allowed scientists to transmit data from the air to the ground, where other scientists analyzed and compared information. Breakthroughs came fast and furiously. Still, scientists dreamed of reaching ever higher.

Rogerio Soud

Out in Space, Looking Back Home

In the late twentieth century, advances in aeronautics led to more powerful rockets that lifted satellites into orbit around Earth. From these heights, scientists could study the **composition** and relative thinness of our layered atmosphere. Since meteorologists could analyze multiple factors at once, the accuracy of their weather predictions improved dramatically.

NASA **launched** dozens of satellites into orbit in the following years. Some stared back at Earth, while others peered deep into endless space. They gathered astronomical data about the ages of planets and galaxies. Sensors and supercomputers measured things such as Earth's diameter with incredible accuracy.

Because of this technology, scientists could develop more reliable models about Earth's systems. For example, they could form theories to show how climate might change over time.

Space missions continue to **venture** farther from home. Even so, nothing compares to seeing Earth the old way, with our own eyes. Views of our planet from space inspire awe in nearly all people who have seen them, even in photographs. "With all the arguments . . . for going to the Moon," said astronaut Joseph Allen, "no one suggested that we should do it to look at the Earth. But that may in fact be the most important reason."

Satellites launched into orbit only last for a limited number of years and then must be replaced.

Brand X Pictures/PunchStock

Make Connections

What were some effects of flight on our knowledge about Earth? **ESSENTIAL QUESTION**

How has your knowledge of Earth changed over time? What effect has this change had on you? **TEXT TO SELF**

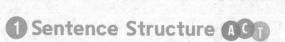

Text Evidence

1 Sentence Structure Ⓐ Ⓒ Ⓣ

Reread the second sentence in the second paragraph. Circle the text that the pronouns *some* and *others* refer to.

2 Comprehension
Cause and Effect

Reread the second paragraph. Underline the cause that resulted in scientists developing more reliable models. Write about the cause.

_____

_____

COLLABORATE

3 Talk About It

Reread the last paragraph. Explain what Joseph Allen thinks was the most important reason for going to the Moon. Justify your answer.

_____

_____

305

Partner Discussion Work with a partner. Answer the questions. Discuss what you learned about "Changing Views of Earth" Write the page numbers where you found text evidence.

What was people's view of Earth in the past?

Text Evidence 🔍

I read that long ago people thought the Sun _____

_____.

Page(s): _____

However, Galileo and Copernicus helped to change _____

_____.

Page(s): _____

How has technology helped scientists make new discoveries?

Text Evidence 🔍

In the 1700s, scientists sent _____.

Page(s): _____

In the 1900s, scientists used _____.

Page(s): _____

To gather information today, scientists use _____

_____.

Page(s): _____

Group Discussion Present your answers to the group. Cite text evidence to justify your thinking. Listen to and discuss the group's opinions about your answers.

Write Review your notes about "Changing Views of Earth." Then write your answer to the Essential Question. Use text evidence to support your answer. Use vocabulary words from this week's reading in your writing.

> **How has scientific knowledge changed our view of Earth over time?**
>
> Long ago, people thought that _____.
>
> Their view has changed because _____
>
> _____.
>
> New technology has helped scientists _____.
>
> Examples include _____.
>
> Today, new technology helps scientists develop _____
>
> _____.

Share Writing Present your writing to the class. Discuss their opinions. Think about what the class has to say. Did they justify their claims? Explain why you agree or disagree with their claims.

I agree with _____ because _____.

I disagree because _____

April

Take Notes About the Text I took notes on the chart to answer the question: *How have people changed the way they make weather predictions over time?*

pages 302–305

First
Long ago, humans used what they heard and saw to explain weather.

Next
Scientists used tools such as thermometers and barometers.

Then
In the mid-1700s, scientists sent tools into the sky on kites and hot air balloons.

Last
From the 1900s to today, scientists use airplanes and satellites.

Write About the Text I used notes from my chart to write
an informative paragraph predicting weather.

Student Model: *Informative Text*

Long ago, people used what they saw and
heard to predict weather. Then, scientists used
new tools, such as thermometers and barometers,
to understand weather patterns. However, these
tools were used only on the ground. Then, in the
mid-1700s, scientists used kites and balloons to
send tools into the sky. In 1900s, airplanes were
invented. People invented satellites, too. Now,
scientists can use information about the Earth's
atmosphere to study weather. Predicting weather
is more accurate now than it was long ago.

TALK ABOUT IT

Text Evidence

Circle a sentence that comes from the notes.
How does April use this information?

Grammar

Underline a comparative adjective. How does
April use the adjective ?

Condense Ideas

Draw a box around the sentences that tell
about what happened in the 1900s. How can
you condense the sentences to create a more
precise sentence?

Your Turn

Why did the author use Joseph
Allen's quote? Use text evidence in
your writing.

>> *Go Digital!*
Write your response online. Use your editing checklist.

TALK ABOUT IT

Weekly Concept Scientific Viewpoints

?

Essential Question

How do natural events and human activities affect the environment?

>> *Go Digital*

COLLABORATE

What is the man's job? How do bees help him? How does he help the bees? What natural and human activities affect the environment? Write words in the chart.

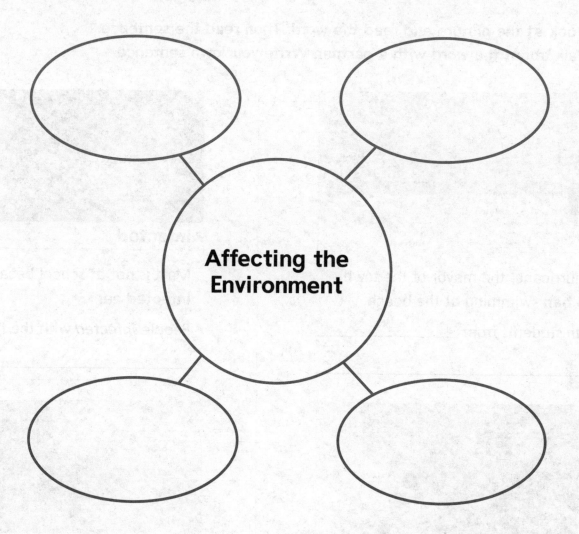

Affecting the Environment

Discuss how natural and human activities affect the environment. Use words from the chart. You can say:

The man helps bees by _____. The bees help the man by the

_____. Activities that affect the environment are _____.

COLLABORATE

Look at the picture and read the word. Then read the sentence.
Talk about the word with a partner. Write your own sentence.

ban

After the hurricane, the mayor of the town decided to **ban** swimming at the beach.

Schools *ban* students from _____

_____.

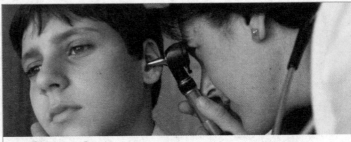

infected

Matt is not at school because he has an **infected** ear.

People *infected* with the flu may feel

_____.

benefit

Computers **benefit** students by helping students learn.

Sleeping 8 hours a day helps me at school

because _____.

nuisance

The loud noise is a **nuisance** to Salina.

Something that is a *nuisance* makes people feel

_____.

originated

Sailors saw that the light **originated** from the lighthouse.

Another word for *originated* is _____

_____.

overwhelm

A big group of ants **overwhelmed** the picnic grounds.

Another word for *overwhelm* is _____

_____.

Words and Phrases
Adverb Phrases

just about = almost or nearly
Tanya got <u>just about</u> every answer correct on the test.

on purpose = intentionally, not by accident
Rudy let his little brother win <u>on purpose</u>.

Read the sentences below. Write the phrase that means the same as the underlined words.

Jose is <u>almost</u> finished with his homework.

Jose is _____ finished with his homework.

Anna wants people to laugh, so she makes funny faces <u>intentionally</u>.

Anna wants people to laugh, so she makes funny

faces _____.

>> *Go Digital* **Add the phrases *just about* and *on purpose* to your New Words notebook. Write a sentence to show the meaning of each.**

olaser/E+/Getty Images; Scott Harms/Getty Images

COLLABORATE

1 Talk About It

Read the title. Talk about what you see. Write your ideas.

What does the title tell you?

_____

_____

_____

_____

Where do oranges grow?

_____

_____

_____

_____

Take notes as you read the text.

Essential Question

? How do natural events and human activities affect the environment?

Read two different views on the arrival of new species into the United States.

It's hard to imagine life without oranges and chickens, which are examples of nonnative species.

Kirk Weddle/Photodisc/Getty Images

Should Plants and Animals from Other Places Live Here?

New Arrivals Welcome

Nonnative species are good for the economy—and they taste good, too!

Some of America's most important immigrants are plants and animals. Called *nonnative species*, these creatures arrive here from other regions or countries. Nonnative species are known as *invasive* when they harm the environment, our health, or the economy. Invasive species often take over a widespread area and **overwhelm** native wildlife. The population of some native species has declined because of a few newcomers, but the news is not all bad. We would be a lot worse off without some of them.

In Florida, for example, about 2,000 species of familiar plants and animals are nonnative. These include oranges, chickens, and sugarcane. In fact, 90 percent of farm sales can be traced directly to nonnative species.

Nonnative species help to control insects and other pests that harm crops. Some scientists identify a pest's natural enemy and bring in nonnative enemy species, such as insects, to kill the pests. Killing the pests is a good thing, and an even better result is that pesticide use is reduced. Vedalia beetles were transported here from Australia to eat insects that killed citrus fruit. The beetles completed their mission without any side effects. They also help keep citrus farmers in business!

Not all new arrivals **benefit** humans. However, many nonnative species are just what the doctor ordered. Many of the dogs and cats we love so much **originated** in other parts of the world. Would you want to **ban** Labrador retrievers and Siamese cats? Creatures like these surely make our lives and our nation better!

Text Evidence

1 Sentence Structure (A)(C)(T)

Reread the second and third sentences. Circle the text that tells the difference between nonnative and invasive species.

Invasive species are _____

_____.

2 Specific Vocabulary (A)(C)(T)

The idiom *just what the doctor ordered* means "exactly what is needed." Underline the text that tells what the phrase refers to.

The phrase refers to _____

_____.

3 Comprehension
Author's Point of View

Reread the last paragraph. Put a box around the words the author uses to tell the point of view.

The author uses words _____

_____

_____.

315

Text Evidence

1 Specific Vocabulary ACT

The word *unintentionally* means "not done on purpose." Circle what was unintentionally introduced. What effects did it have?

_____

_____

2 Comprehension

Author's Point of View

Reread the second paragraph. Put a box around the evidence the author uses to tell the point of view. Write about it.

_____

_____

COLLABORATE

3 Talk About It

Discuss whether you agree or disagree with the author's point of view. Justify your answer.

_____

_____

COUNTERPOINT

A Growing Problem

Thousands of foreign plant and animal species threaten our country.

Visitors to the Florida Everglades expect to see alligators, not pythons. These huge snakes are native to Southeast Asia. But about 150,000 of the reptiles are crawling through the Everglades. The probable reason they got there is that pet owners dumped the snakes in the wild. Now the nonnative pythons have become a widespread menace, threatening to reduce the population of endangered native species.

Some nonnative species may be useful, but others are harmful to the nation. It costs the U.S. $137 billion each year to repair the damage these species cause to the environment. The trouble occurs when nonnative species become invasive. Invasive species are a **nuisance** just about everywhere in the nation. For example, the Asian carp, which was introduced unintentionally to the U.S., has been able to thrive in the Mississippi River and now threatens the Great Lakes ecosystem. Because of its large appetite, the population of native fish has gone down.

Some germs are also invasive species, and they are especially harmful to humans. One, the avian influenza virus, came to the U.S. carried by birds. This microbe can cause a serious lung disorder in **infected** people.

Some agricultural experts have introduced nonnative species on purpose to improve the environment. However, this can sometimes create unexpected problems. A hundred years ago, melaleuca trees were brought to Florida from Australia to stabilize swampy areas. Now millions of the trees blanket the land, crowding out native plants and harming endangered plants and animals.

The facts about this alien invasion lead to one conclusion: We must remove invasive species and keep new ones from our shores.

Jeff Greenberg/Alamy

Nonnative Species: Benefits and Costs

Over the years, about 50,000 nonnative species have entered the U.S. These four examples show the positive and negative impacts they can have.

SPECIES	NATIVE LAND	WHEN AND HOW INTRODUCED TO U.S.	POSITIVE IMPACT	NEGATIVE IMPACT
Horse	Europe	Early 1500s, on purpose	Used for work, transportation, and recreation	Made large-scale wars possible
Kudzu	Asia	Early 1800s, on purpose	Stops soil erosion	Crowds out native plants
Olives	Middle East and Europe	Early 1700s, on purpose, cultivation began in 1800s	Major food and cooking oil source, important industry in California	Most olives must be imported because they do not grow everywhere.
Mediterranean Fruit Fly	Sub-Saharan Africa	1929 (first recorded), accidentally	May be a food source for creatures such as spiders	Destroys 400 species of plants, including citrus and vegetable crops

This community is trying to control the invasive melaleuca plant that has taken over this marsh.

Make Connections

Talk about the uses and harmful effects of species introduced into the United States. **ESSENTIAL QUESTION**

Would you give up eating or using a species if you discovered it was nonnative? Explain your reasons. **TEXT TO SELF**

Text Evidence

1 Sentence Structure ACT

Read the second sentence. Underline the text that the phrase *they can have* refers to. How do you know that the word *impacts* is used as a noun and not a verb.

Impact is used as a noun because

_____.

2 Comprehension

Reread the chart. Circle the nonnative species that threaten the native species. Then write about it.

_____

_____

COLLABORATE

3 Talk About It

Choose one nonnative species and discuss whether it is invasive or not. Justify your answer. Write about it.

_____

_____

CAUTION
MELALEUCA CONTROL PROJECT

Respond to the Text

Partner Discussion Work with a partner. Answer the questions. Discuss what you learned about "Should Plants and Animals from Other Places Live Here?" Write the page numbers where you found text evidence.

How do nonnative species help us?

I read that in Florida most plants and animals are _____.

Some nonnative species control _____.

Common pets, such as _____, are _____ species.

Text Evidence 🔍

Page(s): _____

Page(s): _____

Page(s): _____

How do nonnative species cause harm?

Some nonnative species cause harm to _____.

Nonnative species become invasive _____

_____.

One example of invasive species is _____.

Text Evidence 🔍

Page(s): _____

Page(s): _____

Page(s): _____

Group Discussion Present your answers to the group. Cite text evidence to justify your thinking. Listen to and discuss the group's opinions about your answers.

COLLABORATE

Write Review your notes about "Should Plants and Animals from Other Places Live Here?" Then write your answer to the Essential Question. Use text evidence to support your answer. Use vocabulary words from this week's reading in your writing.

How do nonnative species affect the environment?

Nonnative species are brought into the country to _____

_____.

Nonnative species are called invasive if _____

_____.

Nonnative species have had positive and negative effects because _____

_____.

COLLABORATE

Share Writing Present your writing to the class. Discuss their opinions. Think about what the class has to say. Did they justify their claims? Explain why you agree or disagree with their claims.

I agree with _____ because _____.

I disagree because _____.

Write to Sources

pages 314–317

Take Notes About the Text I took notes about the text on the idea web to answer the question: *In your opinion, should nonnative species be introduced to the United States?*

Vince

Evidence
Vedalia beetles from Australia came to Florida to eat insects that ate citrus fruit.

Evidence
Vedalia beetles ate citrus pests and helped citrus farmers. No pesticides were used.

Opinion
Nonnative species should be introduced to the United States.

Evidence
Florida has around 2,000 nonnative species that are familiar to us.

Evidence
Many pets are nonnative species.

320

Write About the Text I used notes from my idea web to write my opinion about nonnative species.

Nonnative species should be introduced into the United States. They can have a positive result. For example, the introduction of Vedalia beetles into Florida's citrus crop helped many citrus farmers. The beetles ate the pests that were killing the citrus plants. Farmers did not have to use pesticides. Many of the familiar plants and animals are nonnative species, such as oranges and chickens. Also, many pets are nonnative species. There are many benefits to having nonnative species come into our country.

TALK ABOUT IT

Text Evidence
Draw a box around a sentence that comes from the notes. How does the information support Vince's opinion?

Grammar
Circle past-tense and present-tense verbs. Why does Vince use the different tenses?

Condense Ideas
Underline the sentences about Vedalia beetles. How can you combine the sentences into one detailed sentence?

Your Turn

In your opinion, which nonnative species has been the most helpful to the United States? Use the chart on page 317 for text evidence in your writing.

>> Go Digital
Write your response online. Use your editing checklist.

Linked In

The Big Idea

How are we all connected?

Bill O'Leary/The Washington Post/Getty Images

323

TALK ABOUT IT

Weekly Concept Joining Forces

? **Essential Question**
How do different groups contribute to a cause?

» *Go Digital*

What are the women working to make? How did women contribute to the cause of the war effort by building airplanes? How can people contribute to a cause? Write words in the chart.

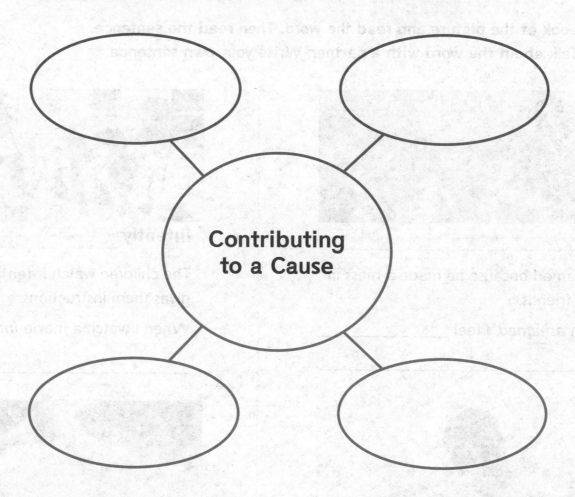

Contributing to a Cause

Discuss how people can contribute to a cause. Use words from the chart. You can say:

Women contributed to the _____ of the war effort

by _____.

People can contribute to a cause by _____.

More Vocabulary

Look at the picture and read the word. Then read the sentence. Talk about the word with a partner. Write your own sentence.

ashamed

Seth is **ashamed** because he made a mess in front of his friends.

When I am *ashamed,* I feel _____

_____ .

intend

Chris did not **intend** to spill the milk on the table.

If I did not *intend* to do something, it means that I _____ .

intently

The children watch **intently** as the teacher gives them instructions.

When I watch a movie *intently,* it means I ___

_____ .

knead

Rachel will **knead** the dough until it is smooth.

To *knead* dough you need to _____

_____ .

mechanic

The **mechanic** fixes the engine.

A *mechanic* fixes machines, such as _____

_____ .

supplies

Before the school year begins, Paul gets his school **supplies**.

School *supplies* that I buy every year are

_____ .

Words and Phrases
Homophones

The words *way* and *weigh* are homophones. Homophones are words that sound the same but have different spellings and meanings.

way = how someone thinks, feels, or does something; how something happens
The teacher smiled in a <u>way</u> that made us feel better.

weigh = to have weight
Apples <u>weigh</u> more than blueberries.

Read the sentences below. Underline the homophone in each sentence.

Ralph uses a scale to weigh the package.

Lexie is tired. She feels that way when she stays up late.

Write your own sentences using *way* and *weigh*.

_____

_____

_____

>> *Go Digital* **Add the words *way* and *weigh* to your New Words notebook. Write a sentence to show the meaning of each.**

COLLABORATE

❶ Talk About It

Read the title. Talk about what you see. Write your ideas.

What does the title tell you?

_____

_____

_____

_____

What do you see in the store window?

_____

_____

_____

_____

Take notes as you read the story.

SHIPPED OUT

Essential Question

? **How do different groups contribute to a cause?**

Read about how a young girl learns how to contribute to the war effort during World War II.

My name is Libby Kendall, and I am a prisoner of war. Well, not really, but some days it feels that way. Just like my dad, I've packed up my things and shipped out. Unlike my dad, however, nothing I do will ever help the Allies win World War II.

My father is a **mechanic** on a battleship in the Pacific Ocean. I'm trapped in a little apartment above my Aunt Lucia's bakery downtown. Mom says it's just for a few months while she works double shifts at the clothing factory. She makes uniforms, mostly sewing pockets on jackets. I asked her once if she snuck things into the pockets for soldiers to find, like little poems written in calligraphy. She said soldiers wore jackets with pockets to hold tools they might need for war survival, not silly things like poetry.

It seems no one appreciates my creative contributions to the war effort, but Aunt Lucia says my help to her is important, since both her workers joined the army.

On my first day with Aunt Lucia, she explained the daily

operations of the bakery. First, we get up before dawn to **knead** the dough. Next, we bake breads and muffins. Then, while I help customers, Lucia makes cakes and cookies for sale in the afternoon. Whenever the phone rings, she races from the back room to intercept the call. She's always worried that it might be bad news, so she wants to be the first to hear it.

After dinner, Aunt Lucia invites neighbors over to listen to the radio. Some are immigrants from a wide diversity of backgrounds. Lucia and others help translate the news into several languages for everyone to understand. I always listen closely for any bulletin about fighting in the Pacific.

Sean Qualls

1 Specific Vocabulary Ⓐ Ⓒ Ⓣ

The word *snuck* means "secretly put something somewhere." Circle the context clue that helps to tell the meaning.

2 Sentence Structure Ⓐ Ⓒ Ⓣ

Reread the last sentence in the fourth paragraph. The sentence has two parts. Circle the text the pronoun *it* refers to in the first part. Underline the text *it* refers to in the second part. Why does Aunt Lucia answer all the calls?

_____

_____

3 Comprehension

Reread the last sentence. Put a box around the text that tells why Libby always listens for news about the Pacific. Write about it.

_____

_____

329

1 Specific Vocabulary ACT

The idiom *stormed off* means "to walk away angrily." Underline the text that tells why Libby stormed off. Write about it.

She stormed off because _____

_____.

2 Sentence Structure ACT

Reread the last sentence of the third paragraph. Circle the text the pronoun *that* refers to. Compare how Libby felt then and now.

_____

_____

3 Talk About It

Reread the last paragraph. Discuss why Aunt Lucia asks Libby to help when she knows that Libby is feeling down. Justify your answer.

I remember how **intently** my parents read reports about the war, which I rarely understood. They often whispered to one another, and I'd shout out something like, "Speak up! I can't hear you!" They'd frown and leave me alone to talk in private.

One night, they came into the living room and turned off the radio. At first I was angry, but they had serious expressions on their faces. "Our country's at war," Dad said. "The military will be looking for new recruits. I know something about boats and ship engines, so I **intend** to join the navy."

My face grew hot, but my hands felt cold. "You can't just leave," I said. I stomped on the floor for emphasis and stormed off to my bedroom. Looking back on that now, I feel **ashamed** of how selfishly I had acted.

This morning, Aunt Lucia can tell I'm feeling down. She asks me to help her decorate cupcakes for a fundraiser tonight. At first I'm not interested. I just slather on frosting and plop a berry on top. Then I realize that I can make red stripes out of strawberries and a patch of blue from blueberries. Soon I have a whole tray of cupcakes decorated like flags to show Aunt Lucia.

Sean Qualls

"These are wonderful!" Lucia says. "I'm sure they'll sell better than anything else!"

For the first time in weeks, I feel like I've done something right. I think of all the money we might make at the sale, and how it may buy **supplies** for my father.

"I enlisted in the navy to help restore democracy in the world," my dad said on the day he left. "Now you be a good navy daughter and sail straight, young lady." I promised I would. As he went out the door, I slipped a little poem into his coat pocket. "Here's a little rhyme to pass the day," it said. "I love you back in the U.S.A.!"

I look at the cupcakes and wish I could send one to my dad. Instead, I'll draw a platter on which they're piled high and send the picture off to the Pacific with a letter. That way, my dad will have plenty to share with everyone there.

1 Specific Vocabulary Ⓐ Ⓒ Ⓣ

The idiom *sail straight* means "to be good" and the word *sail* refers to traveling on the sea. Circle context clues that tell why Libby's dad uses words related to the sea.

2 Sentence Structure Ⓐ Ⓒ Ⓣ

Reread the last sentence. Circle the text the phrase *That way* refers to. How will that way help Dad share with everyone? Write about it.

_____

_____

3 Comprehension

Theme

Read the last paragraph. Underline Libby's actions. How do her actions help the war effort? Justify your answer.

_____

_____

_____

Make Connections

? What kinds of contributions to the war effort do characters make in this story? **ESSENTIAL QUESTION**

Think about an event in your own life that required contributions from others. How did they all work together? **TEXT TO SELF**

Respond to the Text

Partner Discussion Work with a partner. Answer the questions. Discuss what you learned about "Shipped Out." Write the page numbers where you found text evidence.

How do members of Libby's family help with the war effort?

I read that Libby's dad joined _____,

while Libby's mom _____.

Aunt Lucia helps by _____.

Text Evidence 🔍

Page(s): _____

Page(s): _____

Page(s): _____

How does Libby help with the war effort?

Libby helps Aunt Lucia at the bakery by _____

_____.

For the fundraiser Libby _____.

Libby decides to send her father _____

_____.

Text Evidence 🔍

Page(s): _____

Page(s): _____

Page(s): _____

Group Discussion Present your answers to the group. Cite text evidence to justify your thinking. Listen to and discuss the group's opinions about your answers.

Write Review your notes about "Shipped Out." Then write your answer to the Essential Question. Use text evidence to support your answer. Use vocabulary words from this week's reading in your writing.

How does Libby's family contribute to the war effort?

To help the war effort, each member contributes _____.

Libby's dad _____.

Libby's mom _____.

Aunt Lucia and Libby _____

_____.

Libby decides to _____

_____.

Share Writing Present your writing to the class. Discuss their opinions. Think about what the class has to say. Did they justify their claims? Explain why you agree or disagree with their claims.

I agree with _____ because _____.

I disagree because _____.

pages 328–331

Roberto

Take Notes About the Text I took notes about the text on the chart to respond to the prompt: *Add a new event to the story. Write about Libby's family before her dad joined the navy.*

Text Clue	New Event
Libby's father is a mechanic on a ship.	Libby's father worked as a mechanic before the war.
Mom and Libby moved in with Aunt Lucia for a few months.	Libby's family lived together before her dad left, near Aunt Lucia's bakery and apartment.
Mom started working at the factory. She will work for few months.	Mom did not work before the war.
Aunt Lucia's workers left the bakery to join the army. So, Libby works at the bakery.	Libby used to visit the bakery with her parents.
Libby was upset when Dad told her he joined the navy.	Libby and her Dad spent time together before the war.

Write About the Text I used notes from my chart to write a paragraph about Libby's family before the war.

Student Model: *Narrative Text*

Life was very different for Libby and her family before the war. Libby's father worked as a mechanic. He fixed engines on cars, buses, and motorcycles. Libby lived with her parents in a sunny apartment near Aunt Lucia. Libby used to visit Aunt Lucia's bakery with her parents. She ate bread. At the same time, her parents talked with Aunt Lucia. Libby's mom didn't work, and Libby's father didn't work on weekends, so the whole family did a lot of things together. Then one day, her father told Libby that he joined the navy. Libby was very upset.

TALK ABOUT IT

COLLABORATE

Text Evidence
Draw a box around a sentence that comes from the notes. How did Roberto use the text clue to write the sentence?

Grammar
Circle the three prepositional phrases in the fourth sentence. What do they describe?

Connect Ideas
Underline the two sentences that tell about the family's visit to the bakery. How can you combine the sentences?

Your Turn
COLLABORATE

Add a new event. Write about what happens when Libby receives a letter from her father. Use text evidence in your writing.

>> *Go Digital!*
Write your response online. Use your editing checklist.

335

TALK ABOUT IT

? **Essential Question**
What actions can we take
to get along with others?

>> *Go Digital*

336

COLLABORATE

How do you know the animals in the photograph are getting along? How do people get along? Write words in the chart.

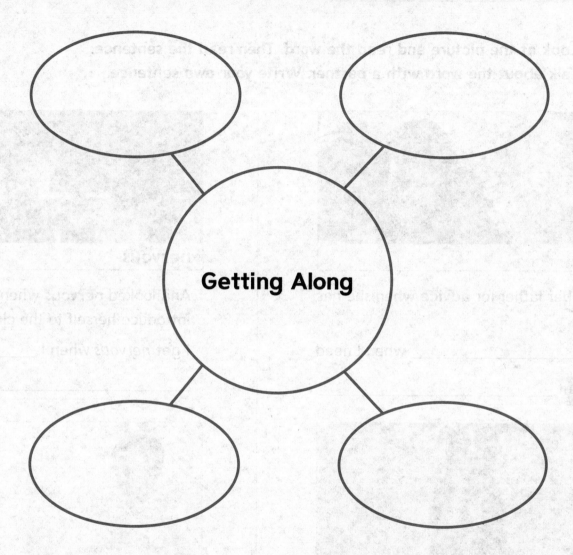

Getting Along

Discuss how people get along. Use words from the chart. Complete the sentences.

The animals get along with each other by _____.

People get along by _____

More Vocabulary

Look at the picture and read the word. Then read the sentence.
Talk about the word with a partner. Write your own sentence.

advice

Tanya asks her father for **advice** when she has a problem.

I talk with _____ when I need

advice about _____.

defend

Our dog **defends** the family against burglars.

When I *defend* a friend against a bully, I _____

_____.

nervous

Ana looked **nervous** when she had to introduce herself to the class.

I get *nervous* when I _____

_____.

offenses

Gus received punishment for his **offenses** of starting a food fight in the lunchroom.

An example of an *offense* in school is _____

_____.

338

proud

Tyler's family is **proud** of him for getting an award.

My parents are *proud* of me when I _____
_____.

relief

The girl got **relief** from the heat by drinking water.

During summer, a good way to get *relief* from the heat is _____.

Words and Phrases
Phrasal Verbs

picked on = laughed at or made fun of
Some older kids <u>picked on</u> Kyle because he is not a good athlete.

stand up to = face someone or something without fear
Carol will <u>stand up to</u> anyone to laughs at her speech.

Read the sentences below. Write the phrase that means the same as the underlined words.

Emily felt badly because she <u>made fun of</u> her little brother.

Emily felt badly because she _____ her little brother.

The kitten will <u>bravely face</u> the puppy that took her toy.

The kitten will _____ the puppy that took her toy.

>> *Go Digital* Add the phrases *picked on* and *stand up to* to your New Words notebook. Write a sentence to show the meaning of each.

The Bully

Marcelo Baez

COLLABORATE

1 Talk About It

Look at the picture. Read the title. Talk about what you see. Write your ideas.

What does the title tell you?

_____

_____

Who is the bully in the picture?

_____

_____

What is the bully doing?

_____

_____

_____

_____

Take notes as you read the story.

Essential Question

? **What actions can we take to get along with others?**

Read about how one student tries to deal with a bully.

Michael saw the trouble coming from all the way at the end of the school hallway. There standing by the stairs was J.T., the school bully who enjoyed taunting anyone he felt like at any given moment. J.T. was tall and strong, so few of his victims were willing to stand up to him and **defend** themselves. Michael hated the idea that he let J.T. get away with these **offenses**. Yet like most of the other kids who were picked on, he just took it quietly and waited for the unpleasant moment to pass.

J.T. walked directly toward Michael, his eyes locked on the books that Michael carried under his arms. When they met in the middle of the hallway, J.T. stopped abruptly and snapped at Michael, "Hey, let me see those books!" A group of students watched as Michael held out the books he was carrying, trying not to tremble to reveal how **nervous** he was.

J.T. grabbed a math book, looked inside for a second, and then shoved the book at Michael, who dropped all the books he held. "Hey, those books are school property," J.T. barked, "so don't let them fall to the floor!" Then he walked away, laughing loudly.

Michael, his cheeks turning red, half kicked the fallen books. Suddenly a hand appeared beside Michael and picked up an adventure novel as it slid away. "You look like you could use an ally," a friendly voice said with a laugh.

Text Evidence

1 Sentence Structure ⒶⒸⓉ

Reread the fourth sentence. Circle the text that tells what the phrase *these offenses* refers to. How do you know that Michael lets J. T. get away? Justify your answer.

I know because _____

_____.

2 Specific Vocabulary ⒶⒸⓉ

The word *took* means "accepted." Underline the text that tells what Michael took. Why did he take it quietly?

He took it quietly because _____

_____.

3 Comprehension

Reread the third paragraph. Put a box around the words that describe the actions of a bully.

_____

_____

_____

1 Sentence Structure (A)(C)(T)

Reread fourth and fifth paragraphs. The pronouns *that* and *It* refer to the same thing. Underline the text the pronouns refer to.

The pronouns refer to _____

_____.

2 Specific Vocabulary (A)(C)(T)

The phrase *leave me alone* means "stop bothering me." Circle the text that tells why Michael wants J.T. to leave him alone.

_____

_____

3 Comprehension
Theme

Reread the seventh paragraph. Underline the text Ramon says is vinegar. Why does he say this? Justify your answer.

_____

_____

Michael turned around and saw that it was Ramon. He was the school's star baseball player, basketball player, and everything-else-player you could name. Michael couldn't believe that Ramon was stopping to help him. The two had barely spoken to each other since the school year began.

"Thanks," Michael sighed with **relief**. "It's so confusing. I don't know what his problem is."

"I've been watching you in the halls," Ramon said, "and as I see it, you need to find a way to end this conflict with J.T." Michael nodded, stuck for what to say. "Well," Ramon continued, "I can tell you what my grandmother used to tell me whenever I had a problem with someone. She'd say, 'You can catch more flies with honey than with vinegar.'"

Looking puzzled, Michael asked, "What does that mean?"

"It means that being kind to your enemies may be more effective than being angry at them," Ramon explained.

"What if you just intervene and tell J.T. to stop picking on me?" Michael suggested. "I think he'd leave me alone if you threatened him."

"That's vinegar," Ramon laughed as he walked away. "Try honey instead."

That night, Michael thought about the **advice** that Ramon had given him. It sounded like a good plan, but deep down Michael wasn't very confident that it would actually work with J.T.

The next day in school brought Michael's usual misery. There stood J.T., and Michael knew it would be just a matter of seconds before the two of them collided in the middle of the hall.

Marcelo Baez

As J.T. came nearer, Michael wished he had Ramon's protective arm to stop the bully from attacking. Then, suddenly, the unexpected happened. J.T. accidentally tripped. He fell down, and his own armful of books went flying across the floor.

For a moment, all was silent. The crowd of students in the hallway froze, waiting to see what J.T. would do next. As J.T. slowly stood up, Michael had an idea. He bent down, quickly picked up J.T.'s books from the floor, and offered them to him.

Michael said, "You look like you could use an ally."

J.T. was speechless, completely thrown by Michael's act of kindness. He took the books and muttered quickly, "Uh, thanks."

As J.T. walked away, Michael caught Ramon in the corner of his eye. Ramon gave him a big smile and a "thumbs-up." "My grandmother would be **proud** of you," Ramon said.

"It's just honey," Michael grinned. "I hope it sticks."

Make Connections

Talk about how Ramon's advice affected Michael's problem with J.T. **ESSENTIAL QUESTION**

What advice would you give to someone being bullied? Give reasons to support your opinion. **TEXT TO SELF**

1 **Specific Vocabulary** Ⓐ Ⓒ Ⓣ

The word *protective* has the suffix *-ive*, which means "having the quality of." Write the meaning of protective. Circle context clues that help you figure out the meaning.

The word *protective* means _____

_____.

COLLABORATE

2 **Talk About It**

Explain why Ramon's grandmother would be proud of Michael. Use text evidence to justify your answer.

3 **Comprehension**
Theme

Reread the last sentence. Underline the text that tells what *honey* refers to. Why does Michael say this?

_____

_____

_____

343

Respond to the Text

Partner Discussion Work with a partner. Answer the questions. Discuss what you learned about "The Bully." Write the page numbers where you found text evidence.

What was the conflict between Michael and J.T.?

J.T. was the school _____.

Page(s): _____

When Michael was carrying his books, J.T. _____

_____.

Page(s): _____

Text Evidence 🔍

How did Ramon help Michael stand up to J.T.?

Ramon told Michael about his grandmother's advice which _____

_____.

Page(s): _____

When J.T. tripped in the hallway, Michael _____

_____.

Page(s): _____

Ramon was proud of Michael because _____

_____.

Page(s): _____

Text Evidence 🔍

Group Discussion Present your answers to the group. Cite text evidence to justify your thinking. Listen to and discuss the group's opinions about your answers.

Write Review your notes about "The Bully." Then write your answer to the Essential Question. Use text evidence to support your answer. Use vocabulary words from this week's reading in your writing.

What did Michael do to get along with J.T.?

J.T. was a bully, so Michael felt _____

_____.

Ramon gave Michael advice to _____

_____.

When J.T. needed help, Michael _____

_____.

By helping J.T., Michael realized that _____

_____.

Share Writing Present your writing to the class. Discuss their opinions. Think about what the class has to say. Did they justify their claims? Explain why you agree or disagree with their claims.

I agree with _____ because _____.

I disagree because _____.

Write to Sources

pages 340–343

Paco

Take Notes About the Text I took notes about the text on the chart to answer the question: *Should Ramon have tried to stop J. T. from bullying Michael? Write your opinion using evidence from the text.*

Text Evidence	Conclusion
Ramon is a star baseball and basketball player at school.	Ramon is probably strong and popular. J.T. would probably listen to Ramon.
Ramon tells Michael that it is better to be kind than angry to your enemies.	Ramon thinks Michael should be kind to J.T., instead of being mean.
Michael wants Ramon to threaten J. T. but Ramon refuses and tells Michael to be nice to J.T.	Ramon thinks Michael needs to solve the problem by himself.
Michael shows kindness to J.T. when he trips in the hallway. J.T. does not bully Michael.	Michael takes Ramon's advice and solves his problem by himself.

346

Write About the Text I used notes from my chart to write an opinion about what Ramon did.

Student Model: *Opinion*

Ramon could have helped Michael more but he wanted Michael to solve his problem by himself. Ramon is a strong athlete and popular in school. J. T. would have listened to Ramon because he might have been scared of Ramon. However, Ramon believes that it is better to be kind to your enemies. Ramon thought Michael should solve his problem with J.T. Ramon gave Michael advice, but did not speak out for him. In the end, Michael took Ramon's advice. He was kind to J.T., and J.T. did not bully him. Michael solved his problem by himself.

TALK ABOUT IT

COLLABORATE

Text Evidence
Draw a box around a sentence that comes from the notes. How did Paco use the information to support his opinion?

Grammar
Circle a reflexive pronoun. How is a reflexive pronoun different from other pronouns? Why does Paco use this pronoun?

Connect Ideas
Underline the two sentences that describe what Ramon believes. How can you combine the sentences to connect the ideas?

Your Turn

COLLABORATE

In your opinion, will J. T. be nice to Michael in the future? Use text evidence in your writing.

>> Go Digital!
Write your response online. Use your editing checklist.

TALK ABOUT IT

Weekly Concept Adaptations

? **Essential Question**
**How are living things adapted
to their environment?**

>> *Go Digital*

How do the thorns help the lizard survive? What adaptations do animals and people have? How do adaptations help people and animals survive? Write words in the chart.

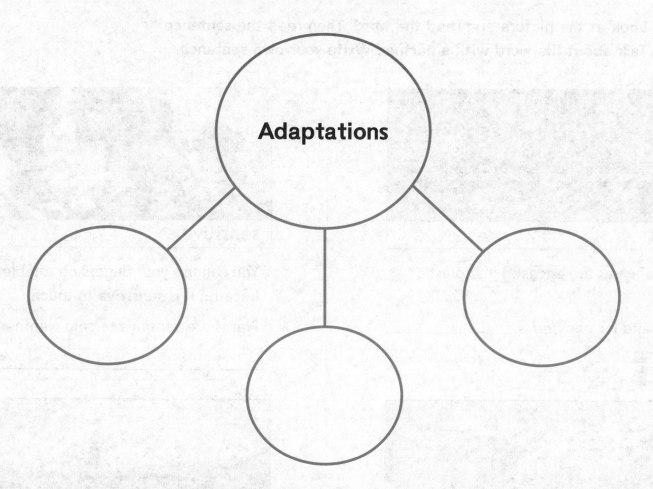

Adaptations

Discuss how adaptations help animals and people survive. Use words from the chart. Complete the sentences.

The thorns help lizards survive by _____.

Adaptations help animals and people survive by _____

_____.

More Vocabulary

Look at the picture and read the word. Then read the sentence.
Talk about the word with a partner. Write your own sentence.

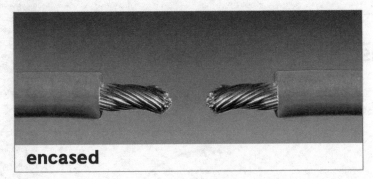

encased

The copper wires are **encased** in a plastic tube.

Another word for *encased* is _____.

sensitive

You can use your fingers on a tablet computer because it is **sensitive** to touch.

Plants are *sensitive* to cold weather because

_____.

odyssey

The explorers are on an **odyssey** to study icebergs in the ocean.

I would like to take an *odyssey* to _____

_____.

sparse

On chilly days, visitors are **sparse** at the beach.

I notice that _____ are

sparse when _____.

teem

During summer, outdoor markets **teem** with visitors.

One time I saw _____ *teem*

with _____.

vast

This prairie has **vast** plains of tall grass.

Something is *vast* when it _____

_____.

Words and Phrases
Adverb Phrases

not only = also, in addition to
Laura plays <u>not only</u> volleyball but also softball.

only because = for no other reason than
Thomas wakes up <u>only because</u> the dog is barking.

Read the sentences below. Rewrite the sentence using the phrase that best completes each sentence.

Peter delivers newspapers. He wants to earn money.

Peter delivers newspapers _____ he wants to earn money.

George speaks English. George speaks Spanish.

George speaks _____ English but also Spanish.

>> Go Digital Add the phrases *not only* and *only because* to your New Words notebook. Write a sentence to show the meaning of each.

COLLABORATE

1 Talk About It

Read the title. Talk about what you see. Write your ideas.

What does the title tell you?

_____

_____

_____

_____

What does the caption tell you about the photograph?

_____

_____

_____

_____

Take notes as you read the text.

Mysterious Oceans

Some deep ocean fish are swimming among tube worms. New ocean species are being discovered all the time.

Essential Question

? How are living things adapted to their environment?

Read about the adaptation of sea creatures to the deep ocean.

Dr. Ken MacDonald/Science Photo Library

Deep Diving

It has no mouth, eyes, or stomach. Its soft body is **encased** in a white cylinder and topped with a red plume. It can grow to be eight feet tall. It is a sea creature known as a giant tube worm, and it lives without any sunlight on the deep, dark ocean floor.

What we sometimes call the deep ocean, in contrast to shallow waters, covers almost two-thirds of Earth's surface. On average, oceans are about two miles deep. However, the deepest point known on Earth, Challenger Deep, descends nearly seven miles.

The ocean's floor is **varied**, consisting of **vast** plains, steep canyons, and towering mountains. It includes active, dormant, and extinct volcanoes. This undersea world is a harsh environment because of its frigid temperatures and lack of sunshine.

The deep ocean is also a mysterious environment that remains largely unexplored. Little is known about it or its creatures. Do any of them cache food the way land animals do? Do any ocean species hibernate? As one example among countless mysteries, not a single, live giant squid had ever been spotted until a few years ago. We knew they existed only because their corpses had been found.

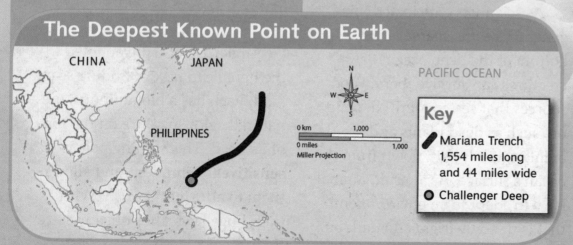

The Challenger Deep is located in an undersea canyon called the Mariana Trench.

The Deepest Known Point on Earth

CHINA

JAPAN

PACIFIC OCEAN

PHILIPPINES

N
W   E
S

0 km   1,000
0 miles   1,000
Miller Projection

Key

Mariana Trench
1,554 miles long
and 44 miles wide

○ Challenger Deep

1 Sentence Structure Ⓐ Ⓒ Ⓣ

Reread the first sentence of the second paragraph. Underline the predicate of the sentence. Circle the text that contrasts the deep ocean. Why is this information included? Justify your answer.

_____

_____

2 Specific Vocabulary Ⓐ Ⓒ Ⓣ

The word *varied* means "includes different types." Circle the text in the paragraph that tells how the ocean floor is varied.

3 Comprehension

Cause and Effect

Reread the last sentence of the third paragraph. Put a box around the factors that cause the undersea to be harsh. Write about it.

_____

_____

Text Evidence

1 Sentence Structure ACT

Reread the first sentence. Underline the text that explains what the scientists needed to explore the deep ocean floor. How is the craft different from others?

_____

_____

2 Specific Vocabulary ACT

A *lure* attracts fish so they can be caught. Circle context clues that help you figure out the meaning of *lure*. How is a lure an adaptation?

A lure is an adaptation because

_____

_____.

COLLABORATE

3 Talk About It

Discuss how creatures have adapted to the environment in the deep ocean. How are the adaptations useful?

This fish, the striated frogfish, lures prey. The nose is an adaptation to life in the deep ocean.

A basket starfish rests in a deep-sea coral reef.

Amazing Adaptations

When a submersible, or submarine, was invented that could descend farther than any other craft, scientists were then able to make the **odyssey** to the deep ocean floor. However, exploration remains difficult, and they have since seen merely five percent of the underwater world.

As scientists anticipated, life generally seems **sparse** at the bottom of the deep ocean. Few creatures can survive there. Food sources that sea creatures depend on, such as dead plants and animals, rarely drift down from the ocean's surface. As a result, animals have to adapt to an environment that is not only frigid and dark but also has little food.

One example of an adaptation to this environment is seen in the starfish. Deep sea starfish grow larger and more aggressive than their shallow water relatives. They can't afford to wait for an occasional snail to pass by. Instead, deep sea starfish are predators that actively forage for food. They reach up their five arms, which have pincers at the ends, to catch meals of agile, fast-moving shrimp.

Anglerfish also are adapted to the herculean task of finding scarce food. Each has a bioluminous, or naturally glowing, **lure** on the top of its head. This shining pole is **sensitive** to vibrations and allows them to attract other fish. With their huge jaws, they quickly seize their prey.

(l) Pixtal/AGE Fotostock; (r) Lophelia II 2009 Expedition, NOAA-OER

Heated Habitats

What has truly surprised scientists, however, is the discovery of another, very different type of environment on the deep ocean floor. They found that cracks, or vents, in Earth's surface exist underwater, just as they do on dry land. Sea water rushes into these vents, where it mingles with chemicals. The water is also heated by magma, or hot melted rock. When the water from the vent bursts back into the ocean, it creates geysers and hot springs.

To scientists' amazement, the habitats around these vents **teem** with life. In addition to tube worms, there are huge clams, eyeless shrimp, crabs, and mussels, along with many kinds of bacteria. One odd creature is the Pompeii worm. It has a **fleece** of bacteria on its back that, as far as scientists can determine, insulates it from heat.

How can so much life exist where there is so little food or sunlight? Scientists have discovered that many creatures transform the chemicals from the vents into food. The process is called chemosynthesis. Because of this process, animals are able to flourish in these remarkable habitats. Creatures that don't use chemosynthesis for food, such as crabs, eat the ones that do.

There are many mysteries to be found and solved at the bottom of the deep sea. In the last few decades alone, scientists have discovered more than 1,500 ocean species! If scientists continue sea exploration, they are bound to discover many more.

Make Connections

Talk about the ways some sea creatures adapt to the deep ocean. **ESSENTIAL QUESTION**

Compare one sea creature adaptation to that of another animal you have seen. **TEXT TO SELF**

Text Evidence

1 **Sentence Structure** **ACT**

Reread the second sentence. Circle the places where cracks appear.

Cracks appear _____

_____

2 **Specific Vocabulary** **ACT**

A *fleece* is a coat made of soft woolly material. Underline the text that tells how the author uses the word to describe the bacteria on the back of the Pompeii worm. Write about it.

_____

_____

3 **Comprehension**
Cause and Effect

Reread the third paragraph. Put a box around the cause that allows the creatures to survive. How do crabs survive?

Crabs survive by _____

_____

Respond to the Text

COLLABORATE

Partner Discussion Work with a partner. Answer the questions. Discuss what you learned about "Mysterious Oceans." Write the page numbers where you found text evidence.

How have creatures in the deep ocean adapted?

Text Evidence 🔍

I read that the ocean floor is _____.

Page(s): _____

Deep sea starfish adapted by _____.

Page(s): _____

Anglerfish has adaptations that _____.

Page(s): _____

What did scientists discover near the vents on the ocean floor?

Text Evidence 🔍

I read that the bottom of the ocean is teeming with _____.

Page(s): _____

Around the vents, there are _____.

Page(s): _____

Many sea creatures survive by _____

Page(s): _____

_____.

COLLABORATE

Group Discussion Present your answers to the group. Cite text evidence to justify your thinking. Listen to and discuss the group's opinions about your answers.

Write Review your notes about "Mysterious Oceans." Then write your answer to the Essential Question. Use text evidence to support your answer. Use vocabulary words from this week's reading in your writing.

How are living things adapted to living in the deep ocean?

Deep sea starfish adapted by _____

_____.

Anglerfish adapted by _____

_____.

The creatures that live near the vents adapted by _____

_____.

Chemosynthesis helps the creatures by _____

_____.

Share Writing Present your writing to the class. Discuss their opinions. Think about what the class has to say. Did they justify their claims? Explain why you agree or disagree with their claims.

I agree with _____ because _____.

I disagree because _____.

357

Write to Sources

Ana

Take Notes About the Text I took notes about the text on the idea web to answer the question: *Why do deep-sea creatures have adaptions? Use text evidence.*

pages 352–355

Topic
Deep-sea animals have adaptations because it is dark and there is little food.

Detail
Deep-sea starfish are aggressive and use arms to catch shrimp.

Detail
Anglerfish use glowing lures to attract and catch fish.

Detail
Animals that live near vents use chemosynthesis. It changes chemicals from the vents into food.

Write About the Text **I used the notes on my idea web to write a paragraph about deep-sea animals.**

Student Model: *Informative Text*

Deep-sea animals have to adapt to live at the bottom of the deep ocean because it is cold and there is very little food. Deep-sea starfish adapted to this environment by being aggressive. They use their arms to catch shrimp. Anglerfish adapted to the dark by using glowing lures to attract and catch fish. Animals that live near vents adapted by using a process called chemosynthesis. The process changes chemicals from the vents into food. These adaptations allow the animals to live at the bottom of the deep ocean.

TALK ABOUT IT

COLLABORATE

Text Evidence

Draw a box around a sentence that comes from the notes. Why does Ana include this information?

Grammar

Circle an irregular noun. How do you know it is an irregular noun?

Connect Ideas

Underline the two sentences about deep-sea starfish. How can you combine the sentences and connect the ideas?

Your Turn

COLLABORATE

Explain the adaptations found in animals living in the environment around deep-sea vents.

>> *Go Digital*
Write your response online. Use your editing checklist.

TALK ABOUT IT

Essential Question

What impact do our actions have on our world?

>> *Go Digital*

COLLABORATE

How does the man take care of the chimpanzees? How does he make a difference? What can people do to make a difference? Write words in the chart.

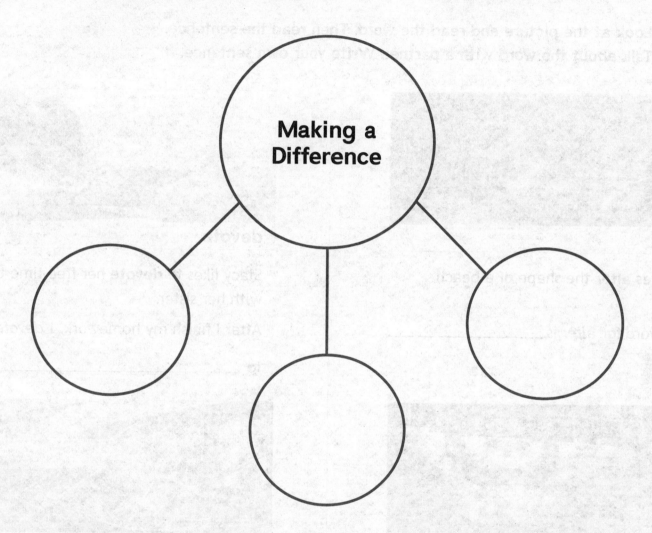

Making a Difference

Discuss how the man's actions make a difference. Use words from the chart. You can say:

The man takes care of the chimpanzees by _____.

To make a difference, people can _____.

More Vocabulary

Look at the picture and read the word. Then read the sentence.
Talk about the word with a partner. Write your own sentence.

alter

Large waves **alter** the shape of a beach over time.

Another word for *alter* is _____.

depict

The family decorates their house on Independence Day to **depict** their patriotism.

Another word for *depict* is _____.

devote

Stacy likes to **devote** her free time to reading with her sister.

After I finish my homework, I *devote* my time

to _____.

foundation

Early airplanes are the **foundation** of modern jets.

Learning to read is a foundation you need to ____

_____.

mocked

Lela **mocked** her sister by sticking out her tongue.

_____ *mocked* me when

_____ .

restrict

The workers **restrict** driving on the road during construction.

My parents *restrict* me from _____

_____ .

Words and Phrases
Adverb Phrases

You can use the phrase *even so* to tell about something that is different from what you just said.
Kyra went to bed early last night. <u>Even so</u>, *she is tired this morning.*

The phrase *in order to* means "so that something can happen." You can use the phrase to tell why you do something.
Robert studies <u>in order to</u> *get good grades.*

Read the sentences below. Rewrite the sentences using the phrase that best completes the sentences.

Carla used an alarm clock. Carla wants to wake up on time.

Carla used an alarm clock _____ wake up on time.

Coach was sick. The soccer team played the game.

Coach was sick. _____, the soccer team played the game.

>> *Go Digital* Add the phrases *in order to* and *even so* to your New Words notebook. Write a sentence to show the meaning of each.

COLLABORATE

❶ Talk About It

Read the title. Talk about what you see. Write your ideas.

What do the title and the subtitle tell you?

_____

_____

_____

_____

What information does the caption tell you about the photograph?

_____

_____

_____

_____

Take notes as you read the text.

Shared Read   Genre • Biography

Words to Save the World

The Work of Rachel Carson

Essential Question

?   **What impact do our actions have on our world?**

Read about how the biologist Rachel Carson used the power of writing to change the world.

Sometimes, the quietest voice can spark the most clamorous outrage. Combining her love of nature with a belief in scientific accuracy, the soft-spoken writer Rachel Carson raised awareness about environmental issues. As a result, the U.S. government strengthened the rules and regulations regarding the use of chemical pesticides. Many people consider Rachel's book *Silent Spring* the **foundation** of today's environmental movement.

Early Influences

Rachel was born in Springdale, Pennsylvania, in 1907. Throughout her childhood, her mother encouraged her to explore the landscape surrounding the family's farm. Often equipped with binoculars, Rachel developed a love of nature that affected many of her decisions. For example, she first chose to study English literature and writing when she went to college. However, she later decided to study biology. While studying at a

◄ **Rachel preferred working alone as she gathered information.**

marine laboratory, she became fascinated by the glistening and shimmering seascape.

From an early age, Rachel had loved to write. These writing skills proved useful to her career. She began by creating radio programs for the U.S. Bureau of Fisheries. She then became an editor and librarian for the agency. While she was working, she submitted her own articles to newspapers and magazines. Rachel eventually published three books about the ocean and its native plants and animals. This trilogy included *Under the Sea-Wind, The Sea Around Us,* and *The Edge of the Sea.*

Rachel supported her ideas with well-researched facts.

Text Evidence

❶ Specific Vocabulary Ⓐ Ⓒ Ⓣ

The word *regulations* means "laws about how something should be done." Circle the synonym of regulations in the paragraph.

❷ Comprehension
Problem and Solution

Reread the first paragraph. Underline the effects of Rachel Carsons' work. Write about it. Rachel Carson's work led to _____

_____

_____.

❸ Sentence Structure Ⓐ Ⓒ Ⓣ

Reread the third sentence in the second paragraph. Circle the text that describes the effect. How did using the binoculars affect Rachel? Write about it.

_____

_____

Text Evidence

❶ Comprehension
Problem and Solution

Reread the first paragraph. Circle the problem DDT solved. Underline the new problem DDT caused. Write about it.

The new problem was _____

_____.

❷ Specific Vocabulary ⒶⒸⓉ

The word *dramatize* means "to make people take notice." Circle the text that tells you how she dramatized the dangers of DDT.

COLLABORATE

❸ Talk About It

Reread the last paragraph. Discuss what Rachel probably said when she testified. Justify your answer. Write about it.

_____

_____

_____

_____

A Call to Action

The success of Rachel's books allowed her to **devote** more time to her own projects. She built a cottage close to the sea on the coast of Maine. Soon, however, a letter arrived from some old friends, Olga and Stuart Huckins. They described problems resulting from the spraying of DDT on their private wildlife sanctuary. Chemical companies had developed DDT as an effective solution to crop-eating insects on farms and plantations. At the Huckins's sanctuary, however, the chemical also seemed to be harming birds.

In response, Rachel hired assistants to help research the Huckins's claim. Worried by the slow pace of their work, she decided to continue alone. By publishing her findings, she hoped to warn about the dangers of these new chemicals. In order to **dramatize** the situation, she urged readers to imagine a world without songbirds.

The book's title, *Silent Spring,* describes this possible result of pesticide abuse.

Silent Spring prompted readers to raise their voices in unison against the chemical corporations. They demanded an investigation into pesticides and implored the government to **restrict** their use. In response, President John Kennedy created a Congressional committee to study the matter. Rachel testified before this group and provided facts and information to influence its decisions.

Though a pesticide may target insects, animals can also feel its effects.

Sample Food Chains

TROPHIC LEVEL	GRASSLAND BIOME	OCEAN BIOME
Primary Producer	grass	phytoplankton
Primary Consumer	grasshopper	zooplankton
Secondary Consumer	rat	fish
Tertiary Consumer	snake	seal

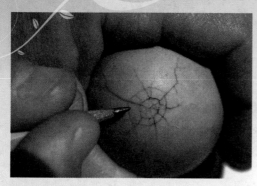

Rachel Carson's research revealed that DDT caused damage to birds and eggs.

A Strong Reaction

Meanwhile, the chemical companies struggled to counter Rachel's claims. Despite her reasonable approach to the problem, they tried to **depict** her accusations as irrational. They published articles and reports that **mocked** her writing style and belittled her ideas. Advertisements on television proclaimed the safety of their products. When these ads did not change public opinion, they pulled financial support from programs that featured Rachel.

Rachel worried that once pesticides poisoned an area, it might be impossible to restore the environment to its original state. "Man's attitude toward nature is today critically important simply because we have now acquired a fateful power to **alter** and destroy nature," she said in an interview. Her testimony led to restrictions on certain pesticides in the United States. Even so, chemical companies continued to produce them for export to other countries.

Rachel Carson died shortly after *Silent Spring* was published, but her voice survives within her books. Her love of nature endures, along with her quiet desire to preserve and protect the natural world.

Make Connections

What impact did the publication of *Silent Spring* have on the makers of pesticides such as DDT? **ESSENTIAL QUESTION**

Think about a time when you wrote or spoke about something that needed to change. What impact did your words have? **TEXT TO SELF**

Text Evidence

1 Specific Vocabulary Ⓐ Ⓒ Ⓣ

The word *counter* means "prove wrong." Underline how the companies tried to counter Rachel's claims. Rewrite the sentence using another word or phrase for *counter*.

_____

_____

2 Sentence Structure Ⓐ Ⓒ Ⓣ

Reread the last sentence in the first paragraph. Circle the word that the pronoun *they* refers to.

3 Comprehension

Problem and Solution

Reread the second paragraph. Put a box around the text that tells the problem has not been solved fully. Justify your answer.

_____

_____

_____

Partner Discussion Work with a partner. Answer the questions. Discuss what you learned about "Words to Save the World." Write the page numbers where you found text evidence.

What effects did pesticides have on the environment?

Chemical companies developed pesticides to _____.

Pesticides solved the problem of _____,

but it also had the effect of _____.

Text Evidence 🔍
Page(s): _____
Page(s): _____

What effect did Rachel Carson have on the use of pesticides?

Rachel researched about the _____.

Rachel published her findings in _____.

She gave testimony before _____.

As a result, the government _____.

Text Evidence 🔍
Page(s): _____
Page(s): _____
Page(s): _____
Page(s): _____

Group Discussion Present your answers to the group. Cite text evidence to justify your thinking. Listen to and discuss the group's opinions about your answers.

Write Review your notes about "Words to Save the World." Then write your answer to the Essential Question. Use text evidence to support your answer. Use vocabulary words from this week's reading in your writing.

> **What impact did Rachel Carson's actions have on the environment?**
>
> Rachel's scientific findings and book inspired people to _____
>
> _____.
>
> As a result, the government responded by _____
>
> _____.
>
> Rachel's actions preserved and protected _____
>
> _____.

Share Writing Present your writing to the class. Discuss their opinions. Think about what the class has to say. Did they justify their claims? Explain why you agree or disagree with their claims.

I agree with _____ because _____.

I disagree because _____.

Write to Sources

Yasmine

Take Notes About the Text I took notes about the text on the chart to answer the question: *In your opinion, is the author against pesticides? Use text evidence.*

Details	Point of View
Author tells about how Rachel did research to get information.	
Author tells that Rachel wrote a book about her discoveries.	
Author tells both good and bad things about pesticides.	The author is not against pesticides. The author describes how the government dealt with pesticides.
Author tells that the government had a Congressional committee study pesticides.	
Author tells the government restricted the use of some pesticides. This shows that pesticides are harmful.	

Write About the Text I used notes from my chart to write an opinion.

Student Model: *Opinion*

The author is not against pesticides. The author describes how Rachel Carson researched about pesticides and then wrote about her discoveries. The author explains the benefits of pesticides. The author also explains the negative effects of pesticides. The author does not say that pesticides are bad. Instead, the author explains that the government had a Congressional committee study pesticides. As a result, the government restricted the use of some pesticides. This shows that pesticides are harmful. It is not because the author is against pesticides.

TALK ABOUT IT
COLLABORATE

Text Evidence
Draw a box around a sentence that comes from the notes. How does Yasmine use the information?

Grammar
Circle the pronoun in the last sentence. What does this pronoun refer to?

Condense Ideas
Underline the two sentences that tell what the author wrote about the effects of pesticides. How can you condense them into one sentence?

Your Turn

COLLABORATE

In your opinion, should DDT be banned in all countries? Use text evidence in your writing.

>> *Go Digital!*
Write your response online. Use your editing checklist.

TALK ABOUT IT

? **Essential Question**

What can our connections to the world teach us?

➤➤ *Go Digital*

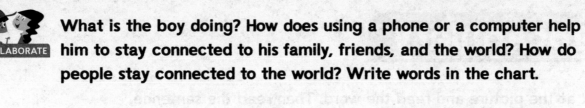

What is the boy doing? How does using a phone or a computer help him to stay connected to his family, friends, and the world? How do people stay connected to the world? Write words in the chart.

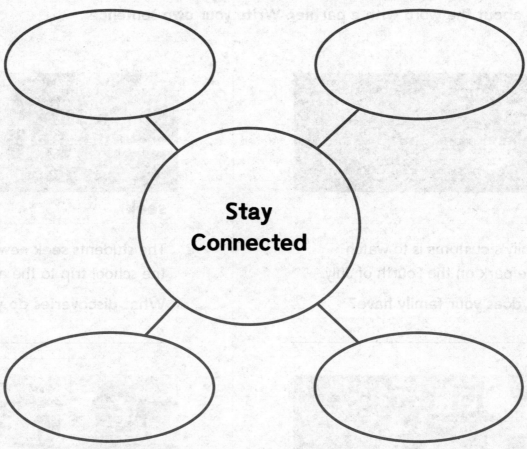

Stay Connected

Discuss how people stay connected to the world. Use words from the chart. Complete the sentences.

Using a phone or a computer helps the boy to stay connected

because _____.

People stay connected by _____.

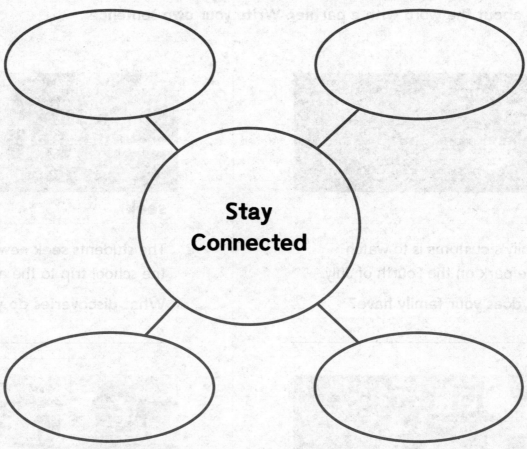

COLLABORATE

Look at the picture and read the word. Then read the sentence. Talk about the word with a partner. Write your own sentence.

customs

One of my family's **customs** is to watch fireworks in the park on the Fourth of July.

What custom does your family have?

_____

seek

The students **seek** new experiences during the school trip to the aquarium.

What discoveries do you seek on a trip?

_____

impatient

After waiting all morning, Jack and Liz are **impatient** for Aunt Tasha to arrive.

When do you get impatient?

_____

sensible

Wearing a helmet while riding a bicycle is a **sensible** way to stay safe.

What is another sensible way to stay safe?

_____

Poetry Terms

assonance

Assonance has words that have the same vowel sound. The long *i* sound is repeated below.

My kite was flying high in the sky.

consonance

Consonance has words that have the same final or middle consonant sound. The /s/ sound is repeated below.

Sissy sells seashells by the seashore.

imagery

Imagery creates a picture in a reader's mind by using words and phrases.

The trees wave to me as I race by on my shiny bike.

personification

Personification tells about objects, animals, or ideas like people.

The thunder clapped loudly through the night.

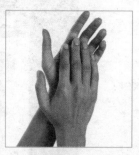

COLLABORATE

Work with a partner. Make up sentences using assonance, consonance, imagery, and personification. Use the words below.

bird   patter
footsteps   heels
kicked   worm

Assonance and personification:

The wind _____

up its _____.

The early _____

catches the _____.

Consonance and imagery:

We heard the pitter

_____ of

tiny _____.

① Sentence Structure (A C T)

Reread lines 1–4. Underline the lines that are not complete sentences. Rewrite lines 3–4 as a complete sentence.

_____

_____

② Literary Element
Personification

Reread lines 5–6 of the second stanza. Circle an example of personification. Write about it.

The poet describes _____

_____.

COLLABORATE

③ Talk About It

Reread the last two lines of the second stanza. Who is the speaker? What does it mean to _live our scenes_? Justify your answers.

To Travel!

To travel! To travel!
To visit distant places;
To leave my corner of the world
To **seek** new names and faces.
Adventure! Adventure!
Exploring foreign lands;
If I can leap across the globe,
My universe expands!

A novel waves her arms to me,
"Come read! Come read!" she cries.
Her pages dance with ancient tales,
A feast for hungry eyes!
The paintings on museum walls
Are begging me to tour:
"Leave your home and live our scenes,
A grand exchange for sure!"

Essential Question

What can our connections to the world teach us?

Read two poems about connecting with other cultures and with nature.

To travel! To travel!
Through timeless books and art,
I enter and experience
A life so far apart.

I sail across the seven seas,
My heart soars like a bird.
And soon I'm hearing languages
I've never, ever heard.

Far across the seven seas,
Aromas fill the air.
Foods I've never, ever tried
Are eaten everywhere!
Music blares a different tune,
And strange, new clothes are worn.
Parents pass on **customs**
To the young ones who are born.

I've traveled! I've traveled!
It's left me more aware;
A valuable connection
To the universe we share.
By reading books and viewing art,
I've learned a thing or two:
The world was made not just for me,
But made for me and you!

— Jad Abbas

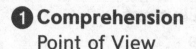

Text Evidence

❶ Comprehension
Point of View

Reread the first stanza. Underline the speaker's point of view. What does the poet mean by *To travel*?

_____

_____

_____

❷ Specific Vocabulary Ⓐ Ⓒ Ⓣ

Aromas are pleasing smells. What aromas fill the air? Circle the text that tells you.

❸ Sentence Structure Ⓐ Ⓒ Ⓣ

Reread lines 1–4 in the last stanza. Circle text that lines 3–4 refer to. What effect does traveling have on the speaker?

_____

_____

_____

1 Literary Element
Assonance

Reread line 3. What vowel sound is repeated to create the feeling of energy? Circle the words that have this sound.

2 Sentence Structure ACT

Reread the third sentence. The sentence has two main clauses. Underline the subject of each clause.

COLLABORATE

3 Talk About It

In your opinion, is the speaker a serious person? Justify your opinion using text evidence from the poem. Then write about it.

_____

_____

_____

_____

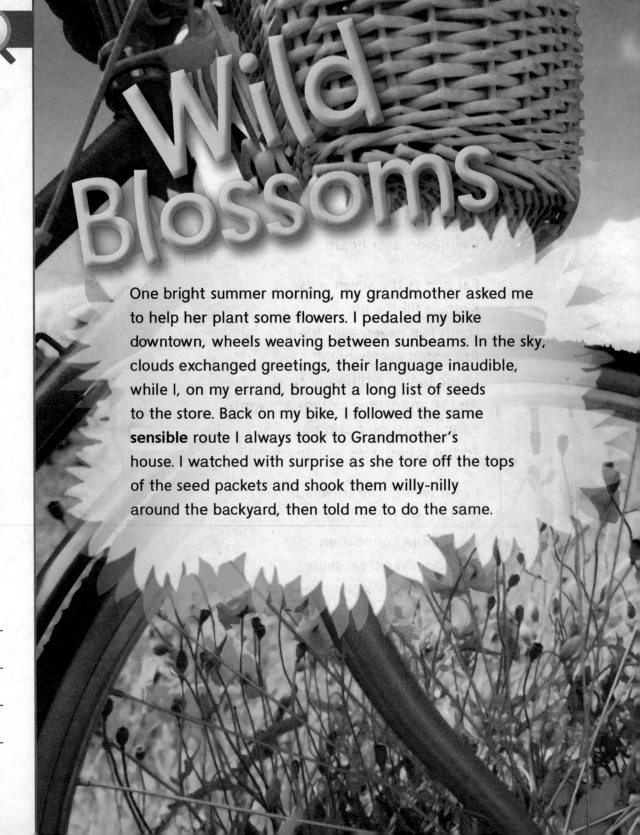

Wild Blossoms

One bright summer morning, my grandmother asked me to help her plant some flowers. I pedaled my bike downtown, wheels weaving between sunbeams. In the sky, clouds exchanged greetings, their language inaudible, while I, on my errand, brought a long list of seeds to the store. Back on my bike, I followed the same **sensible** route I always took to Grandmother's house. I watched with surprise as she tore off the tops of the seed packets and shook them willy-nilly around the backyard, then told me to do the same.

"I thought we were planting a garden," I told her,
"with row after row of flowers." She said, "Oh, no!
I prefer a mountain meadow, one with plenty
of variety." As she talked, bees buzzed about
in excitable flight, **impatient** for blossoms.
Quick swifts and happy sparrows dipped, dove, and darted
after the falling seeds. My grandmother and I
danced about the backyard, arms outstretched, letting seeds
loose on the wind, joyfully dreaming of the wild
beauty that would fill the yard, and us, all summer.

— Amelia Campos

Make Connections

? Describe how the speakers in the poems connect to their worlds. ESSENTIAL QUESTION

How do the connections described in the poems compare with your own experiences? TEXT TO SELF

Text Evidence 🔍

❶ Comprehension
Point of View

What is Grandmother's point of view about gardens? Underline the text that tells you. Write about grandmother's point of view.

_____

_____

❷ Literary Element
Consonance

Reread line 4. Find an example of consonance. Circle the consonant that repeats in each word. Then write the words.

_____

_____

❸ Specific Vocabulary Ⓐ Ⓒ Ⓣ

The word *outstretched* is a compound word. Circle the two shorter words. Based on the shorter words, write the meaning of *outstretched*.

_____

_____

Respond to the Text

Partner Discussion Work with a partner. Answer the questions. Discuss what you learned about "To Travel!" and "Wild Blossoms." Write the page numbers where you found text evidence.

What does the speaker learn in "To Travel!"?

In the poem, the speaker _____.

Studying these things teaches the speaker _____

_____

The speaker learns to connect with _____.

Text Evidence 🔍

Page(s): _____

Page(s): _____

Page(s): _____

What does the speaker learn in "Wild Blossoms"?

In the poem, the speaker helps _____.

Her grandmother teaches her _____.

The speaker learns to connect with _____.

Text Evidence 🔍

Page(s): _____

Page(s): _____

Page(s): _____

Group Discussion Present your answers to the group. Cite text evidence to justify your thinking. Listen to and discuss the group's opinions about your answers.

Write Review your notes about "To Travel!" and "Wild Blossoms." Then write your answer to the Essential Question. Use text evidence to support your answer. Use vocabulary words from this week's reading in your writing.

What do the speakers in the poems "To Travel!" and "Wild Blossoms" learn from their connections to the world?

The speaker in "To Travel!" connects to the world through _____

_____.

This connection teaches him that _____.

The speaker in "Wild Blossoms" connects by _____

_____.

This connection teaches her that _____

_____.

Share Writing Present your writing to the class. Discuss their opinions. Think about what the class has to say. Did they justify their claims? Explain why you agree or disagree with their claims.

I agree with _____ because _____.

I disagree because _____.

Write to Sources

Frank

Take Notes About the Text I took notes about the text on the chart to respond to the prompt: *Write about how the poet uses personification in the poem.*

pages 376–379

Text Clues	What You Know	Inferences
A novel waves her arms to me, "Come read! Come read!" she cries. Her pages dance with ancient tales,	People wave arms to draw attention, so the novel gets your attention. The novel makes the poet want to read the book. "Her pages" refers to the pages in the novel. People dance when they are full of life. So the novel is full of life and exciting.	The poet uses personification to tell about a book. The poet tells that the pages of a novel are full of life.

382

Write About the Text I used notes from my chart to write
an informative paragraph.

Student Model: *Informative Text*

In the poem "To Travel!", the poet uses
personification to describe a novel. The poet
wrote, "A novel waves her arms to me, 'Come
read! Come read!' she cries. Her pages dance
with ancient tales." This is an example of
personification because he describes the novel
as a person. The novel waves its arms and talks
loudly to the speaker. People wave their arms
and talk loudly to get attention. The pages
dance. When people dance, they're full of life.
The poet is saying the stories in novels are full
of life.

TALK ABOUT IT

Text Evidence
Draw a box around a sentence that comes
from the notes. How does Frank use it?

Grammar
Circle the text that tells what the novel cries
out in the poem Why does Frank use single
quotation marks?

Condense Ideas
Underline the sentences that tell about what the
novel does. How can you combine the sentences
into one sentence to condense the ideas?

Your Turn

Identify and explain another example
of personification in the poem. Use
text evidence in your writing.

>> *Go Digital!*
Write your response online. Use your editing checklist.